Postindustrial Peasants

The Illusion of Middle-Class Prosperity

Contemporary Social Issues
George Ritzer, *Series Editor*

Urban Enclaves: Identity and Place in the World, Second Edition
Mark Abrahamson

Hollywood Goes to High School: Cinema, Schools, and American Culture
Robert C. Bulman

Society of Risk-Takers: Living Life on the Edge
William C. Cockerham

Just Revenge: Costs and Consequences of the Death Penalty,
Second Edition
Mark Costanzo

The Wilding of America: Money, Mayhem, and the New American Dream, Fourth Edition
Charles Derber

Global E-Litism: Digital Technology, Social Inequality, and Transnationality
Gili S. Drori

Sex Trafficking: The Global Market in Women and Children
Kathryn Farr

Between Politics and Reason: The Drug Legalization Debate
Erich Goode

The Myth of Self-Esteem: Finding Happiness and Solving Problems in America
John P. Hewitt

Speculative Capitalism: Financial Casinos and Their Consequences
Daniel A. Krier

Sexual Saturation: Sexual Discourse, Pornography, and Erotica in America Today
Kenneth Kammeyer

Coming Soon!
States of Global Insecurity: Policy, Politics, and Society
Daniel Béland

Contemporary Social Issues

Series Editor: George Ritzer, *University of Maryland*

Postindustrial Peasants

The Illusion of Middle-Class Prosperity

Kevin T. Leicht

The University of Iowa

Scott T. Fitzgerald

University of North Carolina at Charlotte

Worth Publishers

Acquisitions Editor: Erik Gilg
Marketing Director: Scott Guile
Production Editor: Benjamin Reynolds
Art Director: Barbara Reingold
Cover Designer: Lyndall Culbertson
Text Designer: Lissi Sigillo
Production Manager: Barbara Anne Seixas
Associate Managing Editor: Tracey Kuehn
Composition: Matrix Publishing Services
Printing and Binding: RR Donnelley
Cover Photo: Stephen Mallon/Photonica/Getty Images

ISBN-13: 978-0-7167-5765-8
ISBN-10: 0-7167-5765-6

© 2007 by Worth Publishers

Printed in the United States of America

First printing 2006

Worth Publishers
41 Madison Avenue
New York, NY 10010
www.worthpublishers.com

To our children

Erika, Curtis, Mariah, and Evan

About the Authors

Kevin T. Leicht is Professor of Sociology and co-director of the Institute for Inequality Studies at the University of Iowa. He received his Ph.D. in Sociology in 1987 from Indiana University, and has had academic appointments at Penn State University and Ohio State University. His research, which examines globalization and economic development and their relationship to the production of social inequality, has appeared in *The American Sociological Review, American Journal of Sociology, Social Forces,* and *The Academy of Management Journal,* and has been funded by the National Science Foundation and the Ford Foundation. He is presently chair of the Organizations, Occupations and Work section of the American Sociological Association and editor of *Research and Social Stratification and Mobility,* a quarterly journal published by Elsevier Science. He formerly edited *The Sociological Quarterly,* the official journal of the Midwest Sociological Society. His books include *Professional Work: A Sociological Approach* (with Mary Fennell), *Analyzing the Labor Force: Concepts, Measures and Trends* (with Clifford Clogg and Scott Eliason), and *Social Change: America and the World* (with Charles Harper). He lives in Iowa City, Iowa with his wife Brenda and his children Erika and Curtis.

Scott T. Fitzgerald is Assistant Professor of Sociology at the University of North Carolina at Charlotte. He received his Ph.D. in Sociology in 2003 from the University of Iowa. His research examines social and economic inequality, religion, and social movements. His research has appeared in *Social Forces, American Behavioral Scientist,* and *Policy Studies Journal,* and has been funded by the National Science Foundation. He lives in Charlotte, North Carolina with his wife Elizabeth and his children Mariah and Evan.

Contents

Foreword

As we move further into the twenty-first century, we confront a seemingly endless array of pressing social issues: urban decay, inequality, ecological threats, rampant consumerism, war, AIDS, inadequate health care, national and personal debt, and many more. Although such problems are regularly dealt with in newspapers, magazines, and trade books, and on radio and television, such popular treatment has severe limitations. By examining these issues systematically through the lens of sociology, we can gain greater insight into them and be better able to deal with them. Each book in the series casts a new and distinctive light on a familiar social issue, while challenging the conventional view, which may obscure as much as it clarifies. Phenomena that seem disparate and unrelated are shown to have many commonalities and to reflect a major, but often unrecognized, trend within the larger society. Or a systematic comparative investigation demonstrates the existence of social causes or consequences that are overlooked by other types of analysis. In uncovering such realities, the books in this series are much more than intellectual exercises; they have powerful practical implications for our lives and for the structure of society.

At another level, this series fills a void in book publishing. There is certainly no shortage of academic titles, but those books tend to be introductory texts for undergraduates or advanced monographs for professional scholars. Missing are broadly accessible, issue-oriented books appropriate for all students (and for general readers). The books in this series occupy that niche somewhere between popular trade books and monographs. Like trade books, they deal with important and interesting social issues, are well written, and are as jargon free as possible. However, they are more rigorous than trade books in meeting academic standards for writing and research. Although they are not textbooks, they often explore topics covered in basic textbooks and therefore are easily integrated into the curriculum of sociology and other disciplines.

Each of the books in the "Contemporary Social Issues" series is a new and distinctive piece of work. I believe that students, serious general readers, and academicians will all find the books to be informative, interesting, thought provoking, and exciting.

—*George Ritzer*

Preface

Before you read our book, we'll give away the ending: The American middle class is in trouble. We did not arrive at this conclusion quickly or easily. It is the culmination of several years of research, teaching, and discussions—always interesting, always informative, and sometimes maddening—with scholars, students, and everyday people throughout the United States. The empirical evidence we've examined largely confirms our nagging suspicion that something is wrong. The economic standing of the American middle class has been slipping during the past thirty years.

As professors, we are amazed that many of our students do not appreciate the current state of the American economy. Bad treatment by employers, low wages, no benefits, and whopping debts seem to be the way of the world, a world that will affect others but not them. Some believe that a college diploma shields people from the ravages of rising inequality. They tend to think that anyone who did not pursue a college degree must be on welfare, and that all labor unions are good for is paying lazy workers to buy another satellite dish. When the types of people that acquire riches in America's new economy are discussed, they naturally feel that they will be among those select few.

so true!

Likewise, those students who have begun to suspect that the early twenty-first century political and social landscape might not provide what it promises are often confused. Concepts like "globalization," "markets," "competitiveness," and "productivity" are so abstract that it is hard for them to see any alternatives to our current economic arrangements, let alone see that there might be human agency behind them. These students see their parents and others consuming as much as ever while shielding themselves from financial crises by using credit.

In this book, we argue that the changes to the middle-class over the past thirty years are a big deal. While the story is complex, our telling of it is not. Through news stories and charts and graphs that are accessible to non-specialists, our book shows that:

1. The middle class has experienced a decline in real purchasing power due to the stagnation of real incomes since the late 1970s.

2. The gaps between the stagnant incomes and consumption aspirations of the middle class are made up through easily available credit—credit that almost magically appeared just as middle-class incomes were stagnating.

3. The use of debt as an instrument for maintaining consumption reminds us of debt peonage and serfdom in agrarian economies. There is a big difference in power and control between an economy in which people consume by borrowing money that they promise to pay back later, and an economy in which people pay for present consumption from steadily rising incomes. The use of debt in place of real income gains has produced the "post-industrial peasant."

4. Very real productivity gains during the late 1980s and 1990s were taken by others instead of redistributed to the workers, fueling a massive increase in wealth and income inequality.

5. The deregulation of consumer credit has led to the socialization of credit risk through the marketing of asset-backed securities. These debt instruments have made credit, and credit cards, more widely available and have fueled the spread of unconventional, sub-prime lending schemes.

6. Many (if not most) of these changes have been politically fueled by the marketing of an illusion—the idea that deregulated markets, federal tax cuts, and the gutting of public infrastructure will benefit everyone, including the middle class. The theoretical evidence supporting this claim was dubious, and the empirical evidence that exactly the opposite has happened is overwhelming. The federal government now exists as a vehicle for redistributing funds to the already prosperous, tax burdens have shifted toward the middle class, and costs for many of the goods that the middle class consumes have been rising. Yet in election after election no candidate seems to point this out in a way that resonates with voters.

7. This gutting of the middle class has led to serious declines in feelings of reciprocity and community, record numbers of personal bankruptcies, and a general "politics of displacement," in which people apparently get angry about virtually anything *except money and wealth*. The contradictions of American politics are now so pervasive that they are self-perpetuating: Unfettered markets destroy jobs, families, and communities; politicians complain about cultural decline while expanding the purview of the unfettered markets that perpetuate it; yet another round of tax cuts and privatizations occurs and still more complaints about cultural decline follow.

Our conclusion does not mince words: Our nation can do better than this. We can reconnect capital accumulation to middle-class prosperity. We can accept that most of us won't really benefit from a capital gains tax cut. We can value families and communities. We can acknowledge that cavernous inequality gaps are corrosive to the political and social order. And we can make better choices as consumers.

Your authors are products of the middle class, the bedrock on which American economic prosperity is based. We believe that future generations of Americans should benefit from the available opportunities promised to this group. American capitalism owes the middle class these opportunities, and the American economy is more internationally competitive, productive, and just when the American middle class is treated fairly.

We welcome any questions or comments you have about this book. Like the economic world we describe, ours is a story that must be constantly updated and rewritten.

Acknowledgments

M any people have contributed to this book in ways both large and small. Erik Gilg has been a tireless advocate and cheerleader for our book, shepherding it through several drafts and patiently requesting changes to make the text more readable and compelling. George Ritzer first approached Kevin Leicht with the idea for this book after watching Leicht's presentation at the American Sociological Association meetings in Anaheim, California in 2002, and Ritzer has diligently stuck with our project and provided commentary on each draft. Ben Reynolds has greatly improved our text with his insightful copyediting. Robert Manning, Stephan Morgan, and Teresa Sullivan provided numerous and detailed comments on a prior draft of our manuscript and we made substantial changes on the basis of their sage advice. Fitzgerald benefited from advice provided by participants in the Department of Sociology and Anthropology research "brown-bag" series at UNCC.

Finally, we would like to thank our families for tolerating the long hours of work it took to bring this book to fruition. It is all too easy for academics in the midst of big projects to become like absentee landlords on feudal estates, only occasionally visiting to commune with family members—an especially tragic outcome in light of the argument in our book!

The Illusion of
Middle-Class Prosperity

I'm in debt up to my eyeballs. Please help me . . .
—a smiling homeowner, riding a lawn tractor in front of a white, four-
bedroom house, in a television commercial for debt consolidation loans

In 1997, the U.S. Council of Economic Advisers painted a relatively rosy
picture of the state of the economy, claiming that a solid foundation had
been laid for future growth, that unemployment was low, and that things
were looking up. President Clinton summed up his economic successes:

> The challenge we faced in January 1993 was to put the economy on a new
> course of fiscal responsibility while continuing to invest in our future. In the
> last four years, the unemployment rate has come down by nearly a third:
> from 7.5 percent to 5.4 percent. The economy has created 11.2 million new
> jobs, and over two-thirds of recent employment growth has been in indus-
> try/occupation groups paying above-median wages. Over the past four years
> inflation has averaged 2.8 percent, lower than in any Administration since
> John F. Kennedy was President. The combination of unemployment and
> inflation is the lowest it has been in three decades. And business investment
> has grown more than 11 percent per year—its fastest pace since the early
> 1960s.
>
> As the economy has grown, the fruits of that growth are being shared
> more equitably among all Americans. Between 1993 and 1995 the poverty
> rate fell from 15.1 percent to 13.8 percent—the largest two-year drop in over
> twenty years. Poverty rates among the elderly and among African-Americans
> are at the lowest level since these data were first collected in 1959.[1]

In September 2004, President Bush's Council of Economic Advisers was
similarly effusive about the recent performance of the American economy:

> In 2004, the U.S. economic recovery blossomed into a full-fledged expansion,
> with strong output growth and steady improvement in the labor market. Real
> gross domestic product (GDP) grew by 4.4 percent in 2004 for the year as a
> whole. About 2.2 million new payroll jobs were created during 2004—the

largest annual gain since 1999. The unemployment rate fell to 5.4 percent by year's end, below the average of each of the past three decades. Inflation remained moderate, especially excluding volatile energy prices. The U.S. economy is on a solid footing for sustained growth in the years to come. This is a marked reversal from the economic situation the Nation faced when President Bush came into office. . . .

Prompt and decisive policy actions helped to counteract the effects of . . . adverse shocks to the economy. Substantial tax relief together with expansionary monetary policy provided stimulus to aggregate demand that softened the recession and helped put the economy on the path to recovery. In addition to providing timely short-term stimulus, the President's pro-growth tax policies have improved incentives for work and capital accumulation, thereby fostering an environment conducive to long-term economic growth.[2]

Yet for many members of the middle class, all was not well—in fact, all has not been well for most of the past thirty to thirty-five years.

The types of people that are having economic difficulties might surprise you. Several recent *New York Times* articles recount hard-luck stories of middle class people forced into dire situations. Jeff Einstein, for example, used to work at a digital media company with 300 employees at a yearly salary of $300,000. After being laid off in 2001 as one of the 21,000 job cuts (41 percent of all jobs) in the computer industry in New York City between 2000 and 2003, he went to work in a Gap outlet on Fifth Avenue, making $10 an hour; it now takes him over two weeks to make what he used to make in a day. Jeff describes the ordeal as a "year-and-a-half long process of dehumanization."[3]

Likewise Lou Casagrande, a Ph.D. chemist and technology consultant in Warren, New Jersey, had trouble paying the mortgage on his house when he lost his job in June 2001. Whereas he and his wife could once afford their $2,700 monthly mortgage payment, they are now delving into his retirement funds and into the money they'd saved to send their three children to college. Lou now works as a substitute teacher in New Jersey and his wife moonlights at Starbucks to make ends meet.

To combat the financial squeeze, middle class Americans are resorting to unorthodox methods of borrowing and brokering their futures, digging even deeper into a pit of debt. Michael Knox, sixty years old and on disability, had run out of ideas for paying his credit card bills when a salesman contacted him and told him he could wipe out his $20,000 debt by taking out a new and bigger mortgage on his house. The broker sent him checks to pay off his creditors, but the payments on the new mortgage devoured 75 percent of his income. He quickly fell behind and the mortgage company moved to repossess his home. Tragically, this seems to have driven Knox, who had suffered for years from clinical depression, to commit suicide.[4]

The crisis affects both young and old members of the middle class. In 2004, James and Doris Stevenson of Espanola, New Mexico, seventy-one and seventy-seven, had twenty-nine years left on a mortgage they'd recently refinanced at a lower interest rate. They purchased the house six years prior by using two-thirds of James's retirement fund for the $35,000 down payment, and the two still work occasional jobs to pay off the remaining $75,000. The debt they have accrued is likely to last until the end of their lives.[5]

When we read the stories of Jeff, Lou, Michael, and the Stevensons, it is easy to write them off as individual accounts of bad luck. We feel bad for them, and we think about friends and family members who are struggling to keep their heads above water. We may even see ourselves in these stories. But we rarely stop to ask ourselves why people who seem to be "playing by the rules" are working so hard just to get by. Why is it that despite all the talk about how prosperous past decades have been, and all our confidence that the United States is a global economic superpower, the middle class doesn't seem to have benefited?

Stories like those recounted above are not simply isolated cases of misfortune, but part of a larger trend. They illustrate important but often overlooked changes that have taken place during the past thirty-five years. Since the early 1970s, the economic and social standing of America's middle class has been changing, often in undesirable ways.

The middle class of the United States—and, to a lesser extent, their Western European counterparts—is the standard by which economic opportunity and prosperity are judged. Large immigrant groups, from eastern and southern Europeans in the late nineteenth and early twentieth centuries to Hispanics and Southeast Asians in the late twentieth and early twenty-first, have come to the United States seeking economic opportunity. While many come hoping to "strike it rich," many more are drawn by the humble idea that the average labors of an average person mean more and are worth more in the United States than anywhere else. Their overwhelming economic perception is that people like them can "get ahead" in America, achieving simple goals: feeding themselves and their families, educating their children so they may lead better lives in this land of opportunity, and experiencing some of the luxuries that make work, saving, and sacrifice worthwhile.

We have written this book to examine critically the economic, political, and social forces shaping America's middle class. We've chosen to focus on the middle class rather than the working class or the poor. Studies that focus solely on the causes of poverty often overlook that many of these same economic and political forces hurt those in the middle. Many people assume that everything is fine for middle-class Americans. But for a growing number of families middle-class prosperity is an illusion rather than a reality.

Our book is not about the hopes, aspirations, dreams, or worldviews of the American middle class;[6] it is about the causes and consequences of their contemporary economic circumstances. Others have talked about social policy and the middle class,[7] the political orientations of the middle class,[8] and concerns about the changing communities of the middle class.[9] What we offer is a broad look at the changes in the economic standing of the middle class, and the social and political consequences of those changes over the past thirty-five years.

Our basic argument is complex, but our conclusion is not: *Middle-class prosperity in the late twentieth and early twenty-first centuries is an illusion.* When we look at the middle class below the surface, aggregate measures of economic vitality hide an ever-widening group of Americans who are struggling just to remain solvent. Worse still, and in contrast to the post-war economic boom of the 1950s and 1960s, there appears to be no institutionalized method for interpreting change, nor is there a new, coherent set of "how-to" rules that describe how to get ahead. Almost all of the conventional rules no longer apply, and prosperity seems illusory or due to luck and being at the right place at the right time.

The rules of the middle-class game used to be simple and stable—in fact, the safeness of these rules helped *define* the American middle class. These rules were passed down from generation to generation and reinforced by popular culture. With the advent of television, families across the nation could see the American Dream played out nightly, with shows like *Ozzie and Harriet* and *Leave It to Beaver* exemplifying middle class family life. To give us some standards for evaluating the changes taking place, let's review the rules:[10]

1. *Find a good, steady job and stick with it.*
2. *Be loyal and hardworking, and your company will reward you with pay raises and promotions.* You can base your current economic decisions regarding debt and consumption on the promise of future compensation.
3. *Get married and settle down.* You will reap the rewards from peace of mind and investment in a community of like-minded fellow travelers.
4. *Buy a house as soon as you can.* Stay in it. Pay off the mortgage before you retire. Your house is your major financial asset and a sign that you are a responsible citizen who has "made it."
5. *Save money for a rainy day.* One day, the furnace will fail or your teenage daughter will wreck the family car, and you will need to

Box 1.1

Who Is Middle-Class?

The term "middle class" has many definitions. For our purposes, when we speak of the middle class we are referring to Americans who annually earn between $35,000 and $75,000, most of which comes from salaries and wages; who work as upper- or lower-level managers, professionals, or small business owners; and who graduated from, or at least attended, a four-year college. The median family income in the United States—the income that separates the top 50 percent of income earners from the bottom 50 percent—was $43,527 in 2003 dollars (see Chapter 2).[11]

We should also define some terms that reflect different dimensions of economic well-being. *Earnings* usually refers to income derived from working. *Income* refers to all forms of monetary compensation including earnings, rents, dividends, and gifts. Policy analysts occasionally speak of *unearned income*, generally referring to income from investments and other assets rather than earnings from a job. *Wealth* refers to economic assets that themselves generate income—stocks, mutual funds, and rental properties, for example—and usually to economic assets that can be sold and turned into income through stock sales, sales of homes, and the like.

crack that nest egg. If you are lucky enough to avoid such calamities, you can retire off this money and use it to do the things you couldn't while you were working. Besides, no one will ever loan you money unless you prove you can save it.

6. *Look forward to retiring in your sixties.* Your company will provide a pension that will fund this period of well-deserved rest, relaxation, and recreation.

7. *Be proud of your hard work, and know that it will be rewarded.* All types of work possess an inherent dignity that is worthy of respect. If your job lacks excitement, it still provides a decent living, and your sacrifices will be rewarded in the long run.

8. *Provide your children with a good education.* Education is vital for your children to get ahead in our society. If your kids can't get scholarships to an Ivy League school, they can still attend the local state university and receive a good education for a modest cost. Between the money you've saved for them, the summer jobs they work, and a financial contribution from your current earnings, your kids can pay for a good college education and good, steady jobs will follow for them.

For reasons that will become clearer, *none* of these rules applies in the globalized, late-modern economic world of the current American middle class. The move from an economy centered on manufacturing to one centered on services, the globalization of markets, and the information age have altered the economic realities of middle-class Americans. In this new post-industrial economic world there has been a shift "from a social world characterized by long-term, stable relationships to one characterized by short-term, temporary relationships."[12] The uncertainty surrounding short-term employment relationships leaves many middle class professionals filled with anxiety. Many members of the middle class intuitively sense this change, but can't put a finger on "what went wrong."[13]

Just ask Silvia Vides, a housekeeper at the Universal City Sheridan Hotel in Los Angeles, who earns $11 an hour:

> "Sometimes I don't know how I pay the bills and food and rent." She has cut back on all nonessential expenditures and she is four months behind on payments on $4,000 in credit-card debt. . . . Ms. Vides ticks off the items of a rising cost of living. She pays $850 a month for a one-bedroom apartment in Panorama City, $25 more a month than last year. The cost of a bus pass rose $10, to $45 a month. The electricity bill is much higher and food costs more. "I've got to do miracles with my salary," she said.

At the same time, the upper echelons of consumer spending—places like Saks Fifth Avenue, Neiman Marcus, and Nordstrom's—report gangbuster business. "I'm surprised by how well we've sold high-priced fashion at this stage," says Pete Nordstrom, President of Nordstrom's full line stores.[14]

The issues faced by Silvia are not the same issues faced by the patrons of Neiman Marcus and Nordstrom's, yet they are inextricably linked by economic and political forces. The affluence of some is assumed to reflect the affluence, or at least comfort, of the many—i.e., the hardworking middle class. Critically discussing these realities is made more difficult by the half-measures and pseudo-solutions that pass for political debate on the status of the middle class.

The empirical trends and practical economic lessons of the past thirty-five years reveal painful economic realities. The general trends are not that complicated, and many average Americans who don't make a living thinking about these things could articulate the lessons drawn from these experiences. These lessons form the "new rules" of middle-class life:

1. *Good, steady jobs that last longer than a year or two are hard to come by.* Many jobs that appear to have long-term potential turn out not to.

Box 1.2

Stock Options and 401(k) Plans

Stock options represent the option to purchase stock at a given price sometime in the future. A stock option gives the owner the right to purchase company stock at a given price by a certain expiration date. The price of the option is usually set at the market price of the stock at the time the option is granted. If the company stock increases in value, the option becomes more valuable. If the stock decreases below the given option price or stays the same, the option becomes worthless.

A _401(k) plan_ is a tax-deferred retirement fund set up by employers or employees to accept employee contributions (up to 25% of eligible payroll). The maximum allowable contribution is 100% of employee compensation, not to exceed $42,000 (the maximum federal tax-deferred allowance). Employer contributions may be vested, requiring specific years of service or other conditions to withdraw benefits.

2. _Companies do not reward employee loyalty, they reward customer loyalty._
   There is no connection between working now and later rewards. At most, if you're lucky, your company will reward you with company stock or stock options, but the future value of these is beyond your control; moreover, vesting rules make it difficult to cash in at critical times (as top executives invariably do when they anticipate changes in the company fortunes). If you work your hardest, you will be rewarded as if you have some control over the company's fate and when and where you can sell your stock, when in fact you probably don't.

3. _Since it is difficult to find a steady job, it is hard to obtain the economic security on which marriage and "settling down" are based._
   Worse than that, two full-time workers' incomes are needed to support a lifestyle that one income used to buy.[15] Two jobs per family are necessary because at any time one of you might be out of a job. This economic uncertainty, the lack of coherent rules for what one should be doing, and larger sets of cultural changes drastically lessen the prospect that your marriage will last. And economic complications stemming from rising divorce rates complicate your economic prospects still further. Your ability to put down roots in a community and stay there is marred by economic instability affecting you and your neighbors.

You spend so much time trying to keep your head above water that you can accomplish nothing else.

4. *Buying a house is increasingly difficult.* Despite historically low interest rates, buying and keeping a house is virtually impossible in an economy in which jobs don't last. Paying off a mortgage becomes an elusive dream. Increasingly, you borrow against the equity in the house to afford the consumer items that are the markers of a middle-class life. Such borrowing acts as a buffer when you're between jobs.

5. *Saving for a rainy day—or any day, for that matter—is impossible.* Your employer may contribute to a retirement package for you, but you won't work for them long enough to accrue any money in the package. Also, the package is only as good as the long-term viability of the company—a rather shaky prospect. So much of your money goes to meet current expenses that no money goes into a savings account or mutual fund for the future. You live from one paycheck to the next, a few missed paydays from bankruptcy.

6. *You may never be able to retire.* Whether you are or not, coping with medical expenses as you age will be your major preoccupation. Medicare doesn't cover very much, and companies can't afford to provide healthcare benefits for their retirees. Chances are you will have so many jobs over the next few decades that it will be impossible to tell which company's retirement healthcare plan you are on anyway. Supplemental insurance is expensive and eats up a substantial portion of the limited retirement benefits you receive.

7. *People who work hard and play by the rules are viewed as "suckers."* Modern television, movies, and music glorify glamorous lifestyles and unconventional, "get rich quick" ways of making money. Politicians ignore you or treat you as a "cow to milk";[16] big investors see you as a consumer who can be duped into borrowing money on easy credit to maintain the appearances of a middle-class lifestyle.

In fact, this lifestyle itself is the subject of debunking by cultural elites. Those who labor diligently at what they do find employers who pay too little, who offload most of their risks and expenses onto employees and communities, who demand too many working hours, who don't follow or openly violate most labor laws, and who vote for political parties that glorify images of 1950s "traditional" lifestyles—lifestyles that this very economic system makes it all but impossible to emulate.[17] Employers move production to places where costs are low, offloading expenses for public infrastructure onto their employees, who must pay higher taxes, user fees, and private fees from their limited, non-growing, non-guaranteed

Box 1.3

Medicare and Medicaid

Medicare is the federal health insurance program for people sixty-five years of age or older, certain younger people with disabilities, and people with End-Stage Renal Disease (sometimes called ESRD—chronic kidney failure treated with dialysis or transplant).

Medicaid is a joint federal and state program that helps with medical costs for some people with low incomes and limited resources. Medicaid programs vary from state to state, but most healthcare costs are covered if you qualify for both Medicare and Medicaid.

Supplemental insurance policies are also known as *Medigap plans*. Most health insurance policies do not cover all expenses, and this is especially true of Medicare. A Medicare supplemental insurance policy is designed to pay for certain expenses not covered by Medicare.

---

paychecks. These same economic elites attempt to convince their employees that taxes are spent on "undeserving, lazy people" and that still lower taxes will benefit them. Yet tax cut after tax cut, the benefits never come.

8. *Your child's college education is paid for by student loans.* Your contribution involves moral support or money from your meager savings. The state you pay taxes to continues to cut support for the state institution your child attends while giving tax breaks to footloose investors. Colleges make up for the cuts to public funding by charging higher tuition and pumping alumni for contributions and research grants. Because the earnings of those who don't go to college have fallen through the floor, everyone wants to go to college whether they belong there or not, putting added strain on the higher education system. The degree your child earns might prevent downward mobility, but it doesn't provide upward mobility.

Some analysts don't see a problem with this almost complete reversal of the traditional rules; social change is, after all, social change. The American middle class has adapted to changes in the past—suburbia, automobiles, urbanization, and the sexual revolution, among others—and they will surely adapt to the new economy. Others have reasons to doubt such sanguine pronouncements, and they point to a variety of factors that are making middle-class life in the United States more precarious.

Globalization and the rise of neoliberalism as a political ideology have a great deal to do with changes in middle-class life.[18] *Neoliberalism* refers to the promotion of free markets, reduced trade barriers, and global movement of capital and labor to different parts of the world. This movement has produced a global "race to the bottom" in which investors search the world for the most favorable investment environments, disinvesting in operations and service delivery in first-world locations such as the United States, Western Europe, and Japan and moving operations to locations in the less developed world, where labor costs are lower and regulations are less burdensome. Neoliberalism incorporates a search for quick profits and the ability to deliver these in the short time frames that investors demand.

The American welfare state is also the least generous in the world. In place of extensive income assistance, universal healthcare, and a universal pension system, Americans face a byzantine system of privatized health insurance, uncertain unemployment benefits, and a tottering social security system that doesn't provide much retirement security. Private pension systems, where they exist, are becoming less generous and are more dependent on the performance of specific companies at specific times. None of this is the lot of the average member of the middle class in any other industrialized nation in the world.[19]

Unions helped define the labor market during the middle-class heydays of the 1950s and 1960s, negotiating contracts with employers in industries that were largely protected from global competition. The wages and benefits negotiated in unionized firms tended to set a pattern for wages and benefits in entire industries and economic sectors. The labor movement could negotiate these contracts because corporations had massive capital investments in specific places that could not be moved: manufacturing was labor-intensive, and technology and the organization of work depended on a stable, competent, happy workforce.[20]

Technology and the information age have altered the social organization of work. These changes include *flatter organizational hierarchies,* as new information technologies eliminate the need for middle layers of management; the growing use of *temporary workers* employed on an as-needed basis to perform specific jobs for the duration of single projects; the extensive use of *subcontracting and outsourcing* to external firms and/or suppliers for products and services once provided by permanent employees; *massive downsizing of the permanent* workforce as organizations need fewer management and support people and replace skilled workers with computer-skilled operators or unskilled machine tenders; a *post-unionized bargaining environment* in which unions have either no place or reduced power and no structural ability to gain a foothold for bargaining with employers; and *virtual organizations* that exist as a web of technologically driven interactions rather than as a distinctive, physical worksite concretely located in a specific place.[21]

The pace of this change accelerated in the 1990s, directly affecting the managerial and professional jobs the white-collar middle class relies on. No longer do layoffs, firings, job instability, ever-shifting earnings, and difficulty paying bills affect only blue-collar workers; these prospects have now "trickled up" into the middle class, where bedrock economic stability was once the norm.[22] As job instability grew, a new variable was added to the middle-class economic equation: easily available consumer credit. Credit has replaced earnings as the major source of middle class purchasing power.

Ironically, this condition has occurred in previous stages of Western civilization: the American middle class is becoming a class of post-industrial peasants. The image of "peasants" in most modern minds conjures pictures of poverty, servitude, abuse by landowners, debt, and injustice. Peasants in most agrarian societies did most of the work, constituted a majority of the population, fought most of the wars, provided most of the labor that landlords (and the church) lived on, paid most of the taxes, and rarely got anything for their trouble other than food (if the harvest was good), shelter (usually a mud or thatched hut), and early death. In some agrarian societies, peasants couldn't marry unless landlords gave their permission, and in most agrarian societies peasants were tied to the land through arrangements that varied from sharecropping to serfdom. The economic elites of agrarian societies, landlords and feudal aristocrats constructed elaborate ideologies of inherent superiority, *noblesse oblige*, and divinely-sanctioned rights to justify their positions and their abuses of the peasantry. It isn't clear if peasants accepted these ideologies or even knew of them.[23] Elite domination of the system was so total, and the locations of the peasants so fragmented, that rebellions against injustice and abuse rarely materialized. If they did, they were quickly and easily crushed.

The American middle class faces stark choices not unlike those faced by the peasants of the agrarian societies of old. In this book, we argue that a wide variety of factors have converged to produce this state of affairs and that the situation is worse than it appears on the surface. Stagnant incomes, rising taxes, the pocketing of productivity gains by the corporate elite, a surplus of available credit, globalization, privatization, and labor market changes have altered what it means to be part of the American middle class. This combination of factors has produced a "post-industrial peasant"—someone who is so in debt that those to whom they owe money (and the employers and economic elites who provide the investment and consumption capital for the system) control them. These elites are the same people who have absconded with productivity gains and paid themselves inflated salaries, benefits, and stock options.

12

Box 1.4

Peasants, Sharecropping, and Serfdom

Peasants are agricultural workers who owe their landlord payments in crops and labor in exchange for access to land and the right to grow crops to feed their families. Historically, peasants could not legally leave the land they cultivated. Though peasants are usually regarded as remnants of our feudal past, there are still many third-world regions that employ exactly this method of employment.

Serfdom refers to the tying of peasants to the specific lands owned and administered by landlords. Serfs were usually required to provide military service and labor on the landlord's property in exchange for land grants.

Sharecropping refers to the practice of leasing land to tenant farmers in exchange for a share of the crops the farmers produce.

To outline our argument: Chapter 2, "The Middle-Class Patient in the Economic Doctor's Office," provides case studies from the contemporary middle class, using composite scenarios created from the economic trends of the past thirty-five years. This chapter also reviews the relationship between elites and workers in pre-industrial economic systems, not as a comprehensive overview of the history of agrarian class relationships but as an analogy for interpreting the data that follows. Chapter 3, "The Income/Credit Squeeze," compares the major macroeconomic theories that have shaped public policy in the twentieth and twenty-first centuries, and documents the stagnation of incomes for the middle class and the rise in available credit that occurred at precisely the same time.

Chapter 4, "Robbing the Productivity Train," examines trends in productivity in the 1980s and 1990s: worker productivity rose and earnings did not. Rather than being distributed to the average worker, revenues financed executive compensation packages and investments in financial markets by the wealthy. We provide statistical simulations that illustrate that the compensation available through productivity gains, if it were paid in wages, would substantially offset the credit advanced to the middle class. To put it bluntly, the American middle class was loaned money they could have received as earnings.

Chapter 5, "Where Did All That Credit Come From?," documents the rise of easily available consumer credit and the ways we use it. Deregulation of the banking industry and a shift in populations targeted by the banking and credit industry drastically changed the availability and implications of consumer credit in the 1980s and 1990s. The widespread availability of personal credit cards (often at exorbitant interest rates), home equity loans, "no money down" car loans, and leases have changed the landscape of middle-class finances. Investors and lenders have profited while the middle class has become trapped in a "work and spend" cycle that shows little hope of abating.

Chapter 6, "From Washington to Wall Street: Marketing the Illusion," argues that it isn't merely advertisers for shampoos, cars, and clothes that peddle a make-believe culture of glamour, riches, and prosperity. The economic struggles of the middle class have been effectively hidden from the public agenda through the promulgation of neoconservative ideology and supply-side economics. While politicians and lobbyists contend that these policies will benefit everyone, the "supply-side miracle" has never materialized for the middle class. Since the 1980s, a combination of tax cuts for the wealthy, deregulation, corporate tax avoidance, and an overall shifting of tax burdens onto earned income and away from unearned income have hurt the economic standing of middle-class Americans. During the same period, the costs of maintaining a middle-class lifestyle have continued to rise, and owning a home, buying a car, paying for college, obtaining healthcare, affording daycare, and retiring have become nearly impossible.

Chapter 7, "The Consequences of Post-Industrial Peonage," explores the consequences of the cycle of stagnant wages, rising debts, high taxes, and political disenfranchisement. The unemployment rate dipped to record lows in the 1990s, but wages barely moved. The debts acquired as a result of stagnant wages mean that no one is available to fight the current system of work, spending, and debt, so employers continue to pocket productivity gains and workers work harder and harder just to remain financially solvent. We identify four important consequences of post-industrial peonage that are corroding the social order: the growing number of personal bankruptcies filed by middle-class Americans, the cultural contradictions of American politics, the fraying of community ties, and the hardening of public discourse and development of a general politics of displacement.

Chapter 8, "What Can We Do?," concludes the book by proposing a "Manifesto for the Middle Class," offering a multilevel recommendation to encourage active individual and collective responses to the development of the post-industrial peasant.

A cursory flip through these pages reveals a number of charts and figures. For readers who generally view charts and figures with fear and loathing, anger, or calloused indifference, we offer the following entreaty. We have done our best to compile a wide range of data from major governmental and academic sources in order to assess important trends during the past thirty-five years. These data provide the empirical evidence

14

Box 1.5

IBM: Cutting Here, but Hiring Over There[24]

IBM Corporation is proceeding with layoffs of 13,000 workers in Europe and the United States while increasing its payroll in India this year by more than 14,000 workers. These numbers are telling evidence of the continued outsourcing of skilled jobs to low-wage countries like India, and IBM as the world's largest technology company is a leader of this trend.

Critics of this trend point out that IBM is a leading example of a corporate strategy of shopping the globe for the cheapest labor in the obsession to find quick profits, to the detriment of wages, benefits and job security in the United States and other developed countries.

Robert W. Moffat, an IBM senior vice president, states that the buildup is due to the surging demand for technology services in the thriving Indian economy and the opportunity for Indian software engineers to work on projects around the world. Lower trade barriers and cheaper telecommunications and computing allow a distant workforce to work on technology projects. Mr. Moffat said that IBM is making the shift from a classical multinational corporation to a truly worldwide company whose work can be divided and parceled out to the most efficient corporations. Mr. Moffat claims that cost is part of the calculation but that outsourcing is mostly about finding skills. "You are no longer competing just with the guy down the street, but also with people around the world," he said.

Most economic studies suggest that such outsourcing has no effect on American jobs as a whole. But changes can be particularly harsh for workers in the west when they are competing against well-educated workers in low-wage countries like India. An experienced software programmer in the United States earnings $75,000 a year can be replaced by an Indian programmer who earns around $15,000.

Joseph Stiglitz, a Nobel-Prize–winning economist and professor at Columbia University and former chief economist for the World Bank, says that job numbers alone understate the potential problem, "What worries me is that it could have an enormous effect on wages, and that could have a wrenching impact on society."

The fact that globalization anxiety about jobs hasn't extended to the executive ranks has stirred resentment among workers. "Maybe shareholders should look offshore for competitive executives who would collect less pay and fewer benefits," said Lee Conrad, national coordinator for Alliance@IBM, a union affiliated group with 6,500 dues-paying members at IBM. "In all this talk about global competitiveness, the burden all falls on the workers."

for, among other things, our rather bold claim that the American middle class are becoming post-industrial peasants. We provide all the charts and figures because they are simple, yet accurate, visual representation of these data and taken together help paint a mental picture of the plight of the

American middle class. Our book can be navigated without paying attention to the charts and graphs, and the basic points will still make sense.

For those who think we are biased, you have our evidence, most of it publicly available and plainly presented, that you can examine to contribute to the debate. No doubt there are sources who can provide individual accounts and stories of wealth, prosperity, and upward mobility during these last few decades, just as we have found individual accounts of downward mobility, rising debt, job instability, and economic despair. But this isn't a debate about who became individually wealthy and individually poor; it's about the continuing economic health of a group of people who were once the bedrock of a very prosperous developed economy.

One final note: It might be tempting to believe that the source of the crisis we discuss is a conspiracy hatched in a smoke-filled conference room on Wall Street, but we are not implying that a particular small group of people are completely responsible for the trends we discuss in this book. No particular set of elites sat down in the late 1970s and said, "By the year 2000, average Americans should be earning less than they are now, they should be working longer hours, and they should be mired in consumer credit that keeps them tied to the exploitative work system we've set up for them. It's a bonanza!" Some of these outcomes are clearly the product of deliberate political and economic decisions by people in power, but others are not.

While there is no conspiracy, there has been change. The economic standing of the American middle class is increasingly precarious. Jeff, Lou, Michael, the Stevensons, and others like them are clearly looking for answers. In these pages, we attempt to provide some.

Sociological imagination?

The Middle-Class Patient in the Economic Doctor's Office

I'm a forty-five-year-old man . . . I should be independent enough to pay my own rent. I feel so grateful to my dad, who literally saved me from becoming homeless . . .

—Steven Fields, a former systems administrator for
Electronic Data Systems in Dallas[1]

America prides itself on the development of a solid middle class; indeed, the American Dream is almost synonymous with middle-class life. But what does it mean to say that someone is middle class? What are the characteristics of a member of the middle class?

In this chapter, we offer a definition of the middle class that focuses on the socioeconomic status of individuals. We also explain why we must examine economic trends and conditions, financial institutions, corporate practices, and public policy to understand the plight of the middle class. We will introduce prototypical families whose stories will reappear in subsequent chapters, putting faces to the larger economic and political story being told. We then provide a brief introduction to agrarian, feudal, and sharecropping economies and the systems of control that marked the lives of workers within these systems. This discussion provides the backdrop for the central analogy of the book: members of the American middle class are becoming post-industrial peasants.

Defining the Middle Class

Most Americans identify themselves as members of the middle class, sometimes qualifying the designation by adding "upper middle" or "lower middle." Nationally representative survey data from the General Social Survey show that "at no time between 1972 and 1994 did more than 10 percent of the American population classify themselves as *either* lower class or upper class."[2] But is it true that the overwhelming majority of Americans are middle class? No

That is difficult to answer because the term "middle class" means different things to different people. For some, you are middle-class if you make more than minimum wage but less than Bill Gates, if you are an office manager rather than a cashier at McDonald's, or if you have graduated from college rather than dropped out of high school. There is also academic and popular disagreement on how to best identify the middle class. Most classification systems rely on three criteria—income and wealth, occupational prestige, and educational level—that sociologists label *socioeconomic status* (SES). In this book, we primarily identify the middle class based on SES characteristics, although we consider cultural factors as well. In general when we speak of the middle class we are referring to those Americans who earn incomes approximately between $35,000 and $75,000 annually;[3] who work as upper- and lower-level managers, professionals, and small business owners; who graduated from or at least attended a four-year college; and whose primary source of wealth is home ownership.

Another sociological approach to identifying classes focuses on culture, examining consumption patterns—i.e., how people spend their money and what they buy—and the beliefs people hold. Thorstein Veblen's *A Theory of the Leisure Class* and Pierre Bourdieu's *Distinction* represent important works in this tradition. From this perspective the American middle class might be those families owning a house in the suburbs, driving an SUV, and believing in the importance of a college education.

Karl Marx (1818–1883), the father of modern class conflict theory, had surprisingly little to say about class. His major contribution to class theory is the claim that *analytically* there are two classes—the owners of the means of production and the non-owners—while *descriptively* there are many classes—for example, lumpenproletariat, petite bourgeoisie, intelligentsia, capitalists, and workers. Max Weber (1864–1920) shared Marx's focus on the importance of ownership and non-ownership, but also claimed that it is important to differentiate the types of productive assets possessed by owners, and the types of labor performed by workers forced to sell their labor. These differences play a key role in determining the market activity of these groups, activity that in turn affects the opportunities and lifestyles of the groups.

More recently neo-Weberians, such as sociologist Anthony Giddens (b. 1938), focus on how economic systems, institutions, individuals, and the state form a nexus of market capacities and life chances. Aage B. Sørensen describes the unearned portion of this nexus—the part that does not result from individual effort—as "rent."[4] Rents accrue to people based on who they know (but not *what* they know), where they live, or because of their social background (SES or race, for example).[5] Charles Tilly perceptively describes how economic systems produce durable inequalities by allowing dominant groups to hoard opportunities for more income and prestige.[6] To understand the realities of the middle class, we must examine the configuration of these forces, looking at economic trends and conditions, financial institutions, corporate practices, and public policy.

To illustrate the plight of the middle class, let's visit two families. Unlike the subjects of the cases in Chapter 1, our protagonists here are characters, constructed from aggregate trends in our data on the middle class. These families represent the current dilemmas of middle class social and economic life, but are not in any sense "sob stories." They have their own assets, liabilities, hopes, and dreams. They strive to "do the right thing," to engage their fellow travelers with honesty and compassion, and to play the economic game by the rules as they understand them. If we asked them to describe their lives to us, they would express gratitude for the opportunities they've had and the luck that has come their way. Yet something is wrong, as we will see.

David and Monica Tread Water

David (thirty-six years old) and Monica (thirty-four) have been married for ten years. They have one two-year-old child, Jennifer, and live in suburban Tampa, Florida, having recently relocated from Minneapolis, Minnesota. David's company, Telemwhat Inc., relocated to Florida after a corporate merger because its corporate managers believed that the business climate was better in Florida than in Minnesota, and because the taxes in Florida are significantly lower. David received relocation assistance from the company, and sold their two-bedroom house in Minneapolis and purchased another in Tampa without great difficulty.

Because David agreed to relocate, he got to keep his job as an office manager, which pays $38,800 a year. Monica quit her job as a secretary in Minneapolis and took a similar job in Tampa for far less pay and no fringe benefits, "starting over" as the subordinate member of a small secretarial staff.

David has put in long hours in the hopes of getting ahead at Telemwhat. His job is considered steady by early twenty-first century standards. He's received one raise, a 3 percent hike three years ago, in the five years he has worked for Telemwhat, and has received several cash bonuses when the company's quarterly profit numbers have looked good. He has purchased shares in the company's stock options plan with these bonuses, but the vesting period on employee shares is five years and the stock price fluctuates wildly. David says he "tries not to think about" which direction his shares are going or what they're worth. *Brutal*

David works about sixty hours a week, and Monica forty. Because of their busy schedules, Jennifer spends about forty hours each week in day-care, which costs the family $800 each month. Even with the flexible benefits package Telemwhat provides, David and Monica's daycare expenses eat up most of what Monica earns, less a few hundred dollars. Because they work at opposite ends of the city, David and Monica have purchased a second car (with no money down) that they make payments on each month, in addition to the minivan that they have two years left to pay off.

In addition to car payments, daycare, and mortgage payments, David and Monica have a substantial amount, over $10,000, of credit card debt. Each month they make minimum payments on their cards, which have interest rates of around thirteen percent, but these payments barely pay the interest. The mortgage on their house, purchased with a 5 percent down payment from the sale of their Minneapolis home, is large, and their payments stretch for a long time into the future before David and Monica will accumulate substantial home equity.

After making these monthly payments, David and Monica don't have much money left to do anything else. This void is filled by further credit card spending. The real estate taxes on their house are lower than they were in Minneapolis, but David wonders where his tax money goes. The ambulance, fire, and police service for his neighborhood is spotty; the highways are overcrowded, there seems to be no rhyme or reason to the development patterns of the city; almost no one he talks to sends their children to the public schools that his tax money pays for, and he pays a private company each month to pick up their trash and dispose of it. David dreams of retirement but can't foresee any way to finance it. Both David and Monica would like to go back to school so they can find better jobs, but they cannot afford to risk their steady incomes and there is barely any time in their daily schedules for anything beyond work and the immediate needs of the family.

Bill and Sheryl Need a Snorkel

Bill and Sheryl, both forty-five years old, have been married for twenty years. They are the proud parents of two children, Dillon (twenty) and Clara (fifteen), one in college and another college-bound. Bill has worked most of his life as a computer software engineer, and Sheryl is a social worker for the county they live in near Cleveland, Ohio. They have a nice four-bedroom house in the suburbs. They have paid off two cars that look a little shabby and have a lot of miles, but Bill manages to keep them running with the help of local mechanics. Bill and Sheryl are active in their local Catholic parish and enjoy having roots in their community. By most middle-class standards, Bill and Sheryl seem to have it made.

However, Bill and Sheryl's economic life is a shambles. Bill was laid off from the large engineering firm he worked for ten years ago—his job was eliminated in a leveraged buyout of corporate management by a takeover specialist—and since then he has not found steady employment, in spite of his considerable skills. He works on different consulting jobs around the area and maintains some semblance of an income this way, but his string of temporary positions provides no fringe benefits and the hours of work are not steady enough to provide a full-time wage approaching the $55,000 a year he used to earn. Worse, Bill gets the impression that the consulting business is reserved for young, eager workers with relatively new and portable skills. His ten years of work experience with his former engineering firm seem to be more a liability than an asset.

Sheryl's job as a social worker for the county at least provides benefits, including health insurance, making Bill and Sheryl relatively fortunate compared to the 40 percent of U.S. workers who have no employer-provided healthcare coverage. However, her state government has declared war on the poor, and the federal government's welfare reform provisions and state and local budget cuts make it harder to do her job. She hasn't received a pay raise in five years and there are signs that her entire unit might be eliminated as the county strives to consolidate its services and do more with less. Still, when Sheryl compares their lives to those of her clients, she thinks they are pretty lucky; "At least we're not sleeping under bridges," she tells the kids.

Bill and Sheryl have been cannibalizing their economic assets to keep their middle-class lifestyle afloat. Bill cashed in his retirement plan from his former employer to provide cash to live on while he was looking for work. They started charging more on their credit cards, including groceries when the local supermarket started taking credit cards, and they now owe $15,000. They took out a second mortgage on their house when their son started college, and they've had a "home equity" line of credit for the past ten years. Between the home equity line of credit and their son's tuition bills at Ohio State, Bill and Sheryl have no equity in their house to call their own, even though they've lived there for fifteen years.

Our Diagnosis

The people in these stories are just folks like us. Yet David, Monica, Bill, and Sheryl are part of a much larger group in the United

States: the declining middle class. The combination of job losses, sketchy and unstable opportunities, consumer perceptions, corporate restructuring, and easy credit have produced an American middle class that is an economic disaster. Bills are paid and appearances maintained by squandering savings and cannibalizing the future to maintain the present. The American economy moves toward a globalized, knowledge-intensive future, while the American people live in a cultural and consumption fantasyland built on the norms, values, and advice of a prior era. Old cultural ideologies die hard, especially when society is bombarded with media and political messages that suggest things are getting better and that you really can own the car or home of your dreams for no money down.

David, Monica, Bill, and Sheryl are trapped in a cycle of work, layoffs, debt, payments, and taxes that will never end. Regardless of the amount they earn at any one moment—and at times their earnings look pretty good—the instability of their job prospects contrasts sharply with their steadily mounting bills, diminished futures, rising debts, and middle-class dreams.

Multiply these stories by several million and you discover a large segment of the U.S. economy, the portion that stimulates aggregate demand and whose rising productivity once stimulated economic growth, that is so desperate just to pay their bills and keep their heads above water that they will work long, nonstandard hours with poor pay, no fringe benefits, and no prospects for advancement. The reasons for this predicament involve globalization and the ability to move productive investment to different parts of the world electronically; the spread of neoliberal economic ideologies that promote free trade, low trade barriers, and reduced government regulations; the inability of the U.S. social safety net to provide insurance against the insecurities produced by the changing labor market and organization of work; national tax and spending policies that favor investors and those that are already well off at the expense of wage earners; and declining protections provided by a labor movement that has seen its ranks decline from 32 percent of the nonagricultural workforce in the 1960s to less than 9 percent today.[7] These circumstances remind us of *agrarian* economies.

Our Feudal Past

Agrarian economies, you say? Subsistence farmers? Homesteaders? *Little House on the Prairie*? John Wayne in *Paint Your Wagon*? No. Most of our American ancestors worked in an *agricultural* economy, not an agrarian economy (though there were some similarities between the two for some particularly unfortunate people). Instead, we're thinking of the agrarian

Box 2.1

Agrarian Economies

In an *agrarian economy*, which relies on fully developed agriculture with plows, draft animals, and fertilizers, most workers are peasants or other dependent cultivators who are politically and economically dependent on landowners.

In *feudalism* or *feudal economy*, the system of economic life that prevailed in the West from the end of the Roman Empire until the development of modern capitalism, landlords cultivated land with peasant labor. In feudal economies, a *fief* was a grant of land in return for military service or mutual protection. *Vassals* were groups of landlords tied together through personal ties or oaths of loyalty. The landlord's land that was dedicated exclusively to his use rather than granted to vassals was his *demesne* (pronounced "de-main").

Freeholding generally refers to the independent cultivation of land by farmers who claim ownership to the land they cultivate.

Indentured servitude is a type of slave labor in which laborers work without pay under contract for a specified period of time in exchange for food, accommodation, or free passage to a new country.

In the feudal or medieval social system, *corporate groups* or *estates* were groups of people, such as landowners, priests, merchants, and peasants, that shared the same position. Membership in a corporate group determined one's social rights and obligations.

Proletarianization, a term first proposed by the German social philosopher Karl Marx, describes the conversion of the multitude of personal arrangements that tied landlords, vassals, and serfs together into a system of employer/employee relationships in which workers are paid in wages.

economies of the Middle Ages, the social order romanticized in the Robin Hood legends and stories of King Arthur and the Knights of the Round Table. Our focus is far from these fanciful tales. Agrarian societies of the Middle Ages produced a distinctive set of relationships between the economically dominant classes and those that worked for them.

Most agrarian societies were built on two economic and political classes—a class of landlords that controlled the rights and access to vast tracts of land, and a class of peasants who worked the land in exchange for protection and control over small plots used to support their families. Other distinctive economic and political positions, such as priests, merchants, and craftsmen, took part in these societies, but the exchanges between landlords and peasants drove the economy, feeding the masses in good times, providing soldiers in wartime, and distributing rations in bad times.

Because agrarian economies were land-rich and money-poor, the exchange between landlords and peasants involved land and labor services. Landlords granted tracts of land to peasants, as individuals, families, or villages, in exchange for a substantial portion of the crop the peasants raised and labor services including harvesting and thrashing the landlord's grain, tending to his livestock, maintaining his manor house, and serving as conscript in his militia.

Under slightly better circumstances, the peasant was a freeholder who paid taxes in the form of crop shares to local elites. This situation provided some leverage for the peasant against potential abuses, but the basic economics of the exchange was not affected and land (or more) could be confiscated from peasants who refused to pay.

The agrarian system provided a measure of security in an uncertain world. The peasant received some protection from roving bands of thieves and marauding invaders, limited communal insurance in the event of crop failures and famine (frequent occurrences), and access to land to feed himself and his family. The landlord received the proceeds from his vast tracts of land without having to work it himself, assurance that his property would be maintained, and access to surplus grain taxes, which he could use as barter for luxury goods produced in towns by craftsmen or brought from distant lands by merchants. He was also assured a regular army of conscripts to defend his property against intruders and to use in brokered alliances with other landlords.

While the peasant life has been idealized in theater and art, theirs was a hard lot:

> On certain days, the tenant brings the lord's steward perhaps a few small silver coins or, more often, sheaves of corn harvested on his fields, chickens from his farmyard, cakes of wax from his beehives. . . . At other times, he works on the arable or the meadows of the demesne. Or we find him carting casks of wine or sacks of corn on behalf of the master to distant residences. His is the labour which repairs the walls or moats of the castle. If the master has guests the peasant strips his own bed to provide the necessary extra bedclothes. When the hunting season comes around, he feeds the pack. If war breaks out he does duty as a foot-soldier or orderly, under the leadership of the reeve of the village. . . . Of all the new "exactions" imposed on tenants, the most characteristic were monopolies of many different kinds . . . Sometimes [the landlord] reserved for himself the right to sell wine or beer at certain times of year. Sometimes he claimed the sole right to provide, in return for payment, the services of bull or boar for stud purposes. . . . More often he forced the peasants to grind their corn at his mill, to bake their bread in his oven, to make their wine in his wine press.[8]

As Gerhard Lenski describes the political philosophy of the feudal system, "The great majority of the political elite sought to use the energies of the peasant to the full, while depriving them of all but the basic necessities of life. The only real disagreement concerned the problem of how this might best be done. . . ."[9]

Rebellions against the system were easily crushed, even though peasants vastly outnumbered landlords, because low population densities made it difficult to communicate across vast distances and landlords could easily come together to protect their rights and privileges.

The landlord's control depended on his ability to control access to land and the rights that came with it. The landlord's massive tracts of land couldn't be sold: there was no money, thus nothing to trade the land for. Clearly the system depended on a large, steady supply of laborers; the more laborers, the better. Any force that interfered with access to this labor force threatened the very existence of the system.

In almost all agrarian societies, there were such forces. Famines, plagues, wars, and anything that reduced the size of the peasant population increased the bargaining power of the peasants that were left.[10] Opportunities in growing towns and rumors of better arrangements could induce peasants to leave rural landed estates and seek their fortunes elsewhere. Landlords tried to prevent such an exodus by imposing serfdom and indentured servitude.

Serfdom took an already exploitative situation and rendered it permanent. Serfs were peasants indentured to a landlord's lands. In principle, serfs could "buy" their freedom by paying huge sums of crop shares years into the future, but in practice, such individual emancipation almost never occurred. The feudal contract that bound serfs to the landlord's property often extended to his heirs, and usually to their heirs as well. The appearance of fixed time commitments was an illusion. In virtually no agrarian society on record were serfs emancipated because their feudal contracts with landlords ended;[11] instead, emancipation resulted when new elites rose up against landed elites to compete for the loyalty of the potential workforce that emancipated serfs represented.[12]

The material relationships among lords, vassals, peasants, and serfs were part of an extensive cultural system that identified social worth with inherited privilege. Historians debate the effectiveness of landlords' psychological attempts to assert ideological control over average peasants,[13] but evidence suggests that whatever else produced social peace in feudal societies, happiness and acceptance of dominant ideologies were not at the top of the list.[14]

Feudal elites and others with significant stakes in the inequalities of the system developed political and social ideologies that organized segments of the population into corporate groups. These groups—landlords, priests, vassals, merchants, peasants, and serfs—consisted of people in different structural positions in the feudal system. One's position in the system of dominance and subordination was determined by one's location in these groups, and these groups were ranked on evaluations of their members' social worthiness or unworthiness. Landlords and priests were on top, vassals and merchants made up the middle ranks, and "commoners" were at the bottom. One's opportunities, choices, marriage partners, family ties, and potential for advancement were defined and circumscribed by group membership.

Along with the obvious and serious social inequalities of this system came elaborate ideologies on the virtues and divine favor of landlords and priests, who were "destined" to administer and control the system. On the other side were ideologies and cultural beliefs about the obvious unworthiness and inferiority of peasants and serfs. Attempts to change the functioning of the system outside the bounds of the existing corporate structure were viewed as assaults on the natural order of human life as conveyed and sanctioned by God.

However, feudal ideology did not completely sanction anything elites decided to do with their inferiors. Each group was subject to a strong set of moral norms defining acceptable and unacceptable behavior. Feudal lords provided protection to their subjects, and organized serfs and peasants to defend their domains against invaders. Attempts to extract uncustomary extra taxes or labor services met with resistance from peasants and serfs who didn't demand the overthrow of the feudal system so much as the return of "good landlords," "just Tzars" and "traditional taxes."[15] Priests were expected to confer legitimacy on the feudal regime and kept feudal lords in line when temptations arose to abuse and overwork peasants and serfs. In most feudal societies, the church was also a landlord with its own sets of peasants and serfs who worked lands and were taxed to support the religious hierarchy. Sanctioned political inequality legitimated the feudal system and the lords and vassals who dominated it.

The transition away from feudalism involved a series of economic changes and one big political change.[16] The economic changes did not come all at once, and were not uniformly beneficial to all members of the elite or detrimental to all commoners. The move toward a capitalist global economy from global empires urged trade in the direction of exchange, away from the traditional system of conquest and tribute that had characterized feudal empire building. The incorporation of outside areas and hinterlands into the global economic system, which took well into the twentieth century, linked even the most remote parts of the world into a system of market transactions tied across continents. The proletarianization of the workforce moved almost all work relationships between employers and workers toward wage exchanges, away from traditional, reciprocal forms of obligation. Finally, people from different corporate groups could privately own, develop, and exploit land as they saw fit. All these economic changes were fueled by the combined push of urban entrepreneurs and others with an interest in maximizing economic opportunities and separating political power from traditional concepts of fealty and landed proprietorship.

These changes coincided with the development of Enlightenment political philosophies in the fourteenth and fifteenth centuries. Enlightenment political philosophy, identified with Descartes, Montaigne, Locke, and Hume, advanced causes of human reason, freedom, and rationalism. Most Enlightenment thinkers were skeptical of traditional justifications of authority, especially those that tied the traditional social order to divine sanction. To Enlightenment thinkers, all truth claims were subject to evaluation by reason, and free inquiry and open intellectual development allowed people to reach their stations in life to which they were best suited. Enlightenment philosophy was often tied to the struggles of Protestantism and merchants against the Catholic Church and traditional nobles and landlords. Enlightenment philosophy inspired developments in France and Britain that hastened the decline of feudalism by providing an emerging urban merchant class with a political ideology to buttress the development of contemporary capitalism and urban labor markets.

Enlightenment philosophy also inspired the founding fathers of the United States and was the intellectual undercurrent for the American Revolution, the Declaration of Independence, and the Constitution. But this did not make the United States a bastion of Enlightenment practice. Freedom and equality developed slowly, and America had its own form of feudalism in the nineteenth-century tenant sharecropping system.

Feudalism in a Contemporary Context: Tenant Farming in the Deep South

In the United States, the experience closest to medieval feudalism was nineteenth- and early twentieth-century tenant farming in the former Confederate states after the Civil War. The Civil War left the states of the Deep South in an economic shambles. Plantation owners survived as landed elites, but had lost the African slaves who performed the labor that maintained their economic position. The currency of the Confederacy, never worth much, was completely devalued. There was almost no banking system to speak of. The remnants of the plantation system included a mass of agricultural laborers with no access to land and a set of plantation owners with no workers and no money to pay them.

Box 2.2

Basic Concepts of the Farm Tenancy System in the American South

In the South, the *farm tenancy system* was an economy of landlords, merchants, and tenant farmers who exchanged dry goods and food for access to land and crops through sharecropping arrangements. This term also usually refers to the legal system that enforced the economic and social superiority of landlords and merchants to farm tenants.

In this system, *crop liens* were legal claims by landlords against current or future crops grown by tenant farmers. Landowners could file liens to seek repayment for bills accrued during the crop season for tenants' clothing and subsistence. Crop liens were often legally enforceable between landlords so that tenants could not move from one landlord to another unless their debts were paid. *Debt peonage* in a sharecropping system was the state of perpetual servitude that resulted from debts accumulated during the crop season that could not be paid off by the tenant's share of the crop at the harvest. Unpaid debts usually required the tenant to remain with their landlord for additional crop seasons, perpetuating the cycle of debt that kept tenants tied to the land.

The practical solution to these problems was a system of tenant farming or *sharecropping*, providing many with access to labor and crops. For most rural laborers, both emancipated blacks and poor whites, it was the only practical way to gain access to food. Yet the transactions involved were extremely exploitative and not greatly different from those of medieval feudalism.[17]

In sharecropping, a landlord exchanged farm implements such as machinery, seed, and fertilizer to a group of tenants so the tenants could sustain themselves during the growing season. In return, the landlord received a percentage of the crop, due as payment to the landlord or merchant at the harvest. Both parties benefited from this arrangement:

1. Landlords didn't have any money to pay wages, so they advanced foodstuffs and dry goods in lieu of these, gaining laborers to work their land.

2. Tenant farmers generally owned no land and most were very poor and often illiterate. Gaining access to subsistence goods in exchange for growing a crop was thus a valuable arrangement.

3. The tenancy system dealt with the practical problem of the lag between the time of the harvest and the winter, when living expenses were incurred (similar to the cash flow problems many of us face in contemporary economic life).

4. In theory, at harvest a percentage of the crop would be handed over and the transaction—the exchange of labor for foodstuffs and dry goods—would be complete. The landlord would have farm produce, usually cotton, to sell; the laborer would have his family provided for. Not a bad arrangement.

But, like many things in life that look good on the surface, the devil was in the details. The foodstuffs and dry goods advanced to the tenant farmer were credited against his portion of the harvest rather than the landlord's. In effect, the tenant farmer was buying subsistence on credit with his portion of the crop as payment. This system was open to abuse. Since the landlord was providing the subsistence goods to the tenant as an exchange, the tenant usually had no idea what the actual cost of the goods was in cash. The landlord could charge substantial markups on these goods in an attempt to gain access to all or most of the tenant's share of the crop. The landlord could set the cash price of the tenant's cotton at the price he would receive at harvest, when there was lots of cotton on the market and prices were low, and confiscate more of the tenant's cotton to pay the debts the landlord inflated. The landlord could then hold the cotton provided by the tenant farmer and sell it at some other time of year when the cotton price was higher, pay his own expenses, and pocket the difference.

Worse, the landlord could construct a pricing scheme for the dry goods he provided and the cotton turned over by the tenant so that the tenant's debts were not paid off at harvest time. At that point, the tenant was obligated to work for the landlord another year to pay off his debt. If the tenant decided to move on, one of three things would happen:

1. local law enforcement officials could track him down and return him to the landlord, requiring him to work to pay off his debts;

2. the landlord could file a lien against any crops raised by the tenant on other landlords' properties, claiming that they had rights of first claim on the labor of the indebted tenant; or

3. other landlords wouldn't hire the wandering tenant once they discovered that he owed debts to other landlords.

The combination of these outcomes made it almost impossible for the tenant to start anew.

The end result was a system of debt peonage in which tenants were tied to the landlord's land, perpetually in debt and perpetually "borrowing" subsistence goods to maintain their households in exchange for cotton crops whose value never managed to pay their bills.

The cultural and ideological underpinning of the sharecropping system was racial superiority and the "southern racial state."[18] Landlords were almost always white. Tenant farmers were not exclusively black, but whites from all economic circumstances identified with racial politics and the alleged inferiority of newly freed African Americans. The elaborate racial etiquette—deference rituals, pecking orders, and "separate" accommodations—of interactions between the races reinforced the cultural and biological superiority of whites, who were "burdened" with their role as overseers of the childlike freed Africans who were not fit to govern their own affairs. The entire criminal justice and legal system rested on the premise that white landowners were privileged elites to whom all others owed their allegiance. As we'll see, some of the racial divisiveness that helped to maintain this system returns in later political ideologies used to justify the policies of late twentieth-century elites.

Comparing Pre-Industrial Peasants to Post-Industrial Peasants

There are important parallels between agrarian systems and the contemporary situation of the American middle class. The most striking is the similarity between the system of debt peonage that emerged in agrarian systems and the system of work, wages, and debt facing the middle class in the past thirty-five years. In agrarian systems, peasants were indebted to specific landlords; in contemporary America, post-industrial peasants are indebted to an economic system. In both cases, workers are locked into arrangements that force them to struggle continuously to make a living with little hope of breaking free from their subordinate positions.

Today, the average middle class worker is mired in stagnant wages, job instability, rising prices, increased work hours, higher taxes, and bigger debts. The net result of these changes are post-industrial peasants, people in such economically precarious positions that their only option is to work harder at jobs that provide relatively low wages, no benefits, and no security (see Table 2.1).

That said, we should be clear about the limits of our analogy. No one we're aware of would trade a middle-class life in the United States for life as a serf in the Middle Ages or a tenant farmer in the nineteenth-century South. No one we're aware of would trade a life as an investor or corporate manager for a life as an agrarian feudal lord or plantation owner. To say that economic situations resemble one another doesn't make them interchangeable.

Table 2.1

A Coincidence? Feudal Peasants, Southern Sharecroppers, and Post-Industrial Peasants

System Characteristics	Feudal Peasants	Southern Sharecroppers	Post-Industrial Peasants
Social classes	Landlords and serfs	Landlords and sharecroppers	Capitalist employers and workers
Government	Landlord alliances	Planter-dominated democracy	Electoral-representative, capitalist-dominated democracy favoring the wealthy
Means of exchange	Land and labor services	Land and labor services	Money
Means of control by dominant classes	Direct coercion	Direct coercion and debt	Market discipline and credit
Type of expropriation	Direct taxation	Direct taxation	Taxation, long work hours, flat wages despite productivity gains
Terms of continued subordination	Control over land	Debt produced by crop liens	Debts from credit cards and financial manipulation

There are several notable achievements of all advanced industrial societies that, by themselves, make life for all but the most unfortunate better now than for most members of agrarian societies. Perhaps the most important of these is that modern societies have unprecedented freedom and political democracy. For all of their imperfections, modern democratic political institutions and philosophical notions of freedom and equality have brought tremendous value to the lives of many people. Even in contemporary public debates on personal rights and responsibilities, everyone assumes that each individual is entitled to the same set of rights and responsibilities and should be left to arrange their affairs as he or she sees fit. This is due to widespread Enlightenment ideologies of democracy and governing with the consent of the governed. Contemporary democratic political ideologies, along with such concepts as self-determination, personal freedom, and political equality, are powerful justifications for the outcomes of American politics. Claims that the political system is slanted in favor of those with wealth, money, and influence must provide proof that contradicts this prevailing ideology. This would not be the case under any feudal regime, in which patrimonial privileges and ideologies— ideas of the inherent superiority and inferiority of groups of people, with beliefs about the social privileges that come with political and economic domination—and inherent inequality is assumed, and private and public privilege are linked.

For all its warts, industrial capitalism (the development of market economies based on manufacturing in the wake of the industrial revolution) has increased the chances that average people can improve their lot. Some of this has to do with the basic structure of the system. The capitalist class is in constant competition for customers and against each other. This has affected in many ways the relationship between capitalists and those who work for them, especially when there are labor shortages. Factories and urbanism increased contact between groups of people, and especially members of the industrial working class. This led to unionization and myriad attempts to improve working conditions. The wide availability of money and an extensive banking system allowed capital investment, wages, and consumption to expand. Politics and economics were separated (at least in theory) so that political elites and economic elites were not the same people. Unlike the landlord in an agrarian society, a capitalist can, and often does, fail. Workers could improve their lot and "move up" into middle-class positions.

Modern societies also have access to an unfathomable surplus of opportunities and basic goods. Mass production may pollute the environment, waste natural resources, and exploit workers, but it also provides enormous amounts of basic consumer items at relatively low prices. One reason that poverty, hunger, and destitution seem so unjust to most of us is that we realize that our global economy has the resources to end such suffering. The sheer economic power that mass production market economies can bring to bear on any situation massively outranks anything an agrarian society could produce.

Modern society has also benefited greatly from the unprecedented levels of creativity and innovation unleashed by economic markets. Benefits of this creativity and innovation are distributed more broadly than people in agrarian societies could ever imagine. This creativity and innovation is expressed in ways both small (micro-lending, changing farm practices) and large (the development of new computer software, space travel).

And lest we forget, one major product of the industrial market economy was the creation of the middle class. No other set of economic arrangements has produced a middle class of the size and general prosperity of the American middle class and its European and Asian counterparts. As we stated in the introduction, the massive immigration of people into these parts of the world doesn't suggest to us that millions of people are greedy and want to make it big (which is not to say they wouldn't take those opportunities if they came up!), but that the economic contributions of "average people like me" are worth more here than they are back home. The aspirations of these migrants often are met. This, in itself, is a major achievement.

But there are also important differences between the post-industrial capitalism in the United States since the 1970s compared to industrial capitalism. These differences have complicated the plight of the middle class. Work has reorganized, with downsizing, outsourcing, temporary work, and flat organizational hierarchies, making it difficult for modern Americans to find steady jobs, establish careers, and build solid financial bases for middle class life. Increasingly the globalized economy is changing the relationships between large corporations and cities as corporations attempt to stay competitive, moving from place to place looking for the most favorable investment conditions and demanding tax and infrastructure concessions from cities and government agencies.[19] The sheer scale of the post-industrial enterprise and the dispersal of functions to different parts of the world make it difficult to determine who is responsible for job creation and community welfare.[20]

Is it really fair to liken the American middle class to peasants? After all, there are plenty of Americans who are in worse economic shape than the middle class. Across our country, hundreds of thousands of homeless men, women, and children live on the streets and in shelters. In 2003, over 35 million Americans lived below the official poverty line.[21] Families of migrant farm workers struggle to eke out a living, and women, primarily recent immigrants, work in sweatshop conditions in our cities. Fourth- and fifth-generation farmers are forced to take second jobs at Wal-Mart to avoid their inevitable slide into bankruptcy. Millions of children grow up in families locked in a vicious cycle of poverty, dead-end minimum wage jobs, and despair.[22] With so many Americans facing these stark realities, why focus on the middle class?

Our focus is driven by two observations. First, by focusing on the lower class, observers implicitly assume that the economic prosperity that we read about in papers and hear on the news must be benefiting everyone else. Second, many observers assume that Americans who are struggling do so because they do not have the skills, motivation, and education to compete in a post-industrial economy. The college-educated professional is held up as the "poster child" of the new economy, and the middle class is said to be profiting from these economic shifts. But what if the very people who are thought to be gaining unprecedented wealth, freedom, and mobility are actually saddled with debt and locked into a system of work that provides little stability, few benefits, and no rewards? In this context, the idea of the post-industrial peasant starts to make sense.

Apart from the use of money and the sophistication of the exchanges involved, the economic position of the U.S. middle class looks much like that of the feudal peasant of the Middle Ages and the Southern share-cropper. While the specific means of control (how the dominant classes or elites maintain their privileged position), type of expropriation (how the dominant classes or elites obtain funds needed to maintain the system), and terms of continued subordination (the condition that keeps the subordinate group under the control of the dominant classes or elites) are different in each system, the overall function is the same. So while it is true that post-industrial peasants are not tied to specific plots of land or specific lords, they *are* tied to a system that keeps them in a perpetual cycle of work and debt.[23]

The analogy of the post-industrial peasant shows us that social and economic relationships are intimately linked and that these trends have changed the rules and realities of middle-class life. The new rules and harsh realities of the middle class have been largely overlooked, downplayed, or outright ignored by economic and political elites.

Who are these people economically? The next chapter addresses their income and credit predicaments. As you'll see, it's not a pretty sight.

The Income/Credit Squeeze

The old system was keeping up with the Joneses. The new system is keeping up with the Gateses.

—Juliet Schor[1]

If we equate economic vigor with economic growth, the vigor of the United States economy over the past twenty years is almost unprecedented. Growth rates (in terms of change in Gross Domestic Product) that were negative in 1974 and 1975 became consistently positive and strong after the 1990/1991 recession, as economic growth was between 2.5 and 4 percent prior to the 2001 recession. The consumer economy depends on the purchasing power of the middle class to fuel economic growth, yet during the past few decades middle class incomes have not risen. How is it that despite the stagnant incomes of the middle class the economy has continued to grow by leaps and bounds?

In this chapter we examine two characteristics of the middle-class predicament: first, the stagnation of real incomes for most members of the middle class, and second, the expansion of easily available consumer credit. These trends are ominous symptoms of middle class decline, and they have been accompanied by other trends including the drastically increased compensation of top executives and a new paradigm for stimulating consumer demand that is tied to destabilizing jobs and loaning domestic consumers money they could otherwise be paid.

To understand these trends we must examine the workings of the consumer economy and theories about the relationship between consumer demand and aggregate economic health. These subjects are the purview of macroeconomics.

Market Economies and Purchasing Power: A Digression into ✓ Macroeconomic Theory

Macroeconomics is the study of the relationship between supply, demand, and income. The major issues macroeconomics addresses are the relationships between inflation, unemployment, wages, and productivity, and between business cycles, employment, and growth. *Business cycles* are the periodic ups and downs that are an inevitable part of market economies. *Inflation* is the upward spiral of wages and prices. *Economic growth* refers to increases in economic output in the economy as a whole, usually measured as change in the Gross Domestic Product. Most macroeconomists, like most of us, assume that less extreme business cycles, more employment, higher wages, relatively big productivity gains, and low inflation are desirable goals. Macroeconomics is policy-oriented, designed to guide government policies on taxation, expenditure, interest rates, and money supply to either stimulate or slow down economic activity. In theory, the correct choice of macroeconomic policy—and, perhaps more important, the political will to pursue it—will promote economic stability and steady growth.

Most macroeconomists believe that government actions affect economic performance, though they differ on which government activities produce the effects and whether the effects are good or bad. All market economies depend on the same activities to distribute needed goods and services:

Investment. In private hands, investment drives the economy forward. Investors, entrepreneurs, venture capitalists, and average people saving

Box 3.1

Basic Macroeconomic Terms

Macroeconomics, a sub-discipline of economics, develops theories and methods to study the relationships between inflation, unemployment, income, and government expenditures and policies.

Fiscal policy refers to the expenditures of the government to provide goods and services, and the methods, such as taxes, bond sales, and borrowing, that governments use to finance these expenditures.

for retirement or a rainy day see an opportunity to provide a good or service and invest in it. The ability to see such opportunities is the result of several signals including personal experience, conversations, and monitoring the investments of others. All macroeconomics assumes that profits motivate investors to invest and that investment returns are a major force driving a prosperous market economy.

Demand. Consumers look at an array of goods and services that investors and their agents provide and "vote" with their money. The demand for different goods, relative to their supply, determines the price. In the absence of demand, markets collapse under the weight of their own unsold goods. Distortions of market signals lead to imbalances of supply and demand, during which consumers look for goods that aren't available and investors provide products no one wants to buy at prices that are too high.

Credit and banking. No market economy can function without credit and banking institutions, which act as intermediaries, providing money for investors and consumers to borrow. In more advanced credit and banking systems, like ours in the United States, investment banks may pool investors' money to engage in various market interventions such as big stock purchases, initial public offerings of stock by companies that are going public, and takeovers of firms that are underperforming.

Banks pool money from individual investors and loan it for investments and consumer purchases that they deem worthy. They charge interest on the money they lend (or, in the case of investment banks, charge fees associated with the size of the investment pool they assemble). Prior to the Federal Reserve Act of 1913, banks issued banknotes directly, regulating the value of money in the economy. Now in the U.S. and almost all other nations, a central bank, like the Federal Reserve Bank in the United States, does this.

But why is credit needed in the first place? Because there are inevitable gaps between when expenditures are needed and when money arrives to pay for them. For investors and firms, new plants and equipment cost millions of dollars but the company rarely has enough ready money to make such investments all at once.[2] For consumers, the overall situation is similar. Most of us do not have $30,000 at hand to pay cash for cars or hundreds of thousands of dollars to pay for houses, and even if we had the cash, such purchases might not be the smartest ways to use our money. Instead, most of us borrow money to make such purchases. Credit institutions determine whether we're good credit risks by looking at our ability to pay off our loans in the future, using our employment record, record of paying past debts, and our current indebtedness as indicators. If they choose to loan money to us, they attach an interest rate, a fee they collect over time for borrowing their money.

To sum up, market economies work by offering credit, allowing investors to borrow money in anticipation of greater returns at some later date, and allowing consumers to purchase goods and services they could not afford because of cash flow problems separating when and how much income is earned and how much consumer goods cost in the here and now. So far, so good. But what's wrong with this picture?

Enter Macroeconomics

Macroeconomics as it is presently understood is a product of the Great Depression precipitated by the stock market crash of October 1929. After the crash, unemployment rose to 25 percent of the labor force; investors lost billions of dollars of wealth, by some estimates over one third of that available; and the economy was stagnant for most of the next ten years. Local conditions were often worse: in Pennsylvania in 1933, for example, only two fifths of the working population had full-time work and over one million state residents were totally unemployed.[3]

The administration of Franklin D. Roosevelt, elected in 1932, promised to take on the Great Depression, claiming that astutely placed government intervention would fuel economic recovery. To stimulate aggregate demand, Roosevelt introduced his "New Deal," a series of government interventions such as the National Industrial Recovery Act, the Wagner—Connery Act, the Social Security Act, agricultural price supports, the Civilian Conservation Corps, and the Works Progress Administration. There is considerable debate about whether these policies worked; at the time Germany invaded Poland in 1939, one of the official starting points for World War II, unemployment in the United States was still at 15 percent.[4]

John Maynard Keynes (1883–1946) provided the rationale for government intervention in his book *The General Theory of Employment, Interest, and Money* (1936), which stated that the government has a responsibility to sustain the levels of aggregate demand necessary to promote full employment and productive capacity, and could adopt policy tools to promote economic growth, to lower inflation and unemployment, and to provide satisfactory levels of economic prosperity.[5] The central purpose of government policy was to close the "Okun gap," named after economist Arthur M. Okun (1928–1980), between the potential and actual output that the aggregate economy could support. Without some attempt to close

Box 3.2

Basic Terms of Keynesian Economics

Keynesian economics, the series of economic theories and policy statements associated with British economist John Maynard Keynes, defines most economic problems as problems of *aggregate demand*—the ability and willingness of individuals and institutions to purchase goods and services in the economy. Aggregate demand is stimulated by income maintenance programs such as unemployment insurance, social security benefits, and other government spending programs. These programs are designed to put money into the pockets of people with a high *marginal propensity to consume*—people who will spend, not invest or save, a large share of their increases in income. (Conversely, many supply-side economic policies are designed to put money in the pockets of people with a *high marginal propensity to invest*—those who will invest or save larger shares of their increases in income.)

In Keynesian economics, boosts to aggregate demand produce demand multiplier effects—more employment and greater national income resulting from greater spending. The major fear in Keynesian economics is that the *laissez-faire economy*, the economy with little or no regulation of the relationship between supply and demand, will produce unacceptable levels of unemployment and poverty. The Keynesian argument, which gained popularity in the 1930s, was that the Depression resulted in a wide gap between potential economic output (what the economy was capable of producing) and actual economic output (what the economy was actually producing). This relationship is referred to as the Okun gap.

this gap, the aggregate economy would be stuck in a "liquidity trap" of insufficient economic activity to promote employment and satisfactory material prosperity. The implications of Keynesian economics, as this macroeconomic school came to be called, were that levels of economic output, inflation, and unemployment were political decisions rather than characteristics set by the "invisible hand" of markets. Keynesian economics drove much of the United States's macroeconomic policy from the 1930s through the 1960s.

The mechanism for altering economic output was to raise *aggregate demand*, the amount of goods and services that consumers and businesses wish to buy. The concrete policies resulting from Keynesian economics attempted to stimulate aggregate demand by putting in people's pockets money that they would spend almost immediately. Income maintenance programs like Social Security, targeted tax cuts (like the Kennedy–Johnson tax cut of 1964–1965),[6] public works spending, and investment to improve infrastructure and provide public works jobs were all major components of the Keynesian strategy. Raising aggregate demand would create new jobs and lower unemployment. The Depression-era assumption was that prices wouldn't rise because output was below capacity—the "maximum" output the economy could produce with a fixed set of capital stock. Such interventions in an otherwise *laissez-faire* economy must be understood in the context of the erosion of political elite's confidence in markets from the 1920s through the 1960s.[7]

The recessions of the 1970s and "stagflation"—high inflation coupled with rising unemployment—led many economists and policy makers to question the further applicability of the Keynesian macroeconomic model.[8] This sparked a revival of and new developments in other theories of macroeconomics, each with their own policy implications. Something was clearly wrong—interest rates were high and rising, inflation was high and rising, unemployment was high and rising, and real purchasing power was declining. New classical, monetarist, and supply-side economics stepped in with their own assumptions and policy remedies for these serious problems.

The Revival of New Classical and Monetarist Economics

The core Keynesian assumptions concerning demand management are rejected in new classical economics, which is defined by the "policy ineffectiveness hypothesis"—the belief that the rational expectations of economic actors will lead them to negate whatever changes government interventions in the economy are intended to produce. This means that almost all forms of economic intervention have unintended consequences, and the intended consequences of any policy choice are not likely to come about.

Specifically, new classical economists believe that unemployment does not respond to government intervention at all; instead, it is affected only by its long-term trend. The rate of economic innovation also is not responsive to government policy to stimulate aggregate demand; instead, government fiscal policy should be directed toward fighting inflation.[9]

Monetarist economics, associated most notably with Milton Friedman, proposes that the money supply helps to explain unemployment rate variations and inflation. In direct contrast to the Keynesian view that unemployment results from the gap between actual and potential output, monetarists claim that growth and contraction in money supply determine inflation and that restrictive fiscal policy (tight interest rates) without slowing expansion in the money supply won't reduce inflation. Unlike new classical economists, monetarists see a relationship between inflation and unemployment: a decline in inflation will make unemployment rise. There is thus a social cost to fighting inflation: slow but steady monetary expansion should make the unemployment rate fall, even though it permanently raises the inflation rate.[10]

Returning to our subject, middle-class families could be either helped by fiscal policy decisions that attempt to close the gap between real and potential output or harmed by attempts to alter aggregate economic performance in ways that can't be controlled, contributing to inflation and the erosion of purchasing power. The debates between Keynesian, new classical, and monetarist economics all boil down to the question of what costs are involved in fighting inflation. To new classical theorists, there is no cost because unemployment is not affected by anything the government does. To Keynesians and monetarists, policies that fight inflation would result in higher unemployment. Supply-side economics attempted to answer this question once and for all.

Supply-Side Economics and the Reagan Revolution

The 1980s brought a set of relatively obscure economic ideas for dealing with stagflation. Supply-side economics and its proponents claimed that the very interventions that Keynesian economics promoted—mechanisms for stimulating aggregate demand to smooth out the business cycle by shrinking the Okun gap—were behind the high-inflation and high-unemployment 1970s. These policies, and the cumulative effect of the federal government's activities in a wide range of areas, produced perverse incentives that made people work less, save less, and invest less. Inflation (directly) and high unemployment (indirectly) were caused by impediments the government erected to increasing productivity in production inputs.

Since supply-side economists define the federal government as the locus of these perverse incentives, the logical conclusion supply-side economists reach is that the incentives that impede productivity growth should be removed. As the Federal government removed disincentives to work, invest, and save, productivity and savings would increase, productivity would improve, inflation would be tamed, and unemployment would eventually decline.

One extension of supply-side economics was the "Laffer curve," named for Stanford economist Arthur Laffer. In 1974, Laffer was having dinner with Jude Wanniski, then associate editor of the *Wall Street Journal*, Donald Rumsfeld, Chief of Staff to President Ford (and later Secretary of Defense under George W. Bush), and Dick Cheney, then Rumsfeld's deputy (and later Vice President). During the course of the evening he sketched out the now famous "Laffer curve" on a napkin.[11] In this variant of supply-side economics, the disincentives produced by the federal government were so great that federal government revenues were actually lower than they would be if these impediments were removed. The temporary deficits the federal government would have as a result of tax cuts and deregulation would be eliminated through the increased government revenues resulting from greater economic growth (see Appendix Figure 3.1). In another variant of supply-side economics, the removal of government disincentives was paired with substantial cuts in the federal budget. These cuts would allow the gap between government expenditures and revenues to close even faster as increased productivity drove economic growth.[12]

The policy tools advocated by supply-side economics differ considerably from those advocated by other macroeconomic perspectives. These policies include the deregulation of heavily regulated industries; the promotion of greater economic competition by lowering trade barriers; the repeal of special subsidies and tax loopholes for specific industries; across-the-board tax cuts, especially for corporations and those with higher marginal income tax rates; and cuts in government domestic spending in an attempt to remove disincentives to work, invest, and save. These policies became hugely influential during the presidency of Ronald Reagan in the 1980s, and many but not all supply-side economic recommendations were implemented. The Reagan administration passed substantial tax cuts on corporate taxes and taxes geared toward high-income tax payers, and continued the trend toward industry deregulation that had begun during the Carter administration. Subsequent administrations have also taken up the deregulation cause (see Table 3.1).

The list below details how this theory is put into action. Note the differences of supply-side economics from other policies for stimulating economic change, and in particular how supply-side economics turns Keynesian economics on its head:

1. Government incentives are targeted toward those with the greatest "marginal propensity to invest"—people and corporations who would save and invest the money returned to them and respond to new incentives by investing in capital goods.

2. As this group responds to the new incentives, investment increases, inflation drops, unemployment drops, and tax revenues rise.

Table 3.1

Industry Deregulation during the Last Five Presidential Administrations

Industry deregulated	New activities allowed
Banking/finance	Fewer restrictions on branch banking; eliminated limitations in interest rates, capital requirements, and loan restrictions
Airlines	Ended route restrictions and requirements; permitted competition on popular routes; ended mandatory service to smaller markets; created the "Hub" airline system
Trucking	Increased fare competition; deregulated truck sizing and weighting
Telecommunications	Allowed competition for local and long-distance telephone service and cable television service
Electricity	Permitted competition for electrical generation in local markets; allowed grid sales of surplus electricity across regions; streamlined authorization for new power plants; eased some environmental restrictions

3. Inflation drops because productivity and productive capacity are rising faster than wages, and increased international competition keeps prices down.

4. Government revenues rise because increased economic activity brings new tax revenues into government coffers. The new incentives "pay for themselves."[13]

The domestic rise of supply-side economics dovetailed with the international spread of *neoliberalism.* Neoliberals believe that international trade and domestic economic activity are best governed by open and free markets, minimal government regulations, and maximum capital and labor movement. In addition, late-twentieth century neoliberalism is identified with spreading markets to ever broader sets of human activities, from healthcare to schools; while these areas were always a concern in other economic theories, neoliberalism was the most effective at treating these in a market-like fashion. Neoliberalism is an outgrowth of nineteenth-century liberalism, in which society and by extension markets should be allowed to develop through processes. Results from processes like market transactions are not to be interfered with, and the outcomes that processes produce are assumed to be the best possible.

Neoliberalism has significant implications for middle class life in the United States. The most important dimensions of neoliberal thought involve the expansion of markets to new spheres of activity; an emphasis on contracts of short duration, including employment contracts; constant assessment and the continual production of performance information; the growth of the financial services sector and the expansion of financial exchanges divorced from the production of actual goods and services; and relentless outsourcing and supplier competition for goods and services (see Table 3.2).

Current U.S. economic policy reflects a combination of supply-side economics and neoliberalism. The drive for privatization and the downsizing of government that accompanied the Reagan administration in the United States and the Thatcher administration in Britain are examples of policies that result from neoliberalism. The actual tenets of neoliberalism, like those of Keynesianism and supply-side economics, have never been fully implemented, but they still have some consequences for post-industrial peasants, including jobs of shorter duration with relentless pressure to work more hours and more time for less pay and fewer benefits; a deregulated financial services sector with a considerable aftermarket for consumer and other forms of debt; and numerous ways for investors to make money that don't involve making anything, providing any service, or employing anyone.

These economic changes in the United States have made the pursuit of financial gain, without any accompanying economic or social obligation, a major component of the political landscape of the last thirty years. Where does this combination of supply-side economics and neoliberalism leave members of the middle class?

Public Policy, Purchasing Power, and the Middle Class

Only Keynesian and supply-side economics have received a "policy hearing" in the sense that they have shaped actual government policy; new classical economics and to a lesser extent monetarist economics have never been practically implemented. Generally the concepts of these theories are unpalatable to voters and politicians. Think about monetarism and new classical economics from the standpoint of a presidential candidate. How inspiring would it be for a candidate to say that he's going to change the way the federal government works by pegging the money supply to an automatic inflator that all economic actors can know in advance, and that's all he's going to do? This would be the monetarist proscription for macroeconomic change. How many candidates could run on the idea that the only thing the federal government should do is fight inflation, and that

Table 3.2

Major Macroeconomic Schools, 1950–Present

Macroeconomic School	Reasons for Stagnation	Solution	Intellectual Leaders
Keynesian	Insufficient aggregate demand	Give money to those who will spend it	John Maynard Keynes (1883–1946), James Tobin (b. 1918)
New classical economics	Policy ineffectiveness/ unintended consequences of policy	Fight inflation; limited government	Robert Lucas Jr. (b. 1937), Thomas Sargent (b. 1943)
Monetarist economics	Inconsistent monetary policy using fiscal policy in place of monetary policy	Controlling money supply in a predictable way	Milton Friedman (b. 1912)
Supply-side economics	Insufficient incentives to work, invest, and save	Tax cuts, deregulation, government spending cuts	Robert Mundell (b. 1932), Arthur Laffer (b. 1940), Jude Wanniski (b. 1936)
Neoliberalism	Trade barriers, fiscal irresponsibility, regulations	Eliminate trade barriers, deregulate labor markets; and subject more societal and individual decisions to market forces	International Monetary Fund, World Bank, Heritage Foundation, Friedrich Hayek (1899–1992)

fighting inflation has no cost because "everyone will adjust"? In spite of the merits of these ideas—and there are some—these don't make for inspiring political messages.

Now think of a presidential candidate running with a real or implied Keynesian or supply-side economics policy position. The typical Keynesian candidate can say that he is interested in "getting America working again" and "maintaining the economic integrity of working Americans" during economic downturns. He can offer incentives from tax cuts, public works programs, and income maintenance programs (for example, unemployment insurance, job training, social security benefits, and interest deductions for incurring consumer debts) that appeal to voters who are down on their luck and who think that economic activity is "too slow." The typical candidate with a supply-side economic platform can claim he's interested in "getting America to invest, save, and work," that he is "getting the government off people's backs," and that his array of tax cuts and deregulation activities will stimulate the economy and bring cheaper consumer goods for all. These are much more inspiring messages, regardless of their merit.[14]

In the 1980 presidential election, the middle class was not offered a choice from these four alternatives. Instead, they were offered a choice between Ronald Reagan's supply-side economics and Jimmy Carter's uncertain and tentative Keynesian economics. Supply-side economics seemed new and attractive; Keynesian economics seemed old and bumbling. When combined with the personalities involved—Reagan appeared decisive; Carter appeared unsure and bumbling—and the high inflation and unemployment of the late 1970s, voters overwhelmingly chose the supply-side alternative.

While interpretations vary on what happened next, the statistics are not in dispute: the political consequences of supply-side economics have been pervasive.

1. For the 1980s and into the 1990s, income inequality increased substantially, more so than during any other peacetime era in America's history.

2. The federal government ran record federal deficits, borrowing more money in the eight years of the Reagan administration than in the history of the U.S. federal government from 1776 to 1980.

3. Tax rates were lowered and tax cuts passed. Federal revenues did not rise fast enough to meet expenditures.

4. The administration had trouble finding domestic program spending cuts that would allow the budget to balance without appearing to be

insensitive to the needs of the poor. (Most government spending does not go to help the poor anyway—see Figure 6.3).[15]

5. Public infrastructure, such as roads, airports, bridges, and dams, began to fall into disrepair as appropriations for their maintenance was trimmed or eliminated.

6. Individual state governments passed "supply-side tax packages" of their own in an attempt to match the federal government at reducing tax rates to increase revenues.[16] This shift in tax burdens hit the middle class especially hard (see Chapter 6).

7. The deregulation of industry included the financial sector—banks and investments—leading to a rash of corporate takeover activity and other unproductive pursuits that were substitutes for saving and investment in actual business enterprise.[17]

8. This same deregulation ushered in the era of easy credit: cars and other consumer items could be purchased with "no money down" (see Chapter 5). Credit cards became much more widely available, and the debts accumulated started to grow as middle class consumers attempted to maintain their lifestyles.[18]

9. The economy never fully recovered until the first Bush administration, and then only tentatively. When Bill Clinton took office in 1992, supply-side economic policies were replaced by a focus on deficit reduction as a federal government priority, and median real family incomes began to rise again (see Figure 3.1 on p. 48). The administration of George W. Bush faced myriad difficulties, passed a large tax cut anyway, and brought back record federal deficits. Bush's projected 2004 budget deficit was $413 billion.[19]

10. Tax cutting and business incentives stimulate new lobbying groups in Washington, all of whom look for special favors for their particular industry or product.[20]

11. The political claim that low taxes stimulate economic growth becomes entrenched in the American political landscape. State and local governments began to compete for footloose and mobile businesses seeking favorable tax treatment and the best economic deals to locate in specific places. The epidemic of tax cutting left state and local governments with reduced revenues, spawning further cuts in public services (see Chapter 6).

12. The view that investors and capitalists don't respond to incentives has been put to the test and found wanting. Not only do they respond to incentives, the incentives produce a new financial elite that does more to manipulate the system to their advantage.

13. Foreign competition makes American products more internationally competitive at the same time it costs the economy hundreds of thousands of jobs.[21]

Many analysts would suggest that Bill, one of our examples from Chapter 2, was a direct victim of the economic manipulations of supply-side economics and the deregulation that came with it. Bill had worked for his engineering firm since he graduated from college, and at the time he was laid off he had put in thirteen years. There were no outward signs that his firm was in financial trouble—there was plenty of work to do, orders and new business came in steadily, and the company had very little debt.

Unfortunately for Bill, these characteristics made his company a prime target to be taken over and dismantled. A group of corporate raiders organized a "hostile takeover" of Bill's firm, offering stockholders double the market price for their stock shares. The interest on the money the raiders borrowed to make this offer was tax deductible—another product of corporate tax reform and deregulation.[22] The offer was too good for the stockholders to refuse, and the corporate managers of Bill's firm, who themselves owned substantial company stock, also would benefit from lucrative severance packages, or "golden parachutes," if they were fired by the new owners.

Bill's company changed hands. Instead of keeping the company intact and attempting to improve its performance, the new owners, a small group of investment bankers and wealthy stockholders, started selling off and closing entire segments of the firm. The manufacturing wing of Bill's firm was sold to an overseas investment consortium. All but a few employees of the engineering wing were let go. "The company can outsource engineering services on the open market," explained the new CEO.

This giant sell-off immediately brought in millions of dollars to the new investors. It cost Bill's company several hundred jobs and its local community hundreds of thousands of dollars in future tax revenues. The small group of investors took their new "downsized" firm and began selling their

Box 3.3

"Golden Parachute" Defined

A *golden parachute*, a clause in the employment contract of an executive-level employee, specifies large benefits in the event the company is acquired or the executive is fired or laid off. These benefits can come in the form of cash, stock options, or both.

shares on the open market. Wall Street loved it: the shares sold for their original asking price and more, netting the set of corporate raiders still more profits for a few months' work.

Perhaps the biggest revelation of this era—amidst rising inequality, financial manipulations, and job insecurity—was that the purchasing power of the middle class was a public good, something that was good for everyone but that nobody had any incentive to help contribute to. This is the root of the "income/credit squeeze" that we turn to next.

Evidence for the Income/Credit Squeeze

The Deflated Income Balloon

One major problem facing the middle class, and a key component of the post-industrial peasant phenomenon, is the decline of real income and purchasing power (see Figure 3.1).

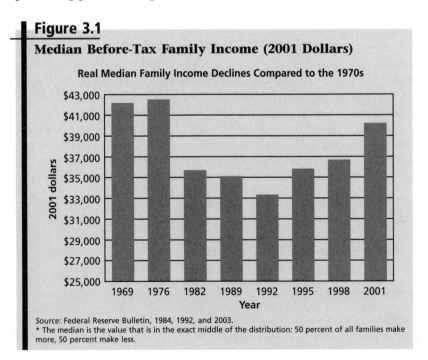

Figure 3.1

Median Before-Tax Family Income (2001 Dollars)

Real Median Family Income Declines Compared to the 1970s

Source: Federal Reserve Bulletin, 1984, 1992, and 2003.
* The median is the value that is in the exact middle of the distribution: 50 percent of all families make more, 50 percent make less.

Box 3.4

The Mean and the Median; or, What Happens When Bill Gates Walks into a Starbucks?

What's the difference between a mean and a median, and why should we care? The *mean* is the arithmetic average of a set of numbers. When discussing income and wealth, the mean is calculated by adding up individual income and wealth and dividing by the number of people. Let's say we have an economy with five workers in it, with earnings of $10,000, $20,000, $30,000, $40,000, and $70,000. To calculate the mean, we add all these values together:

$$10,000 + 20,000 + 30,000 + 40,000 + 70,000 = 170,000$$

And then divide the sum by 5, the number of wage earners in our economy:

$$170,000 \div 5 = 34,000$$

Means are useful calculations, providing the basis for most other advanced statistics by taking into account all values that appear in a population or sample.

The *median* is the middle of a set of numbers, the number that divides the top half of the distribution from the bottom half. The median is less sensitive to extreme scores than the mean and is a better measure of central tendency when the distribution is highly skewed (i.e., different from a normal curve). The median of our distribution of five earnings is simply the number in the middle, in this case $30,000. If the distribution contains an even number of cases, then the median is the mean of the two middle numbers.

Your authors' discussions of income, earnings, and wealth favor medians over means because medians are less sensitive to extreme values. In the case of income, earnings and wealth, distributions are highly skewed, as our figures will show. The mean is much higher than the median because the wealthy and affluent have remarkably greater resources than the middle classes or the poor.

Here's a simple example of how the implications of mean and median calculations are dramatically different. You are sitting in a Starbucks coffee shop with four of your friends. The wealth and assets controlled by all five of you are distributed as follows:

You:	$10,000
Friend 1:	$30,000
Friend 2:	$50,000
Friend 3:	$60,000
Friend 4:	$100,000

The mean of the distribution of wealth and assets in this Starbucks is $50,000, and the median is $50,000. In this case the mean and median are equal, so the impression you get from either figure is the same. The distribution of wealth and assets in this example is much more even than the distribution in most market economies.

Now suppose Bill Gates walks into the Starbucks. For the sake of this calculation, let's say his net wealth and assets are worth $26 billion. What happens to our distribution? To put it mildly, the mean changes drastically in value, but the median barely moves. First let's add Gates's wealth to the distribution and recalculate the median:

You:	$10,000
Friend 1:	$30,000
Friend 2:	$50,000
Friend 3:	$60,000
Friend 4:	$100,000
Bill Gates:	$26 billion

$$(50,000 \div 60,000) \div 2 = \$55,000$$

The median moves from $50,000 to $55,000. We've added $26 billion dollars to our Starbucks economy, but the typical person in our Starbucks economy is worth only $55,000. But look what happens to the mean calculation:

You:	$10,000
Friend 1:	$30,000
Friend 2:	$50,000
Friend 3:	$60,000
Friend 4:	$100,000
Bill Gates:	$26 billion

$$\text{Sum} = \$26,000,250,000 \div 6 = \$433,375,000$$

The mean wealth and assets controlled by everybody in the room is now about *$433 million.*

Does the mean or the median more accurately describe the distribution of wealth and earnings for the typical person at this Starbucks? You and your four friends are much closer to the median's $55,000 than the mean's $433 million—in fact, you aren't even *close* to the mean.

Granted, wealth and asset inequality in a real economy are not distributed this extremely, but the extreme values at the top of the distribution in most market economies make the median represent the status of the middle class people much more effectively than the mean.

By any measure we use, the real earnings (earnings adjusted for inflation) of individuals and the real income of families have undergone a period of stagnation at the middle. Median before-tax family income—the figure that separates the top half of the income distribution from the bottom half—dropped from a high of $42,000 in 1976 to $33,000 in 1992, only to inch upward again by 2001. This evidence suggests that family income for those at the middle of income distribution has not recovered from relatively high levels in the late 1960s and early 1970s.

We can see a similar trend in the average (mean) real yearly earnings of production workers, all non-supervisory, non-agricultural, non–self-employed workers in the economy (Appendix Figures 3.2 and 3.3). Here the dip is less extreme, but the overall lack of growth is obvious—average production worker earnings dropped from $31,054 in 1970 to $28,658 in 1990, a drop of 8 percent. Median weekly real earnings for wage and salary workers (including managers and administrators in addition to non-supervisory workers) dropped as well, from just over $600 per week in 1970 to a low of just over $500 per week in 1990, and recently inched back up toward $600 weekly (approximately $30,000 yearly if the median salaried worker takes two weeks' vacation each year). We see a similar dip in the hourly earnings of non–farm workers as well.[23]

Regardless of who is included in the calculation—individuals, families, wage and salary workers, non-supervisory workers or hourly workers—the trends in real earnings and income at the middle of these distributions suggest that median income and earnings were between $2,300 and $8,000 less at their lowest than they were during the late 1960s and early 1970s. All these figures started to trend upward again in the mid- to late 1990s. A recent study by the Economic Policy Institute finds that earnings fell another .1 percent for workers at the median earnings level and fell 1.2 percent for those at the low end of the earnings distribution (the 10th percentile).[24] These are differences in the real purchasing power of earnings and income accruing to people at or near the middle of earnings and income distributions. Because these are median figures, no one could argue that earnings and income has grown such that most people aren't middle class anymore. Instead, these figures reflect the movement of the middle of the distribution of income and earnings over the past thirty years.

Box 3.5

Real Incomes Using the Personal Consumption Expenditures Price Index

In this chapter, we report income statistics adjusting incomes for the Consumer Price Index (CPI), the traditional adjustment for inflation used to compare economic indicators at different historical periods. Recently, however, the Bureau of Labor Statistics has begun to produce a Personal Consumption Expenditures Price Index. Unlike the CPI, this price index uses contemporary quantities of consumer items as weights, rather than assuming that consumers buy long-standing, unchanging bundles of goods.

Using the personal consumption expenditures deflator rather than the CPI in Figure 3.1 changes the real values of income slightly, but not the overall story. Real median incomes start at $34,429 in 1969, drop to $31,688 in 1989, and rise to $39,079 in 2001. Median incomes still stagnate considerably in the 1980s and start to recover only in the late 1990s.

52

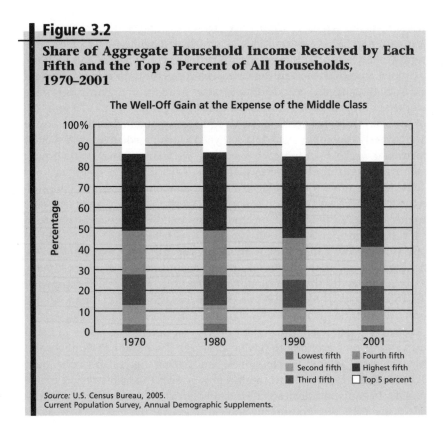

Figure 3.2

Share of Aggregate Household Income Received by Each Fifth and the Top 5 Percent of All Households, 1970–2001

The Well-Off Gain at the Expense of the Middle Class

Legend:
- ■ Lowest fifth
- ■ Second fifth
- ■ Third fifth
- ■ Fourth fifth
- ■ Highest fifth
- □ Top 5 percent

Source: U.S. Census Bureau, 2005.
Current Population Survey, Annual Demographic Supplements.

Stagnant Incomes for the Middle, Rising Incomes for the Top

The stagnant income and earnings at the middle of the distribution mask long-term changes and sharp increases in income inequality (see Figure 3.2).

A standard way to assess the relative equality or inequality in an income distribution is to divide it into parts representing equal shares of the population. Dividing the population into fifths is one popular way of dividing up these distributions. To make statements about inequality, researchers look at the percentage of all income that is awarded to each fifth of the population from the top to the bottom. In the case of "perfect equality," each fifth of the population (20 percent) would get 20 percent of the total income.

Since total equality is an elusive goal most societies never approach, it is useful to compare income distributions over time within the same society or across societies. This way we can judge whether inequality is trending upward or downward over time or whether the income distribution is more or less equal in, for example, Sweden than in the United States.

Income inequality has risen substantially in the United States since 1970. The top 20 percent of all families went from receiving 43.3 percent of the income in 1970 to receiving 50 percent of all family income in 2001. More interesting from our perspective is the change in the relative size of the middle fifth of the family income distribution, those families that made between $41,000 and $62,500 in 2001, whose relative share of the family income distribution has dropped from 17.4 percent to 14.6 percent over the past thirty years. In fact, the shares for all families in the bottom four-fifths of the income distribution have declined relative to the top, suggesting that there has been a strong movement of income in the direction of the nation's richer families.

Another way to look at this trend is to plot the ratio of the middle fifth of the family income distribution to the top two-fifths and to look at the real difference between mean and median family income (see Appendix Figures 3.4 and 3.5). The mean is simply the arithmetical average, summing all household incomes and dividing by the number of households. Unlike the median, which splits the distribution of households exactly in half, the mean takes into account the actual dollars households take in.

The evidence clearly shows that family incomes have ballooned for the upper classes and stagnated for the middle class, the group right in the middle of the family income distribution. The ratio of the middle fifth of family income to the top two-fifths drops from 26 percent to below 20 percent from 1970 to 2000.[25] The difference between real mean and median family income increases from under $10,000 in 1969 to almost $30,000 in 2001.[26] "The fact of the matter is, income trends have favored people at the top of the income distribution," says Gary Burtless, Senior Fellow at the Brookings Institution in Washington. "There is no data source that disagrees with the simple statement. In fact, the better the data, the more that the skew appears."[27]

The preponderance of evidence suggests that middle class purchasing power has eroded as income and earnings have either stalled or declined. Income inequality across households has increased and the relative standing of those we label "middle class" has eroded as well.

What Was Happening at the Top? The Captains of Industry Cash In

Yet another phenomenon is eroding the relative standing of the middle class, involving the rapid rise in the compensation accruing to corporate chief executive officers (CEOs) (see Table 3.3).

Table 3.3

Top CEO Compensation, 1970 to 2002

Company	Name	Title	Annual compensation in thousands of dollars (2002 dollars)
2002			
Oracle	L. J. Ellison	Chair & CEO	260,472
Siebel Systems	T. M. Siebel	Chair & CEO	99,194
CitiGroup	S. I. Weill	Chair & CEO	93,614
MBNA	A. Lerner	Chair & CEO	79,910
Tyco Intl.	L. D. Kozlowski	Chair & CEO	79,403
2000			
Walt Disney	M. D. Eisner	Chair & CEO	243,447
Computer Associates Intl.	C. B. Wang	Chair & CEO	243,137
CitiGroup	S. I. Weill	Chair & CEO	167,913
Computer Associates Intl.	S. Kumar	Pres. & COO	137,176
Tyco Intl.	L. D. Kozlowski	Chair & CEO	125,573
1990			
Walt Disney	M. D. Eisner	Pres. & COO	39,874
Walt Disney	F. G. Wells	Chair & CEO	27,278
Reebok Intl.	P. B. Fireman	Chair, Pres, & CEO	18,750
Paramount Communications	M. S. Davis	Chair & CEO	15,666
Microsoft	J. A. Shirley	Pres. & COO	13,693
1980			
Esmark Inc.	D. Kelly	Pres. & CEO	3,596
CBS Inc.	T. Wyman	Pres.	2,971
Union Oil Co. of California	F. Hartley	Chair & Pres.	2,762
Esmark Inc.	J. Vickers	Chair	2,622
Mobil Oil Corp.	R. Warner, Jr.	Chair	2,244
1970			
International Telephone & Telegraph Co.	Harold Geneen	Chair & Pres.	3,555
Johnson & Johnson	Phillip Hofmann	Chair	2,364
Ford Motor Co.	Henry Ford II	Chair	2,318
Procter & Gamble Co.	Howard Morgens	Pres.	2,254
Ford Motor Co.	Lee Iacocca	Pres.	2,110

Source: Executive Compensation Scorecard, *BusinessWeek*, June 19, 1971: 58–78; *BusinessWeek*, May 11, 1981: 58–78; *BusinessWeek*, May 6, 1991: 96–112; *BusinessWeek*, April 16, 2001: 82–109; *BusinessWeek*, April 21, 2003: 91–101.

In 1970 and 1980, the top CEOs as listed by *BusinessWeek* made between $1.7 million and $3.5 million (in 2002 dollars)—big salaries, to be sure, but not ridiculously high. Since then compensation packages for United States CEOs have spiraled upward at a staggering pace. In 1990, the CEO at the bottom of the *BusinessWeek* list made $8.1 million and Michael Eisner, President and CEO of Walt Disney Studios, was paid $39.9 million (in 2002 dollars); by 2000 and 2002, total compensation packages topped out at about a quarter of a billion dollars in both years and bottomed at $44 to $54 million.

In short, CEO salaries in the United States, already the highest in the world, moved farther away from our economic competitors in Western Europe and Asia since the 1980s while compensation for average workers stagnated or fell.

To reveal how enormous the gap between the salaries of average, middle-class workers and those of CEOs, compare mean CEO pay to average annual production worker pay (see Figure 3.3).

Ratios that started at about 35 to 1 in 1970 (with top CEOs making roughly thirty-five times what the average worker makes) mushroomed to nearly 350 to 1 by 2002. Clearly, the economic landscape for the average worker has shifted and their relative economic standing has slipped.

Figure 3.3

Ratio of Average Top CEO Pay to Average Production Worker Pay, 1970–2000

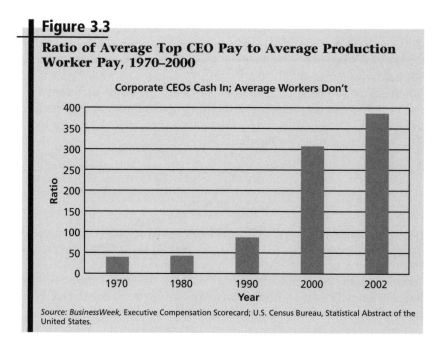

Corporate CEOs Cash In; Average Workers Don't

Source: BusinessWeek, Executive Compensation Scorecard; U.S. Census Bureau, *Statistical Abstract of the United States.*

Lower Wages and Job Instability

There is no denying that these trends exist, but their causes have been widely disputed.[28] The simplest explanation points to globalization and the changing role of international competition in increasing skill-based rewards and technological change.[29] Others point to the massive reorganization of the workplace and the enormous drive to cut employee costs to increase profit margins.[30] Is there any evidence for these explanations?

As skill-biased compensation goes, it is hard to see how a CEO in 2002 can make $400 million when in 1970 he would have made $400,000. It's even more difficult to see how that difference can be justified in real dollars. But if corporate executives are supposed to maximize profits and shareholder value, then plenty of evidence shows that they did just that, especially since 1980. Stock market returns were historically as high from 1980 to 2000 as they were at any time during the post–World War II period. This can also be seen by looking at changes in the Standard and Poor's Stock Index and the Dow Jones Industrial Average. Indeed, it wasn't until the onset of the 2001 recession that these stock market indices turned away from historic highs and unprecedented returns (see Figure 4.1).[31]

But did all this translate into a good corporate bottom line? Definitely. In the 1990s, corporate profits rose to record levels as well. These trends left most CEOs compensated with stock options in great economic shape compared to their average employee.

What happened to this average employee's job? Trends in mass layoffs are difficult to detect; in fact, the U.S. government didn't start tracking what it terms "mass layoff events" until 1996 (see Appendix Figure 3.6). But plenty of anecdotal evidence shows that job instability increased during the 1990s and that middle-class workers were buffeted by the changes produced by globalization.[32] The instability is not only in jobs for individuals, it's in incomes for families:

> Family finances have become much more insecure. Although insecurity dropped in the booms of the late 1980s and late 1990s, the long-term trend is sharply upward. In fact, instability in family incomes was roughly five times greater at its peak in the 1990s than in 1972.[33]

United States balance of payments figures (the difference in the value of what we import compared to what we export) began to look uglier as cheap imports that competed against American-made goods flooded the consumer market (Appendix Figures 3.7 and 3.8). The dollar stayed strong, but now partially because foreign investors invested heavily in U.S. government debt to pay for our budget deficit.[34]

Our picture so far is of economic stagnation and instability among the middle class, and growing economic prosperity among the relatively wealthy. Yet the consumer economy continued to plow on full steam ahead during the mid- to late 1990s. How was this possible? What was fueling all that consumption?

Consumer Credit!

Even though their incomes and earnings stagnated and their CEOs left them in the economic dust, members of the middle class received enhanced purchasing power. They did this by increasing their working hours, reducing their savings, and increasing their debt load.

American workers are supplementing their incomes by working more hours themselves and by bringing a second wage earner, usually a spouse, into the family (see Figure 3.4 and Appendix Figure 3.9).

Figure 3.4

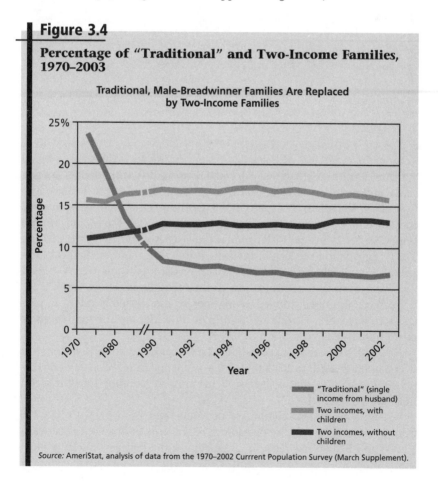

Percentage of "Traditional" and Two-Income Families, 1970–2003

Traditional, Male-Breadwinner Families Are Replaced by Two-Income Families

Legend:
- "Traditional" (single income from husband)
- Two incomes, with children
- Two incomes, without children

Source: AmeriStat, analysis of data from the 1970–2002 Currrent Population Survey (March Supplement).

Figure 3.5

U.S. Net Savings as a Percentage of Gross National Income, 1970–2004

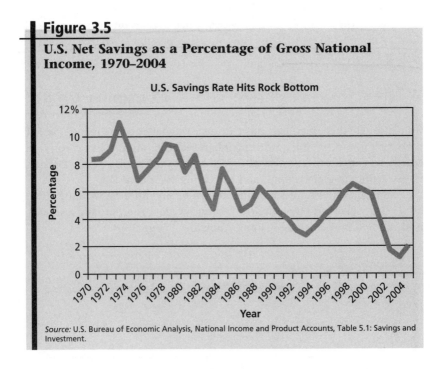

U.S. Savings Rate Hits Rock Bottom

Source: U.S. Bureau of Economic Analysis, National Income and Product Accounts, Table 5.1: Savings and Investment.

From 1970 to 1997, the average for-pay hours per week worked by all married couples rose from 52.5 to 62.8. During this same period the percentage of families in which both husband and wife work for pay rose from 35.9 percent to 59.5 percent[35] In addition, the number of married couples that work more than 100 hours a week (like David and Monica from Chapter 2) has increased dramatically (see Appendix Figures 3.10 and 3.11). Considering the lack of movement in average and median earnings among the middle class over the past three decades, these trends suggest that workers work more hours just to keep their heads above water.

Workers also have stopped saving money and started living from paycheck to paycheck, leaving them little or no buffer against the whims of misfortune (see Figures 3.5 and 3.6).[36]

Not only has real average credit card debt per household risen from just over $4,000 in 1990 to $9,000 in 2003—a change in real dollars of $5,029 (in 2002 dollars)[37]—but college students are also plunging into the credit hole (see Figure 3.7).

The average student credit card debt has risen from $1,222 to $1,770 from 1998 to 2001 and the percentage of students with balances between $3,000 and $7,000 has risen to 23 percent of the college student population (Appendix Figures 3.12 and 3.13).[38] The post-industrial economy

Figure 3.6

Household Debt as a Percentage of After-Tax Income, 1900–2000

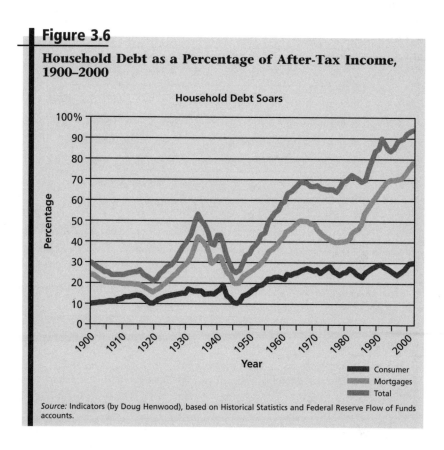

Household Debt Soars

Source: Indicators (by Doug Henwood), based on Historical Statistics and Federal Reserve Flow of Funds accounts.

demands a well-educated workforce, and a college degree has increasingly become the admission ticket to the middle class. But when graduates rack up consumer debt from school loans during their time in college, they enter the labor force already in precarious financial situations.

If we add home mortgages to this equation, household debt as a percentage of personal income has risen steadily since 1980 as well. The costs of homes and credit cards have risen while average incomes have not (see Chapters 5 and 6), so Americans are borrowing more money and a greater percentage of their income and earnings to pay for the goods and services that a middle class lifestyle demands. The debt to income ratio has risen in recent years because debt has gone up and incomes have remained stagnant. Clearly both trends have occurred (see Figure 3.8).

Real average incomes have not kept pace with consumption spending. But that's not the whole story. Because it isn't measured in dollars, the ratio of debt to income isn't sensitive to inflation, which means that the

Figure 3.7

Combined Average Debt of College Students by Class in 2001

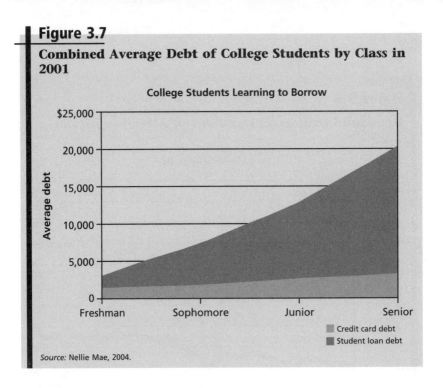

College Students Learning to Borrow

Legend:
- Credit card debt
- Student loan debt

Source: Nellie Mae, 2004.

Figure 3.8

Household Debt as a Percentage of Personal Income: Average Earnings of Production Workers (2002 dollars)

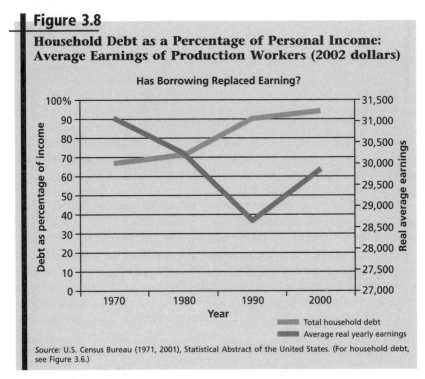

Has Borrowing Replaced Earning?

Legend:
- Total household debt
- Average real yearly earnings

Source: U.S. Census Bureau (1971, 2001), Statistical Abstract of the United States. (For household debt, see Figure 3.6.)

amount of debt the average consumer in the American economy is carrying is much larger than it was twenty years ago.

A new phenomenon was recently reported in the *New York Times*. Credit-card companies seem to be raising interest rates almost at will and on short notice.[39] Ed Schwebel, a retired software engineer from Gilbert, Arizona, saw the interest rate on his $69,000 in credit-card debt change from 9.2 to 18 percent in one month—"I paid my bills the minute the envelope hit the desk," said Mr. Schwebel. "All of a sudden in July, they swapped it to 18 percent. No warning. No reason. It was like I was blindsided." His minimum credit-card payment went from $502 in June to $895 in July. At that rate Ed will be lucky if his credit-card debt is ever paid down.[40]

Credit and debt in the United States far outstrips the incomes of average people. Compared to their counterparts of a generation ago, members of the modern middle class are in greater debt, earn less money, and work more hours at unstable jobs.

Robbing the Productivity Train

—July 2005 *Newsweek* headline to a report on a $113 million payout to Phil
Purcell, ex-CEO of Morgan Stanley, fired for poor performance[1]

So far, we've examined the plight of some typical middle class families and the increasingly problematic relationship between income and credit since the 1980s. In this chapter, we'll look at changes in productivity among American workers and ask where productivity gains went. But first, we need to discuss how productivity is measured.

What Is Productivity?

Productivity is an imprecise concept that yields considerable disagreement among economists, sociologists, and policy analysts. In general terms, productivity is the relative rate at which inputs into a production system turn into outputs. In a market economy, productivity is very important—increases in productivity increase aggregate wealth and income in the economy as a whole. Such increases make wage hikes, extensive fringe benefits, longer vacations, and shorter working hours possible without reducing the overall efficiency of the economy. More to the point, flat or declining productivity renders all competitions over economic output zero-sum, as gains by workers equal losses by employers and vice versa. Those gains that accrue to workers in the form of higher wages are "taken" directly from foregone profits for capitalists or reinvestment capital to keep cutting-edge technologies in place that (in theory) increase productivity. Regular, steady productivity gains ease negotiations between managers and workers: since the pie is getting bigger, everyone can have a slice.

Productivity in economics reflects a technical relationship between outputs and inputs in a production system or process. Box 4.6 on page 77 summarizes some of the more technical issues associated with different measures of productivity, the overall goal of which is to show how efficiently inputs are turned into outputs. The more efficiently raw materials, machinery, utilities, and labor are turned into a product or service and sold, the higher productivity is. Productivity is not strictly associated with increased output or work effort—in fact, some very labor-intensive processes are not very productive (mining for iron ore, for example), and some processes that seem to require little effort are very productive (booking a discount hotel reservation online, for example).

Recent analyses from the National Bureau of Economic Research[2] suggest that productivity measures are wildly inaccurate and tend to underestimate productivity gains in the economy (see the Appendix). Different measures of productivity result in different economic outlooks, with real implications for determining whether the economy is growing and how quickly. In particular, the "difference in growth rates" method used by the Bureau of Labor Statistics (growth in outputs minus the growth in inputs) drastically underestimates productivity growth. In particular, this method fails to take into account changes in technology and the organization of work that occurs when new, more advanced inputs are used. Workers tend to get "excess credit" if productivity rises and "excess blame" if productivity falls. The BLS methodology is the most widely used and quoted, which renders its impressions important for policymakers and business analysts attempting to chart the strength of the economy.

There is no easy way to measure productivity, and the decision of which measure to use is not just an esoteric dispute between academic economists. Measures of productivity are viewed as indicators of the overall health of the economy.[3] If indices suggest that productivity isn't growing, the standard political response by the right (in the United States, at least) is to recommend policies that favor capital investment and profits at the expense of wages and employee welfare. From the supply-side perspective, this makes sense: improving inputs will increase productivity and future productivity gains can be more widely distributed. Other indicators that suggest that productivity is improving could be used as a justification for providing average workers with better pay and benefits packages without necessarily harming investment capital or the investment environment.

Fred Block and Gene Burns illustrate the serious differences in the conclusions reached from slight differences in calculations of productivity.[4] For example, the critical differences come between 1973 and 1979, an era widely recognized as the source of the U.S. Crisis in Productivity (see Appendix Figures 4.1–4.4). Productivity growth before 1973 was between

2 and 3 percent—below the growth rates of the 1960s, but still not bad. But from 1973 to 1979, productivity levels fell to 1 percent, constituting a productivity crisis. Business and political leaders cited the crisis as a symptom of an overregulated, overburdened economy with wages and government spending that were too high, and government regulations that were too burdensome. Productivity rebounded for most of the period from the mid-1980s through 2000, ending most academic and popular press discussion of a productivity crisis.

As a society, we long for simple calculations to tell us how we're doing, as the standard National Income and Product Accounting methods do. Productivity growth stems from a variety of sources, all of which affect how work is organized and compensated, with implications for the middle class.[5] Increases in the quantity of capital, energy, intermediate goods, and services are all (in theory) measurable—they involve a simple calculation of "more" or "less."

But this simple measurement is complicated by other changes that affect productivity, almost all for the better and some in drastic ways. These include technological innovations (replacing an old, antiquated, expensive technology with a relatively cheap, new, and efficient one), economies of scale (lower production costs for big producers), improvements in management techniques and the organization of work (teamwork, quality circles, continuous quality improvement, and workplace changes designed

Box 4.1

Productivity, Economies of Scale, and Reinvestment

Productivity, the relationship between production output and the resource inputs used to generate that output, is usually expressed as the ratio of output per unit of input over time. For labor inputs, productivity is usually measured as outputs per person-hour worked.

The *National Income and Product Accounts* (NIPA) provide a national-level view of usages of the nation's output and income derived from production. The two most widely-used measures from the NIPA are gross domestic product (GDP) and gross domestic income (GDI). The NIPA was revised by the Bureau of Economic Analysis in 1999 and again in 2003.

Economies of scale represent the increase in efficiency that results from producing more goods. Generally, average costs per unit decline as production increases because fixed costs—the costs of plants, buildings, equipment, and materials—are spread over a larger number of finished products.

Reinvestment refers to taking profits from specific activities and (usually) investing them in those same activities or businesses to improve efficiency and remain competitive.

to harness the creativity of the workforce), and improvements to the efficiency and productivity of the labor force. These factors make measuring productivity an inexact science.

Do increases in productivity cost workers their jobs? This debate has raged for many years. The Luddites of the English Industrial Revolution, for example, destroyed weaving machines believing that technological improvements led to unemployment and massive social dislocation. Some policy analysts claim that the current "jobless recovery" in the United States is a product of increased productivity. Plants and offices that use labor efficiently don't necessarily need to hire more workers as demand for products grows and orders increase. This is especially true if, as we said in Chapter 3, there is unused existing capacity or "slack" in the economy.

Still, productivity increases are supposed to improve the economy, producing profits for investors and companies at the same time they generate wages and benefits for employees and tax revenues for governments to provide public goods.

Profits and Reinvestment: The Other Activities that Productivity Gains Support

In a market economy, productivity gains can be and are used for a variety of purposes, not all of which are for the best. For prosperity to be maintained in a market economy, the gains must be reinvested in the enterprises they came from. Without this reinvestment, output starts to grind to a halt as machines wear out, computers and other electronic devices become obsolete, and the technologies that make a modern economy work fall into disrepair. Such setbacks reduce workplace productivity and reduce the gains that can go to other activities such as profits, consumption, and wages.

Reinvestment maintains the momentum of productivity increases. Since the 1930s, many governments have maintained good investment environments, following certain guidelines. These guidelines have recently been reinforced as state socialist economies have begun to move slowly toward becoming market economies. Specifically, economies need a sound banking system, sound currency, fiscally responsible government spending, consistently collected and preferably low taxes, and social stability.

Unfortunately, reinvestment also produces worker displacement. Some of this displacement is probably inevitable, and it is impossible to tell how many workers have been technologically displaced rather than laid off for other reasons. But as we saw with Bill's company in Chapter 2, and as we'll see below, the activities responsible for the huge job losses of the past thirty years had little to do with productive reinvestment.

66

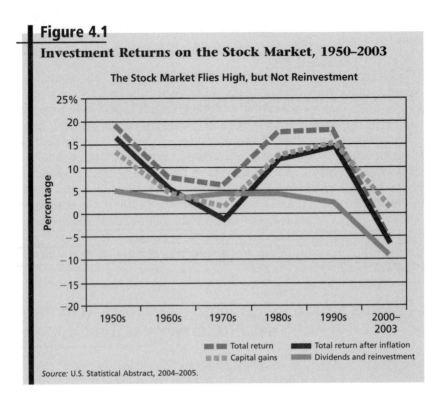

Figure 4.1

Investment Returns on the Stock Market, 1950–2003

The Stock Market Flies High, but Not Reinvestment

Legend:
- ▬ ▬ Total return
- ▬ Total return after inflation
- ▪ ▪ ▪ Capital gains
- ▬ Dividends and reinvestment

Source: U.S. Statistical Abstract, 2004–2005.

What Did Corporate America Do with Profits and Productivity Gains?

Instead of investing in new technologies to spawn further productivity gains corporate managers overpaid themselves, doled out cash to investors, consumed luxury items, and engaged in corporate takeovers and mergers and acquisitions (see Figure 4.1). Whether or not these activities contribute to the overall productive capacity of the American economy is, to say the least, an open question.

Corporate profits during the 1990s hit near-record levels, peaking at above $500 billion in 1997 (see Figure 4.2). The Standard and Poor's (S&P) index and the Dow Jones Industrial Average, the standard indices of stock market performance, increased over 1,000 percent during the 1990s, and stocks did better during the 1990s than at any time since World War II (see Appendix Figures 4.5 and 4.6).[6] By any standard, these are tremendous changes in the wealth and profit available for redistribution, consumption, or investment. But the rate of dividend payment and reinvest-

Figure 4.2

Corporate Profits

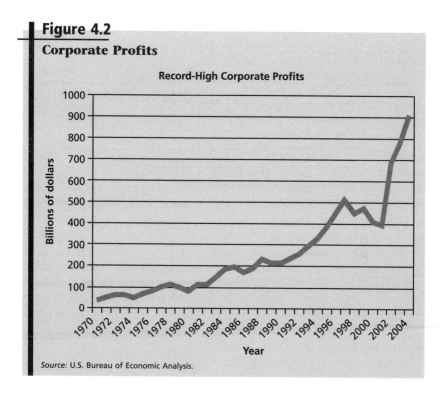

Record-High Corporate Profits

Source: U.S. Bureau of Economic Analysis.

ment, never high in the first place, *declined* through the 1980s, 1990s, and even after that. Isn't this where the funds come from to invest in new technologies? And what about those record-high corporate profits?

So Some People Got Rich! Doesn't Everyone Own Stock These Days?

Without question, the overall level of activity in the U.S. stock market has risen dramatically. But how have these gains been distributed? The answer is clear: not very equitably.

Only 21 percent of all U.S. households have direct stock holdings,[7] and the overwhelming majority of stocks are owned by an extremely small percent of wealthy people (see Appendix Figure 4.7).[8] In 2001, the bottom 80 percent of stockowners *combined* owned just 10.6 percent of total stock value. Of course, stock holdings aren't the only measure of wealth, nor are they the one most Americans rely on, so let's look at broader indicators of wealth and its distribution.

The more complete story is told by looking at changes in family net worth, the total value of the wealth held by different classes of wealth holders (see Figure 4.3).

In spite of the spectacular gains in the U.S. stock market since the 1970s, median net worth for all Americans barely moved. However, mean family net worth (the average value of a family's assets, minus its liabilities) increased substantially to almost $400,000. Since these changes are in real dollars, they represent improvements in the wealth profile of Americans. But since the median doesn't move, the numbers suggest big wealth gains among those who already possess wealth and not much movement near the middle of the wealth distribution. More ominously, it suggests that the wealth profiles of a substantial percentage of Americans probably didn't move at all.

These suspicions are borne out by an examination of distributions of net worth. The growth in wealth displayed by the change in median family net worth is overwhelmingly concentrated at the top of the income and wealth distributions. The median family net worth in the top tenth of the family income distribution almost doubles during the stock market boom of the late 1990s, rising from around $500,000 per household to $850,000 per household (see Appendix Figure 4.8). There are more modest changes in the next two quintiles of the earnings distribution as median net worth rises from $184,000 to $261,000 for those in the

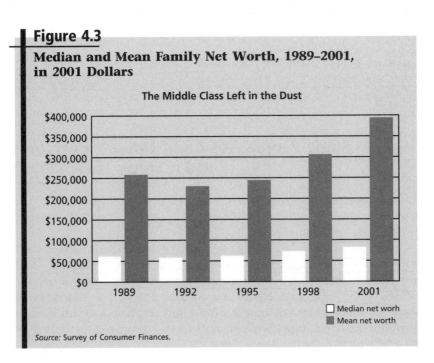

Figure 4.3

Median and Mean Family Net Worth, 1989–2001, in 2001 Dollars

The Middle Class Left in the Dust

Legend: ☐ Median net worh ■ Mean net worth

Source: Survey of Consumer Finances.

Box 4.2

Distributions of Wealth and Income

One way of measuring distributions of income and wealth across populations is to rank everyone on their level of income or wealth, divide the population into equal-sized groups, and then figure out what percentage of the income and wealth each group controls. One way to do this is to divide the population into *quintiles*, equal fifths in terms of population size, with each quintile representing 20 percent of the population; you can also use *quartiles*, groups that represent 25 percent of the population.

Ranking the population this way and determining what percentage of the economy each segment controls provide an easy way to chart the distribution of income and wealth over time. They also allow for rough comparisons of wealth and income distributions between nations that don't use the same currencies.

second highest quintile and from $92,000 to $140,000 for the middle quintile (the people we define as "middle-class" for our purposes).

The rise of wealth inequality in the 1990s is even more apparent when we examine the distribution of wealth by quartiles (see Appendix Figure 4.9). Here the changes are much more stark and inequality much more apparent. Specifically, the bottom quartile of the wealth distribution essentially controls no wealth at all. After that, wealth does grow at all quintiles of the wealth distribution, but it grows disproportionately at the top: the median wealth holder in the top tenth of the distribution is worth over $1 million by 2001.[9]

One consumer manifestation of changes in wealth and income has been a boom in luxury retail sales (see Appendix Figure 4.10). During the 1990s, the sales index among luxury retailers doubled as affluent consumers rushed to spend their new gains on the latest luxury goods from Tiffany's, Gucci, Saks, and Waterford. The rise in consumption from these luxury retailers is a sign that relatively wealthy Americans were reaping the consumption benefits of their newfound income and wealth.[10]

Corporate Takeovers as a Competitive Strategy

Aside from luxury goods, much of the enormous capital raised during the 1990s expansion went toward merger and acquisition activity and corporate takeovers. The value, size, and amount of merger and acquisition activity in the U.S. and in cross-border transactions increased substantially during the 1990s, as did the number of bank mergers and acquisitions (see

Figure 4.4

Merger and Acquisition Activity, 1970–2004, Number of Deals and Deal Value in Billions of Dollars

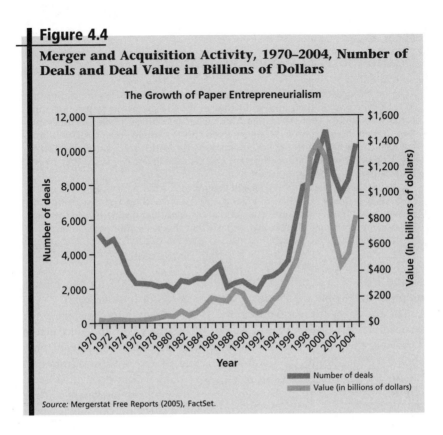

The Growth of Paper Entrepreneurialism

Source: Mergerstat Free Reports (2005), FactSet.

Figure 4.4 and Appendix Figures 4.11 and 4.12). The deregulation of financial services is largely responsible for these changes.

Favorable tax policies played a huge role in the increase of mergers and acquisitions of the 1980s and 1990s. Federal tax laws allow corporations to write off all the debt they assume as a result of merger and acquisition activity.[11] Thus, there are incentives for corporations to engage in takeover activity to hide cash surpluses, lower tax bills, and potentially make money from selling off the pieces of acquired companies for more than the acquired corporation cost in the first place.

Debate rages on the merits of corporate merger and acquisition activity, but several patterns resulting from it are clear:

1. To engage in merger and acquisition activity, corporations often take on massive debts they can't pay. This creates enormous pressure to "squeeze" average employees—through pay cuts, slashing benefits, or adding work hours—to find new sources of cash.[12]

Box 4.3

Merger and Acquisition Activity

Merger and acquisition activity (sometimes referred to as "M&A") is the act of buying, selling, and merging existing businesses through stock and equity exchanges. Business owners and stockholders engage in such activity to merge companies that profit from combining operations, while investors do so to direct management practices. Merger and acquisition activity almost always changes the value of stock shares as investors buy up publicly held stock in an attempt to take over or merge with an existing company.

In some cases, corporations take on debt and other liabilities ("poison pills") to make themselves unattractive takeover targets. In others, investors and corporate leaders borrow money from investment bankers to engage in merger and acquisition activity themselves.

Merger and acquisition activity is part of an advanced, globalized market economy, but it becomes problematic as corporate officers (CEOs, CFOs, and other executives) are awarded stock options. If stock options allow executives to purchase company shares at a predetermined price and merger and acquisition activity drive up that price, executives have a built-in incentive to see their company's stock become a target for merger and acquisition activity: they can sell their stock option shares when the price is at its peak and pocket (in many cases) millions of dollars without changing the underlying productive standing of their company at all. The existence of stock option compensation packages along with merger and acquisition activity is one reason for the massive rise in CEO salaries documented in Chapter 3.

2. Companies are rarely acquired and kept intact; instead, they are sold off, either in whole or in part. For average workers, layoffs often result from this practice.

3. Many of these transactions allow companies to pay little or no income tax.[13] In fact, the corporate debt assembled through merger and acquisition activity is tax deductible!

By the year 2000, the Dow rose past 10,000 and some observers confidently claimed it would keep on soaring.[14] Investors, particularly in technology stocks, were getting richer by the minute. To many observers it seemed that happy days were here again. But, just as the "housing bubble" had done in the 1980s, the "tech bubble" eventually burst, leaving high-skilled workers jobless and with worthless stock options. The stock market continued to climb, but a series of corporate scandals and large bankruptcies were just around the corner. Though several of these took place during President Bush's first administration, the seeds had been planted during the Clinton administration, which backed the continued

Box 4.4

Tyco, MCI-WorldCom, and Enron

L. Dennis Kozlowski and Mark H. Swartz, both top executives at Tyco International, were convicted in the summer of 2005 of looting the company of over $150 million and were sentenced to eight to twenty-five years in a New York State Prison. These sentences followed the conviction and sentencing of Bernard J. Ebbers of WorldCom to twenty-five years in prison and John J. Rigas of Adelphia Communications to fifteen years in prison for financial frauds that allowed them to pocket millions of dollars in compensation. Kenneth L. Lay and Jeffrey K. Skilling, former executives at the now-defunct Enron, were convicted in May 2006 on multiple counts of securities fraud and conspiracy.

These cases expose common problems resulting from the payment of executives in stock options and the obsession of Wall Street traders with ever-growing and immediate profit margins. In a deregulated financial environment, it was possible for these executives to represent their companies as making money hand over fist when in fact profits and performance were either more down-to-earth or, in the case of Enron, nonexistent. With each public announcement of the latest achievement in corporate performance, the price of the company's stock went up and top executives could sell their shares, making millions in immediate profits. The transactions were so fast and so complex that arms-length investors had no idea what was happening. It was only after outsiders began questioning accounting statements that the extent of the fraud in each case was exposed. In the meantime, investors lost millions, tens of thousands of workers lost jobs, and many employees lost their entire retirement funds (see Chapter 6).

deregulation of electricity, telecommunications, and finance.[15] The deregulation of these industries encouraged a range of corporate activities designed to boost stock prices and create added wealth for investors. Unfortunately, many of these practices turned out to be smoke and mirrors, artificially inflating profits and stock prices,[16] and eventually leading to the collapse of several gigantic corporations. On December 2, 2001, Enron filed the biggest Chapter 11 bankruptcy in U.S. history; at the time of filing, the company reported $62 billion in assets. Enron's ignominious title was held only until the next summer, when WorldCom filed for bankruptcy with assets totaling $100 billion.

As Joseph Stiglitz, winner of the Nobel Prize in Economics and chairman of President Clinton's Council of Economic Advisors, points out, Enron and WorldCom were products of deregulation. Enron's growth was fueled by deregulation of the energy industry, and WorldCom's from deregulation of telecommunications. Both businesses benefited from and adapted to financial industry deregulation, which provided incentives for mergers and other techniques to maximize short-term profits.[17] Deregulation also set the stage for questionable, deceptive, and outright fraudulent accounting practices. Many referred to these practices as "aggressive accounting," but as Jim Hightower writes, "That's the same as saying that robbing 7-Elevens is 'aggressive consumerism.'"[18]

Clearly, the productivity gains of the 1990s went to those with considerable income and wealth, or were used by corporations to engage in activities designed to bolster their immediate bottom line. They were not used to improve the lot of average workers, who received no increase in their average paychecks.

What If Wages Were Indexed to Productivity?

What would the distribution of earnings for average workers look like if some of those productivity gains had been distributed to them rather than spent on these other activities? There are complications involved in answering this question. For one thing, workers could be rewarded for increased productivity in several ways, including working fewer hours and taking increased leisure time. (Evidence indicates that this has not happened: Americans now work more hours than anyone else in the industrialized world except for the Japanese.)

Another complication is that, rather than increasing the compensation of existing workers that produce productivity gains, employers could choose to hire more workers at existing wage rates and distribute those gains over more workers. Indeed, in the 1990s the United States saw an impressive trend in job growth.[19] However, if the number of available jobs grew rapidly and the workforce did not grow at the same pace, then there should have been pressure for upward wage movement even if productivity stayed the same—more employers would have chased relatively fewer workers. Since productivity was growing, this should have eased pressure on employer hiring as fewer workers could do the work that more workers did before.

Because of these complications, judging the distribution of productivity gains to average workers accurately is difficult.[20] To do so, we'll make a series of assumptions and then see how earnings would change if those assumptions hold.

Radically oriented economists and social scientists would argue that wages should rise in direct proportion to productivity. This is not the same as saying that all productivity gains should be redistributed completely to

Box 4.5

Marginal Workers and the Productivity Index

A *marginal worker* makes the last positive contribution to production. All workers added after the last marginal worker are surplus workers whose overall effect is to lower productivity, as in an overstaffed bureaucracy.

The *productivity index* (used in the rest of the chapter, from the Bureau of Labor Statistics) measures output per labor input per unit time, indexed so that 1992 = 100. An index of 150, for example, suggests that an economy is producing one third more per unit of labor input than in 1992. An index of 50 suggests that an economy is producing 50 percent less per unit of labor input than in 1992—a truly catastrophic result.

workers; instead, workers' earnings should rise as productivity does, in equal proportion. We'll call this the 100 percent solution.

Others would argue that most if not all productivity gains are necessary to keep up with technological changes and to remain competitive. Under this assumption, the costs of no wage gains should be compensated for by increased investment in new equipment and the organization of work—investments that would yield more employment and higher wages later on. Since those who produced the productivity gains should receive something for their trouble, we'll give them a quarter of the productivity boost as wages. We'll call this scenario the 25 percent solution.

Still others would argue that productivity gains are equally the product of labor and capital, and should be split accordingly. This argument assumes that both investors and workers make sacrifices during bad times— not a safe assumption, given the last twenty years—and should both be rewarded in good times. We'll call this the 50 percent solution.

Before we present the results of the simulations, a reminder of the real hourly earnings changes for average workers. For manufacturing and non–farm business workers in non-supervisory positions, real hourly wages declined for most of the 1980s and 1990s, and started to rise again only around 1997 (Appendix Figure 4.13). Hourly earnings in non–farm business never again came close to their 1970 real value, regardless of when we look. Manufacturing hourly earnings come close to returning to their 1970 levels in real dollars. It is also clear that real wages have declined as productivity has increased (see Figure 4.5).

For manufacturing, we can plot this change only since the late 1980s, but for non–farm business we can go all the way back to 1970 (see Appendix Figure 4.14). In both cases, real hourly wages decline as productivity rises, indicating that there are considerable revenues and profits

Figure 4.5

Non–Farm Business Wages in 1992 Dollars and Productivity Index*

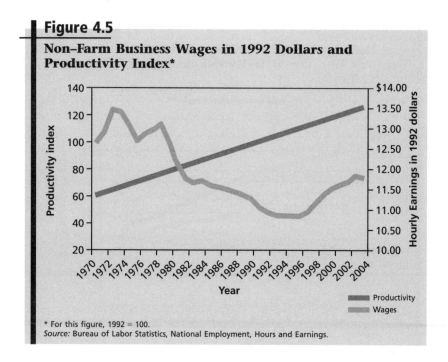

* For this figure, 1992 = 100.
Source: Bureau of Labor Statistics, National Employment, Hours and Earnings.

to redistribute, as we've suggested. The result of our simulation is presented in Figure 4.6.

By any standard we use, from the 25 percent solution to the 100 percent solution, the lot of the average worker would be much improved were they allowed to share in at least some of the productivity gains they've helped produce. The changes would be in real dollars accounting for inflation, representing boosts in standard of living and purchasing power. Even using the most modest proposal, the 25 percent solution, the average non-farm, non-supervisory worker who made $23,560 in 2003 ($11.78 per hour × 40 hours per week × 50 weeks per year) would have made $24,400 ($12.20 per hour × 40 hours per week × 50 weeks per year), a 3.6 percent raise or an additional $840 per year. That difference increases to $3,040 in 2003 if workers received the 50 percent solution, enough money to afford a $250 monthly car payment (on a car you buy—more on this in Chapter 5). Simply allowing raises that are the size of productivity increases in the 100 percent solution would yield an extra $7,160 per year in 2003— almost equal to the average amount of credit-card debt per household in the United States for 2003. Changes in real wages in manufacturing would be even more dramatic (see Appendix Figure 4.15).

Figure 4.6

Real Hourly Wages for Non-Farm, Non-Supervisory Workers, Plus Productivity Enhanced Wages, in 1992 Dollars

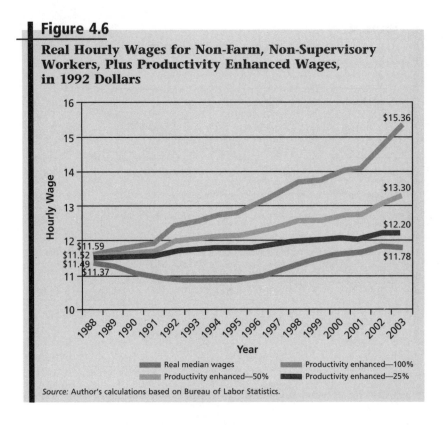

Source: Author's calculations based on Bureau of Labor Statistics.

The productivity-enhanced wage gains of the 100 percent solution would almost equal the amount of money the average consumer carries in credit-card debt. When companies invest profits in financial markets by purchasing asset-backed securities (see Chapter 5), the money that could have been given to workers as increased compensation provides the financial backing for lending institutions to extend credit. This directly supports our contention that the middle class has been loaned money it could have been paid. Of course, it is often not technically the same money. In other situations, such as when companies use revenues to finance executive compensation packages rather than increase average workers' wages, the gains go directly into executive pockets. Workers appear to be relying on consumer credit to provide income that they may not have needed if their wages were higher. (Of course, it is possible that the multi-trillion dollar advertising and credit industry would create additional "needs" for the American middle class to pursue, keeping the household debt rate about the same despite the increased wages.)

Box 4.6

Productivity: An Elusive Concept

In the abstract, productivity measures are divided into *single-factor* and *multi-factor productivity*. Single factor productivity measures usually have focused on labor productivity and are measured as

$$Output \div hours\ worked$$

"Output" in this context varies from one industry to another and even from one workplace to another. In some service-related and high-technology firms, discreet units of output might not exist at all. But this indicator has the advantage of easy measurement, and data of this kind are generally collected by almost all workplaces for internal purposes. The downside of measures like this is that they don't measure the contribution of labor alone. Virtually all changes that increase the efficiency of the production process are "credited" to labor and appear as productivity change.[21] More importantly from our standpoint, non-labor contributions to productivity can deteriorate, and this will appear as declines in labor's contribution to productivity.[22]

The development of the specific measure of productivity favored by the U.S. Department of Labor resulted from the economic and political environment surrounding the adoption of Keynesian economics during the Roosevelt administration of the 1930s.[23] Specifically, economists and policy analysts at the Works Progress Administration (WPA) and other federal agencies were convinced that wages lagged behind productivity gains in the 1920s, and that the resulting "underconsumption" was a drag on the U.S. economy. But at the time there was no statistical mechanism for measuring aggregate productivity in the economy, so convincing arguments that wages lagged behind productivity relied solely on speculation.

Economists developing measures of productivity had another problem on their hands: output units were specific to specific industries (for example, tons of steel, number of cars assembled, and reams of paper manufactured) and were thus incomparable. Though productivity within industries over time could be compared, doing so provided policymakers with little useful information on how aggregate productivity was changing across the economy. No measure of productivity could deal with the different capital inputs and changes in the organization of work that affected aggregate, single-factor productivity measures in ways that had little to do with whether labor inputs improved.

Beginning in 1947, the U.S. government published the National Income and Product Accounts,[24] introducing the measure of Gross National Product (or GNP) that converted the measurement of output from physical inputs (tons of steel, for example) to dollar values. The Bureau of Economic Analysis furthered the development and use of GNP measures by publishing them by industry, tying the production of national output to shares contributed by various sectors of the economy. This virtually eliminated any attempt at measuring physical outputs, instead measuring output in dollars.

This measurement, however, often reflects the "deflation" problem: as output is more efficiently made, the price may drop faster than unit labor costs drop, making productivity look artificially low. Most output measures attempt to

(continued)

measure output in real (inflation adjusted) dollars to take this change into account. Inflation adjustment can adjust for deflation (actual drops in the price of goods and services) as well as for other increases in prices.

Multifactor productivity measures try to avoid some problems of single factor productivity measures by taking into account combined inputs (for example, capital, labor, energy, raw materials, and purchased services).[25] But the problems here are no less daunting than the problems of using single factor productivity measures. Figuring out what the relevant inputs are and assigning the correct values to them are serious challenges. Further, most policy analysts and some economists are interested in the relative contributions of different inputs for increasing productivity.

William Nordhaus proposes that we use a "chain-weighted index" of sectoral productivity growth in place of the standard output per hours worked measure of productivity that is part of NIPA.[26] This method says mathematically that, output and productivity in one sector of the economy is critically bound to productivity in other sectors. Further, the productivity in the entire economy changes as investment grows in one sector of the economy and not another— industries with slow investment growth usually have slow productivity growth, and vice versa. And productivity changes as employment shares shift from high (or low) productivity industries and sectors to low (or high) productivity industries or sectors. Our current aggregate measures of productivity bottle up all these changes and attribute them to changes in output per hour worked.

For reasons that Nordhaus explains, from a social welfare standpoint the traditional measure of productivity needs to be supplemented by the addition of changes due to changing expenditure shares on productivity across industries. If capital investment increases at different rates across industries, then productivity will lag. This second component of a productivity measure places emphasis on increased capital inputs in addition to standard output per unit input.

Current productivity measures do not represent differences in inputs across industries well, so including these two factors while excluding the portion accounted for by shifts in employment is justified. The level of productivity (as opposed to changes in productivity) varies by a factor of over 100 across industries![27] Capital intensive and human capital (educated) sectors of the economy have high levels of productivity. Labor intensive and low-skilled areas of the economy (private household workers, for example) have low levels of productivity. In practice, relative productivity levels almost never move, but industries do change their ability to convert inputs into outputs. That change in ability is what newer measures of productivity try to capture.

How effective are new capital investments at increasing productivity, and do these investments pay off in terms of increased efficiency? If new capital investments don't produce their intended results unless work routines are reorganized, then capital investments by themselves may do relatively little to boost aggregate productivity. If work routines are changed but workers are required to use antiquated equipment that breaks down frequently and requires extensive maintenance, then increased worker inputs won't yield the expected efficiency gains. Without those efficiency gains, the division of the economic pie between investment, profits, and compensation is a fight over who will get theirs at the expense of others. Such confrontations rarely lead to long-term harmony.

The average worker could accomplish much with such gains in purchasing power. The average worker with employer-provided health insurance now pays almost $200 per month,[28] and $600 a month would allow workers whose employers don't provide health insurance to afford a healthcare plan of their own. Putting some of this money in savings and retirement accounts would be the difference between retiring comfortably and retiring on social security. Saving this money would provide workers' children with college educations, especially if savings accrued over several years in interest-bearing accounts.

The results of our calculations may seem large, but the average worker is owed even more money than we've suggested. Productivity enhanced wages are cumulative and accrue for each year that the median real wage is below the productivity enhanced wage, and each year that workers are not paid the productivity enhanced wage, the workers lose the productivity enhanced wage for that year and all raises based on the enhanced wage for the years after that. The cumulative effect over the fifteen-year stretch from 1988 to 2003 in even the most conservative scenario would be $15,420 real 1992 dollars or $20,663 2004 dollars. This is the difference between paying for a new car in 2003 with cash or leasing it from diminished earnings, giving children substantial boosts toward college funds, enhancing health insurance, saving for retirement, or simply having a nice vacation.

Even the 100 percent calculation, which raises real earnings in proportion to productivity growth, assumes that the division of proceeds among employers, investors, and workers was equitable to begin with. We took for granted the prevailing split among workers, profits, and reinvestment that existed in 1988. If we question this relationship between employers and workers, wage and benefit gains are greater still.

But of course, the distribution of productivity gains over the past thirty-five years has not come close to any of these solutions. Without these gains to benefit them, middle-class Americans rely instead on substantial credit. But where did all this credit come from? That's the subject of our next chapter.

5

Where Did All That Credit Come From?

For two months now, federal banking regulators have signaled their discomfort about the explosive rise in risky mortgage loans. . . . The impact so far? Almost nil.

—*New York Times*, July 15, 2005[1]

We can show that productivity has reached its highest levels since the 1960s, but tracing where these gains have gone is tricky. Evidence suggests that these gains have been siphoned by corporate executives in big pay packages and investors and speculators looking for deals. Incomes and earnings have stagnated and wage inequality has risen, yet American consumers are buying products and services at unprecedented rates, and consumer confidence has remained high.[2] To understand this paradox, we must examine the rapidly expanding pool of credit provided by the financial services industry. Basic changes in this industry have allowed for the rapid expansion of credit of all kinds, miring the middle class in ever-expanding debt.

The deregulation of the banking industry during the 1980s set the stage for the transformation of the consumer credit landscape. Limits on the maximum interest rates that lenders could charge were lifted, constraints on securities dealings were removed, and interstate branch banking was allowed. These changes led to a dramatic rise in the types of credit available to consumers and the profitability of lending. The number of credit card users and the levels of debt carried on credit cards have skyrocketed since the 1980s. Home equity loans, leased vehicles, car title loans, pawnshops, and rent-to-own stores have become popular ways for middle-class Americans to access credit and fall further into debt. Investors have fueled the lending industry by purchasing asset-backed securities that help lenders spread the risk of lending and further maximize profits. The post-industrial peasant is trapped in a work and spend cycle.

Box 5.1

A Primer on Banking and Finance Terms

The banking and financial services industry uses various terms to describe different types of credit instruments and the relationships between what you borrow, what you pay, and their resulting profit or loss. Some of these terms describe unscrupulous and questionable practices that consumers should be on the lookout for. The list below covers most of the terms that are used in this chapter.

Annual percentage rate (APR)—an interest rate designed to measure the true cost of loans, including fees and pre-paid interest. Lenders are required to disclose the annual percentage rates on loans as part of Federal Truth in Lending laws.

Asset-backed securities—bonds that represent pools of loans of similar types, duration, and interest rates. Individual lenders such as banks and financial-service companies recover cash quickly by selling their loans to asset-backed securities packagers. Home equity loans and credit cards accounted for 46 percent of the asset-backed securities market in 2004.

Bank spread—the difference between the interest rate a bank charges borrowers and the interest rate they pay to depositors, or the interest rate they pay on the money they borrow.

Car-title loans—loans extended with car titles used as collateral. Interest rates on car-title loans are usually much higher than rates on conventional loans and credit cards. To qualify, the loan applicant must own a car.

Close-end lease—a fixed-rate lease (usually for cars) in which the leaser agrees to fixed-lease payments representing the depreciation of the car over the duration of the lease. If the vehicle depreciates more than the amount covered by the lease, the car dealership is responsible for that loss. In an open-end lease, the person leasing the car is responsible for the loss.

Credit-card rate—the interest rate that credit card issuers charge users on their balances.

Credit securitization—the process of packaging, underwriting, and selling loans in the form of securities.

Equity stripping—depleting the borrower's equity (ownership) in property through deceptive loan practices, refinancing, and fee packing. Through equity stripping practices, the borrower's equity is transferred to the lender.

Federal Deposit Insurance Corporation (FDIC)—an independent U.S. Federal Executive Agency that insures individual bank deposits up to $100,000. The FDIC was created in 1933 to avoid the economic consequences of bank failures during the Great Depression, when banks could not return money deposited in them. The FDIC is managed by a five-member board of directors, appointed by the President with the consent of the Senate. Deposits are covered in banks, the Federal Reserve System, and some state banks.

Federal Reserve rate—the interest rate the Federal Reserve Bank charges banks for "overnight" borrowing from the Federal Reserve Bank. This particular number receives a lot of press because it reflects the Federal Reserve Bank's

(continued)

estimate of how the economy is working overall. Increases in Federal Reserve rates usually signal that the Federal Reserve (or "Fed") thinks the economy needs to slow down because inflation is threatening. Decreases in Federal Reserve rates are designed to stimulate borrowing and more economic activity.

Federal Savings and Loan Insurance Corporation (FSLIC)—formerly a government corporation under the direction of the former Federal Home Loan Bank Board, the FSLIC insured deposits at savings institutions. Congress authorized the FSLIC in the National Housing Act of 1934, and under the Financial Institutions Reform, Recovery, and Enforcement Act of 1989, it was abolished. Its deposit insurance function was assumed by a new insurance fund, the Savings Association Insurance Fund (SAIF), administered by the Federal Deposit Insurance Corporation (FDIC).

Fee packing—attaching excessive fees and ancillary products onto loans in an attempt to increase the lenders' profit.

Home equity credit—credit offered to a borrower based on the amount of equity the borrower has in his house (the portion of the house the borrower owns or has paid off, usually reflecting the principal of the mortgage plus any appreciation or increase in value of the property).

Installment credit—credit that is paid off in a fixed number of installments, to cover the principal and interest for the loan. Payments are usually the same amount per installment period (normally months).

Loan flipping—the repeated refinancing of existing loans so that lenders can earn more fees.

Loan-to-value (LTV) ratio—a value determined by dividing the total amount of the loan by the appraised value of the property. For lenders, high LTV ratios represent more risky loans than low LTV ratios. Loans for more money than an appraised property is worth (for example, a "125 percent mortgage") have loan-to-value ratios greater than 1.

Prime rate—interest rates charged by banks and financial service lenders to their most credit-worthy customers.

Self banking—refers to people who do not have checking or savings accounts at banks or savings-and-loan institutions.

Subprime loans—loans offered at an interest rate above the prime lending rate to people who do not quality for prime rate loans.

The Evolution of Consumer Credit

Prostitution may be the world's oldest profession, but in ubiquity and longevity the practice of extending credit surely comes in a close second. Since the time of the Bible, lenders have played an important role in the expansion of commerce and nations. Columbus never would have "sailed the ocean blue" if not for funds provided by Queen Isabella and the Spanish government. Early American pioneers never could have survived harsh prairie life if not for general stores extending personal credit lines to be repaid after the harvest, allowing struggling farmers to purchase seed, tools, and other supplies. In growing cities across the country during the first half of the twentieth century, installment plans allowed cash-poor urban dwellers to fill their homes with furniture as they pursued the American Dream.

Throughout World War II, many businesses offered payment cards and/or installment plans to customers to encourage and facilitate the purchase of their products. Credit cards that could be used at a wide range of unaffiliated businesses were practically nonexistent; not until the Diners Club International Card was issued in 1950, followed by American Express and Carte Blanche in 1958, did this practice take off on a large scale.[3] These early forms of "plastic" were charge cards, requiring payment of bills upon receipt, rather than credit cards. The creation of credit card giants like Visa and MasterCard in the mid-1960s revolutionized the credit industry. Their cards could be used at a variety of establishments and their balances did not have to be paid each month but could instead be rolled over to the next payment cycle.[4]

As Robert Manning points out, in post-industrial society the economic balance of power has shifted from industry to banking: "General Electric's GE Capital (consumer credit) division generates higher profits than its core manufacturing division."[5] Deregulation of the banking industry in the 1980s led to increased interstate banking, consolidation of the financial industry, and a dramatic increase in the maximum interest rates and fees that lenders could charge. Lenders scrambled to capitalize on this favorable financial environment by issuing more credit cards and expanding the pool of potential borrowers by developing other forms of lending. These other forms include personal credit cards, home equity loans, "no money down" car loans and leases, rent-to-own plans, title loans, check cashing, and other "fringe banking" practices. To understand why Americans now have so many different ways to borrow money, we must examine how the banking industry has changed in the last century.

The Deregulation of the Banking Industry: A Sleepy Industry Wakes Up

Until the 1980s, the banking industry was guided and regulated by Depression-era laws that limited the types of loans banks could issue, the reserves that banks were required to have on hand to cover their deposits and loans, the interest rates they could charge, and their ability to open branch banks. This legislation also produced the Federal Deposit Insurance Corporation (FDIC, for banks) and the Federal Savings and Loan Insurance Corporation (for Savings and Loans).

The 1978 Supreme Court decision in *Marquette National Bank of Minneapolis v. First Omaha Service Corp.*, which ruled that lenders could charge the highest interest rate allowed in their state regardless of a lower rate limitation in the customer's state of residence,[6] had a profound impact on consumer lending and usury laws. The practical effect of the *Marquette* decision was to force states to relax their usury laws or risk losing banking business as banks moved to states with higher rate ceilings. This decision, coupled with the legislative changes to the banking industry discussed below, set the stage for the current state of the industry. "The average 18 percent rate that consumers have been paying on credit cards would have landed the credit company executives in the penitentiary twenty years ago. Today it lands the same executives in flattering profile stories in *Forbes* and *BusinessWeek*."[7]

 The formal deregulation of the banking industry led to three important changes: maximum interest rates on bank deposits were eliminated, constraints on securities dealing were removed, and interstate branch banking blossomed.[8] The 1956 Bank Holding Company Act prohibited out-of-state holding companies from operating in several states unless both states involved explicitly allowed it. Interstate banking was effectively prohibited from the mid-1950s until 1980.[9] From the 1960s until the late 1990s the number of bank branches, including supermarket branches—i.e., branches that provide a reduced set of banking products—grew dramatically.[10]

Since the 1980s there has been steady consolidation of the banking industry. We can see this trend in the growing number of mergers and the amount of assets acquired in these acquisitions. In 1980 a total of 190 acquisitions took place, with a value of about $10 billion; in 1990 there were 366, at approximately $45 billion; and in 1998, 518, at nearly $630 billion.[11] Mergers between banks, brokerages, and investment banks—for example, the $21 billion merger of Morgan Stanley and Dean Witter Discover in 1997—have further consolidated the financial industry.[12] The majority of bank mergers represented attempts to break into new geographic markets by extending the markets served (see Appendix Figure 5.1).[13]

Savings and Loan (S&L) associations were also affected by this deregulation, leading to a debacle in the late 1980s that cost taxpayers dearly.[14] At the start of the decade, federally chartered S&Ls had to keep almost all their loans in relatively stable and safe home mortgages. Changes to federal law in 1982 reduced restrictions on how S&Ls invested; for example, they could now invest completely in commercial real estate ventures—a much riskier form of investment than home mortgages.[15]

S&Ls gambled with their federally guaranteed deposits as they tried to cash in on the changes. As a result, the industry collapsed as thousands of S&Ls became insolvent. The federal government bailed out these failing S&Ls—with taxpayers footing the bill, at an estimated total cost of $300–$500 billion.[16] More recent legislation—for example, the Gramm–Leach–Bliley Act of 2000[17]—has opened the door for further industry consolidation by allowing banking, securities, and insurance activities to be housed together.

Deregulation has also further split first-tier ("traditional") and second-tier ("fringe") banking. As first-tier banks across the country left inner cities to pursue the higher debt ceilings offered in other states, they were quickly replaced by a variety of companies seeking to fill the void and to profit while doing so. These second-tier financial companies, such as check cashing and payday loan services, pawnshops, and rent-to-own companies, appeal to customers who do not have access to traditional banks either because traditional banks have left the area or because of previous credit problems. This type of lending is very profitable: "Consumer-finance companies earn profits that make most businesses jealous. They routinely produce returns on assets that are three to four times what banks produce."[18]

Traditional banks have not completely forgotten the growing population of "self-banked" households, those without bank accounts: many first-tier banks provide fringe banks with the funds they need to operate.

> The reality, of course, is that Citigroup is making large profits reselling subprime loans through its Salomon Smith Barney subsidiary. Other banks such as Wells Fargo, Union Planters, Fleet Capital, Eagle National, and Goleta National are making huge profits on payday loans and providing the lines of credit for check-cashing and car-title pawn operations. In addition, brokerage companies are making millions of dollars in commissions selling the stocks and bonds of second tier banks, and mutual fund managers are eager to benefit from their appreciating stock portfolio of fringe banks.[19]

In addition to expanding the availability and types of credit, banking deregulation has also contributed to fraudulent and disturbing lending practices. Federal Reserve Board Governor Edward Gramlich states, "The growth in numbers and types of subprime credit has been accompanied by disturbing reports of abusive mortgage practices. . . . Many incidents of fraud and abuse have been reported and in certain sections of large cities, mortgage foreclosures are rising to worrisome heights."[20] These practices include loan flipping (the repeated refinancing of existing loans to generate more fees to be paid by the borrower), fee packing (placing additional fees into a mortgage without the borrower's knowledge or understanding), and equity stripping (extending credit when the borrower does not have the ability to repay, then foreclosing on the home when the borrower can't keep up with payments).

In *Merchants of Misery*, Michael Hudson describes the deceptive practices some predatory lenders use. Wilma Jean Henderson, mother of seven children and stepchildren, borrowed $2,000 from Associates Financial Services to fix her 1987 Blazer. During the deal, "the loan officer flipped through the papers so that only the signature portion of the document showed, and some of the numbers on one document had not been filled in until after she signed it. She didn't read anything, she said, because 'I trusted him—to do right.'" She later learned that in addition to the $2,000 loan, she owed another $1,200 for three kinds of credit insurance and an auto club membership—"add-ons" that she knew nothing about.[21]

It doesn't take such fraudulent lending practices to trap borrowers in a cycle of debt. Most borrowers are eager to apply for credit that can help them stay afloat.

A Credit Card for Everybody

Credit cards have become status symbols. If you want to show the world that you've made it, whip out your Platinum Visa; if you want to show your commitment to the environment, use your Sierra Club MasterCard the next time you buy a cup of organic, shade-grown, fair-trade coffee. Though credit cards were originally intended for those with high incomes, since the 1980s their issuers have dramatically expanded the market by targeting different groups and offering different products. Marketers first went after the middle class, and then the working class, including many of the blue- and white-collar workers who lost their jobs as a result of the trends discussed in Chapters 3 and 4. When these markets proved highly profitable, the industry shifted its attention to the poor, the elderly, and most recently students. Robert Manning observes, "Ironically, it is easier for college students to obtain a credit card while in school than after they graduate and begin an entry-level job."[22] He also points out that "for the first time, we're going to see students routinely with $5,000 and $10,000 in credit card debt, which is subsidized by their ability to rotate into federally subsidized student loans, who are going to be entering a job market maxed out before they begin looking for a job."[23]

Credit-card issuing banks aggressively market to college students. As soon as students step onto campus to begin their academic career, they are often met by companies offering "freebies" with brand logos and "great deals" on credit cards. The low teaser rates, free-tchotchkes, and the lure of financial ease encourage students to get their cards quickly and to use them right away. Universities play an important role in setting up their students for future peonage by signing lucrative contracts with credit-card issuing banks that grant access to students.[24] The aggressive marketing of credit cards to students is problematic, in part, because of the very low levels of financial literacy among students and youth.[25] Mandell's study

---

Box 5.2

Should Students Have Limited Access to Credit Cards?

A bill recently introduced in the House of Representatives (HB 1208) would restrict the marketing of credit cards to college students under the age of twenty-one. The bill, sponsored by Louise McIntosh Slaughter (D-New York) and John Duncan Jr. (R-Tennessee), would limit the total amount of credit offered to college students to 20 percent of the gross annual income of the student or the product of $500 times the number of full years since the credit card account was opened, not to exceed $2,000. No increase in the student's line of credit could occur without parents' written approval and an agreement to assume joint liability, and no creditor could offer a credit card account to a student with no gross income or to students who already have credit cards.

"There are kids out there who graduate with as much credit-card debt as college loans, said Eric Burns, Slaughter's press secretary. "A lot of them can never get out from under it."

Not everyone is keen on this idea. The *Daily Iowan*, the student newspaper of the University of Iowa, ran an editorial against the new bill, stating, "Young people are not the only ones with credit problems; the law should not be age-discriminatory and should instead target any person in danger of bad credit."

Representatives of the credit card industry even recycled an old line once used by student radicals. "As an adult in college, someone who is old enough to fight and die for this country is old enough to manage a credit card," said Tracy Mills, the senior manager of public relations for the American Bankers Association. She recommends financial literacy classes for young people as an alternative.

But even some students think the bill makes sense and that students shouldn't have credit cards until after graduation. "It is just common sense," says University of Iowa sophomore Michele Crouch. "If you have a job where you make lots of money, you can spend more. If you don't, you shouldn't spend the money anyway."[26]

Figure 5.1

Consumer Credit Outstanding, 1971–2005, in Millions of Dollars

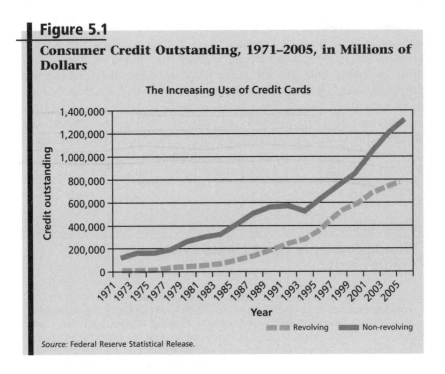

The Increasing Use of Credit Cards

Source: Federal Reserve Statistical Release.

of American twelfth graders reveals that students who use credit cards have no more "financial literacy" about them than those who don't use them.[27]

Some companies have even turned their attention to children. In 2004, Sanrio announced the introduction of a "Hello Kitty" brand debit card. Ads for the card on their Web site bubbled, "Freedom! You can use the Hello Kitty Debit MasterCard to shop 'til you drop!" The senior vice president of licensing for Sanrio, Bruce Giuliano, stated, "We think our target group will be from ten to fourteen, although it could certainly go younger."[28]

As a result of this aggressive marketing, the American youth is being socialized to live on debt, developing spending behaviors disconnected from financial realities. As discussed in Chapter 3, many graduates leave college already in a financial quagmire, with large credit-card debts and student loan payments. Their financial difficulties can be made even worse as they struggle to find a job: employers can and often do look at credit scores during the hiring process.

In 1998, credit card companies mailed out nearly 3.5 billion "preapproved" offers to approximately 75 percent of U.S. households (see Figure 5.1). So, depending on your consumption activities and debt levels, you can expect to receive between thirty-five and seventy-five such offers each year.[29]

Figure 5.2

Average U.S. Credit-Card Debt Per Household

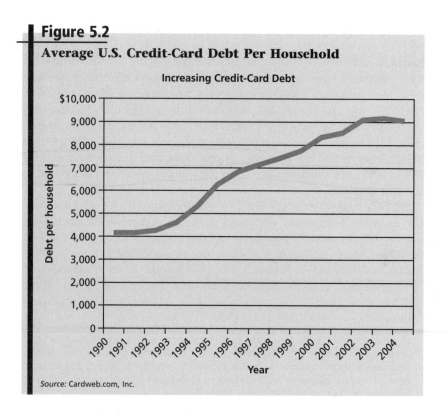

Increasing Credit-Card Debt

Source: Cardweb.com, Inc.

By "emphasizing financial independence and social indulgence, banks enabled cardholders to maintain the image of middle-class respectability and the material accoutrements of economic success even as they struggled simply to stay afloat."[30]

We can see the dramatic rise of the credit card industry by examining the percentage of U.S. families using general-purpose credit cards. In 1970 about half of all families used these cards, but by 2001 usage had jumped by 50 percent to approximately three quarters of all families. In 2001, 60 percent of credit-card users with incomes between $25,000 and $49,999 were carrying a balance (see Figure 5.2 and Appendix Figures 5.2 and 5.3).

The credit-card industry distinguishes between two types of credit-card users: revolvers and convenience users. Revolvers carry debt from one month to the next, while convenience users pay off the outstanding debt at the end of each billing cycle. In 2004, there were 185 million bank credit card holders in the U.S. About 62 percent (115 million) of these users were revolvers and about 38 percent (70 million) were convenience users.[31]

Convenience users are derided as "deadbeats" by some in the industry because they do not produce the revenues revolvers do;[32] by paying their balances each month, these customers avoid paying interest or fees on their purchases. In essence, convenience users receive an interest-free loan from the card issuer for up to four weeks, the length of the billing cycle. Even so, credit card companies profit from convenience users because merchants pay issuing companies a fee based on a percentage of every purchase made with their card. If all credit card users were convenience users the industry would not be nearly as profitable, and it is unlikely that we would have seen the dramatic rise in the number of credit cards issued in the past decades.

Lenders profit from revolvers through climbing interest rates and fees. For example, a borrower who pays only the minimum payment each month (usually either 2 percent or $10, whichever is higher) on a $4,000 credit-card loan at 21 percent APR will pay about $5,592 in interest alone. At this rate, this $4,000 loan will cost $9,952 and take ten years to repay. But paying more than the minimum payment due, or even paying off the full debt each month, does not guarantee protection from increased rates or fees:

> A provision now built into most card agreements allows the companies to reset anyone's interest rate based on the size and status of other debts. And improvements in information technology and a change in federal law have spurred card companies in the last couple of years to check their customer's data regularly, not only when they review applications or notice missed payments.[33]

Credit-card firms often argue that high fees and interest rates are necessary to cover losses due to fraud. This excuse is not valid, however; in 1993, "the cost of fraud [to Visa and MasterCard] comes to a little more than $2 per card per year. A surcharge of $2 or $3 per card per year would

---

Box 5.3

Banking Regulators Propose Increases in Minimum Credit-Card Payments

Bank regulators in the United States in the summer of 2005 proposed increasing the minimum monthly payments on credit cards from 2.5 percent of the outstanding balance to 4 percent. Since the average American family owes $8,400, this change would increase their minimum payment from $210 to $336. Since 2004 was another year of stagnant wage growth (inflation rose 3.1% for the entire year while wages grew only 2.1%), and the personal savings rate was close to zero, average consumers felt the pinch.[34]

Figure 5.3

Average Annual Rates of Credit and Bank Spread, 1980–2000

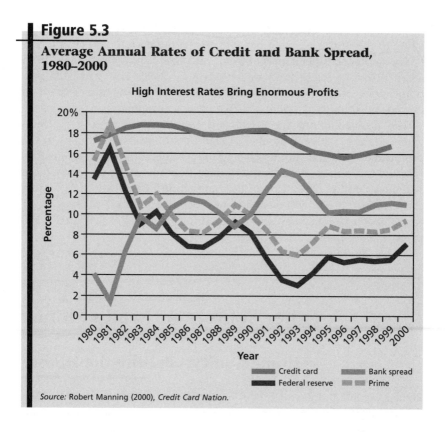

High Interest Rates Bring Enormous Profits

Legend: Credit card | Bank spread | Federal reserve | Prime

Source: Robert Manning (2000), *Credit Card Nation.*

have paid for the cost of fraud to those companies. . . . Nevertheless, fraud offers the credit card industry a convenient excuse for high fees and interest rates."[35]

Another reason the credit-card industry has become so profitable can be seen by looking at the "spread." (see Figure 5.3).

Four key figures affect industry profits: the credit cards rate (the interest rate charged by lenders on credit-card loans), the Federal Reserve rate (the interest rate charged by banks to other banks that need overnight loans), the prime rate (the base rate banks use in pricing commercial loans to their customers), and the bank spread (the difference between the rate banks charge to credit-card borrowers and the rate they pay to borrow money from other banks to cover their needs). As Figure 5.3 shows, the prime rate follows closely the pattern of the Federal Reserve rate; this is because the prime rate is based on the Federal Reserve rate. Both these rates reached their peaks in the early 1980s, dropped dramatically through the mid-1990s, and then rose slightly after that. While the Fed and prime rate dropped, the credit-card rate began this period around 18 percent (close to the prime rate) and has remained around 16 to 18 percent.

For banks and other issuers of credit cards, the bank spread ranged from about 8 to 14 percent from mid-1980s until 2000. This translated into tremendous profits for the issuers of credit cards and drove them to extend the amount of credit available to new consumers.

The profitability of the credit-card industry, the volume of credit extended, and the sheer number of credit cards available all point to the proliferation of credit-card usage over the past decades. The ease of credit-card use can also create a "temptation to imprudence": people buy more and more because of the ease of the transactions. Ritzer writes, "Consider the introduction of credit cards into fast-food restaurants. The use of credit cards leads to more sales and transactions that are 60 percent to 100 percent larger than cash transactions."[36]

Other Sources of Ready Money

Home Equity—Betting the House?

Remember Bill and Sheryl from Chapter 2? Like millions of middle-class Americans, they are caught in a web of financial precariousness and debt. Having already acquired $15,000 in revolving credit-card debt, they took out a second mortgage to help cover their sons' college tuition. Let's look at how this type of credit works and what it means for Bill and Sheryl's financial future.

There are two types of home equity credit. The first type, closed-end loans (traditionally called "home improvement" loans or second mortgages), provide borrowers with a fixed amount of money to perform improvements or repairs to their homes (although the money can be put toward a variety of uses—for example, buying a car, paying college tuition, or consolidating debt). These loans are repaid in installments over a three- to five-year period. The second type, the home equity line of credit, is similar to credit cards: consumers receive a credit limit based on the value of their homes. Home equity lines of credit can be tapped at any time during the designated life of the credit line, and can be paid back in part or fully at any time.[37]

Between 1996 and 1998, more than four million households shifted approximately $26 billion from credit-card debt to home equity loans. Households use home equity loans for a wide range of purposes, the

Figure 5.4

Home Equity Debt Outstanding, 1990–1998

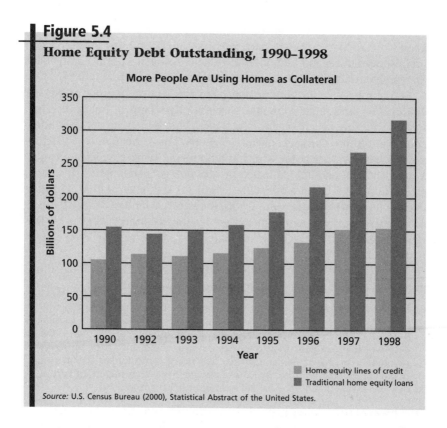

More People Are Using Homes as Collateral

Source: U.S. Census Bureau (2000), *Statistical Abstract of the United States.*

most common being debt consolidation, followed by home improvements, automobile financing, and education.[38] In 1997, almost 50 percent of home equity lines of credit borrowers used these funds to pay off other debts, while over 60 percent of traditional home equity borrowers did so.[39] Home equity loans represented 30 percent of the asset-backed securities market in 1997 and had a total value of $64 billion for that year (see Figure 5.4).[40]

Bill and Sheryl chose a home equity loan for a few different reasons. For one, there are tax benefits to this type of loan. The ability to deduct interest payments was once available for both mortgages and non-real estate consumer loans, but the Tax Reform Act of 1986 phased out tax deductions for non–real estate consumer loans, leaving this benefit in place for home equity credit lines. Home equity lines of credit are appealing also because their interest rates are considerably lower than those of credit cards, even at subprime home equity lenders.[41] And by the mid-1990s, lenders began to market home equity credit lines aggressively, dramatically increasing the ease of obtaining a loan and, in some cases, extending credit beyond the value of the borrower's home, sometimes up to 200 percent above the value.[42] These characteristics—flexibility, tax breaks, lower interest rates, ease, and high loan-to-value ratio—make home equity loans extremely attractive.

Offering home equity loans is attractive to lenders because of the low delinquency and foreclosure rate.[43] Financially strapped Americans often have to decide which creditors get paid and which don't, and home equity and home mortgage payments get paid most frequently: collection managers report that home equity and home mortgage payments are most frequently paid on time, followed by auto loans, installment loans, retail credit, and bank credit cards. One reason for this may be that mortgage lenders do not have the same flexibility as other lenders when it comes to payment options; requirements set by the secondary market on this type of asset-backed security stipulates that they cannot even accept partial payments.[44]

However, if homeowners' overall debt becomes overwhelming, mortgages and second mortgages may lead to personal bankruptcy.

> Homeownership is one of the most visible signs of participation in the middle class. Families in bankruptcy often want desperately to hold on to their homes, and their bankruptcy filings may be an attempt to clear out other debts so they can pour their often shrinking incomes into their mortgage payments. For many, hanging on to their home is no longer a matter of economic rationality; it has become a struggle to save an important part of their lives, one that a financial adviser might tell them to let go.[45]

The threat of bankruptcy may become even more common as certain types of home mortgages become more popular. In June 2005, Federal Reserve Chairman Alan Greenspan told Congress of his concern over the "dramatic increase in the prevalence of interest-only loans, as well as the introduction of other relatively exotic forms of adjustable-rate mortgages." Interest-only loans accounted for "at least 40 percent of purchase loans over $360,000 in areas with fast-rising home prices, like San Diego, Washington, Seattle, Reno, Atlanta and much of Northern California."[46] These loans allow people to buy more expensive houses than they perhaps should because payments are much lower than those of more traditional mortgages. However, the payments may eventually jump, and unless their incomes have done so as well, they may default on their loans and lose their houses.

Auto Leasing—Renting the Car

Over 85 percent of the U.S. population owns one or more vehicles,[47] and for most Americans owning a car is an economic and cultural necessity.

New vehicles come with dazzling features marketed to the "responsible middle-class family." Since the early 1990s, leasing instead of buying has become an increasingly popular way to get "that new car smell" (see Appendix Figure 5.5). Leasing a vehicle basically finances the use of the vehicle instead of the purchase, offering customers a new vehicle every two or three years with no major repair risks. The most common type of vehicle lease is the closed-end lease.[48] Up-front costs when leasing may include the first month's payment, a refundable security deposit, capitalized cost reduction (basically a down payment), taxes, registration, and other fees, plus additional charges such as "gap insurance." The lease is for a set period of time and the cost is based on the anticipated depreciation of the vehicle, calculated by assigning a limit (generally about 10,000 to 12,000 miles a year) to the miles driven during the period of the lease, with any overage penalized an additional 12 to 25 cents per mile.

A closed-end lease allows the buyer to walk away at the end of the contract after returning the vehicle and paying any final costs, or to re-lease or buy the vehicle. While monthly lease payments are almost always lower than vehicle loan payments on the same vehicle, in the long run leasing is considerably more expensive. To buy a car and continue to drive it after the loan is paid off is always less expensive than leasing: the longer an owner drives a paid-off car, the more he saves.

As Figure 5.5 illustrates, despite its greater expense, more and more Americans—especially in the middle class—are turning to leasing. In 1989, there were too few households with annual incomes more than $25,000 but less than $50,000 that leased vehicles even to be counted. By 1995, 3.4 percent of these households were leasing, and by 1998, this percentage grew to five percent. Households with annual incomes between $50,000 and $99,999 demonstrate a similar increase. In 1989, slightly over six percent of these households leased vehicles; by 1998, 9.5 percent did (Appendix Figure 5.5).

Pawnshops: No Longer for Gamblers and Winos

Bill and Sheryl's finances have gotten worse, and they have tapped out their credit card and home equity lines of credit. Their credit rating is shot and they need cash quickly to pay for an unexpected trip to the emergency room. What are their options?

One option is a trip to the pawnshop. The number of pawnshops nearly tripled since the start of banking deregulation in the 1980s. In 1985 there were 4,849 pawnshops in the United States; by the late 1990s the number

96

Figure 5.5

New Passenger Car Leases as a Percentage of All Passenger Car Sales

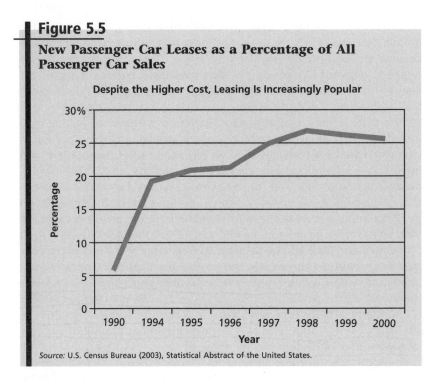

Despite the Higher Cost, Leasing Is Increasingly Popular

Source: U.S. Census Bureau (2003), *Statistical Abstract of the United States.*

grew to approximately 14,000. A drive through any major city reveals that this growth has taken place both in poor urban neighborhoods and the suburbs alike. Suburban strip malls and inner-city blocks are dotted with the red, white, and blue awnings of Cash America and other pawnshops.

Pawnshops used to be known as dark and dangerous, but now many are clean and well-lit. Still, their basic premise remains: they provide short-term loans based on collateral provided by the customer. Collateral can be guitars and other musical instruments, jewelry, stereo equipment, guns, leather jackets, watches, power tools—just about anything that has value.

All Bill and Sheryl need to do is to take something of value—for example, the guitar Sheryl bought Bill for his thirty-fifth birthday—to the pawnshop, and walk out with a cash loan, generally 25–30 percent of the item's appraised value, without having to go through a credit check or waiting to get approved by a loan officer. A typical loan is for 120 days, after which Bill and Sheryl can repay the loan in full (plus interest) and get the guitar back. If they do not have that much money, they can just pay the interest due and receive a "new" loan. If they default on the loan but not paying at least the interest due after 120 days, the pawnshop keeps the guitar and resells it to cover the original loan plus some profit. If this happens, Bill and Sheryl lose the guitar, but no further damage has been done to their credit rating and there are no additional fees or penalties.

Taking Your Pay before You Earn It: Check Cashing, Payday Loans, and Title Loans

Another outgrowth of banking deregulation is the propagation of check-cashing outlets (CCOs). In 2001, nearly 13 percent of Americans did not have a checking account, and as members of the "self-banked" population, they relied on check-cashing outlets to turn paychecks into cash. Cash-checking outlets typically charge between 1 and 3.25 percent to cash government, payroll, and bank checks. Some also provide "payday loans," short-term loans generally between $100 and $300 given for a fixed fee payable to the lender that represents the finance charge, often ranging from 300 to 1,000 percent APR.[49]

Bill and Sheryl have pawned the possessions they can easily do without, but they still need another $100 in cash. To get a payday loan, Sheryl brings in some personal documents—her driver's license, checking account information, paycheck stubs, and a recent utility bill—and if her minimal requirements are met, she then writes a check for $115 (the amount of the loan plus the fee charged by the lender, in this case 391 percent APR) to the lender, who agrees to hold the check until her next payday. The good news is Sheryl now has $100 cash in her pocket; the bad news is at the end of the two weeks if she cannot pay off the loan plus interest, she will have to pay another $15 in fees to roll over the loan. Assuming she is able to pay off the loan by the next due date, she has already paid $30 in fees for this $100 loan.

Once a consumer falls into the debt trap, lenders will use various methods of ensuring repayment. Most lenders threaten to cash the check that secures the loan. Since these borrowers may not have sufficient money in their account, the check will bounce, cause overdraft fees, and prevent them from using their checking account to pay other bills. Lenders also report borrowers to check reporting agencies, thus effectively barring them from writing checks at local stores.[50]

The number of payday lenders has exploded from fewer than 500 in the early 1990s to approximately 12,000 in 2002 and over 15,000 in 2004.[51] The payday loan industry is extremely profitable; the Federal Reserve estimates that payday loan fee revenues were close to $2 billion in 2000.[52]

In 2002, there were an estimated 180 million payday loans in the United States with a gross dollar volume of $45 billion.[53]

A typical payday loan customer makes eleven transactions a year.[54] Who uses payday loans? The answer might surprise you. In 2004, the Community Financial Services Association of America, a trade group of the payday loan industry, released customer profile data revealing that 52 percent of payday loan users have incomes between $25,000 and $50,000, while an additional 25 percent have incomes greater than $50,000. The majority of payday loan users are married couples with children; 42 percent own their own homes and 94 percent have at least a high school diploma.[55] Watchdog groups such as the Consumers Union warn borrowers "to avoid payday lenders at all costs":[56]

> Payday lenders claim they are the only option for debt-strapped consumers. **But borrowing more money at triple-digit interest rates is never the right solution for people in debt.** Instead, payday loans make problems worse. As the data shows, virtually everyone takes more than one payday loan and thus the loans are similar to an addiction. This is not a legitimate loan product that benefits consumers. In fact, because most consumers believe they could be prosecuted for passing a bad check, the payday loan suddenly becomes their priority debt. Thus, the original debt problems that brought them to the lender often cannot be resolved.[57]

Car Title Loans

Bob and Sheryl need still more money, now to cover the cost of some necessary home repairs, so they put up the title to their car as collateral. As with a payday loan, Bob and Sheryl sign over the title of their vehicle to the lender. If at the end of the loan term they are unable to repay the loan or pay minimum financing fees, the car is confiscated.

Companies like FastCash and Fast Title Loan, which offer car title loans, now dot the United States, particularly in the South. Title loans are legal in twenty-five states, and are thriving in twelve.[58] These loans can be particularly dangerous for financially precarious households, because when the cars are confiscated to penalize for late payments, the household's source of transportation is gone, making transportation to work difficult or impossible.

Rent-to-Own or Rent-to-Drown?

Yet another way financially strapped Americans can maintain a middle-class lifestyle is through rent-to-own stores. According to the Association for Progressive Rental Organizations, a national trade association devoted to the rental-purchase industry, the $5.6 billion rent-to-own industry, with over 8,300 stores, serves approximately 2.9 million customers a year.[59] The rent-to-own industry began in the 1960s and differs from traditional retail credit sales. Customers rent items such as furniture, appliances, computers, or jewelry without credit checks or interest charges and retain the right to return the merchandise at any time. Customers can also purchase the merchandise at any time during the rental agreement (which is typically for either one week or one month). Renters pay as they go and credit is not extended, so customers do not acquire debt by engaging in rent-to-own agreements.

However, the costs of this tactic are extremely high: renters who rent to own a new stereo will pay approximately 3.5 times more for the stereo than if they bought it all at once from a chain retailer like Circuit City or Best Buy. A $200 television at Circuit City will cost nearly $800 through rent-to-own.[60]

Again, the types of consumers who use this approach to purchasing may surprise you. According to industry statistics, 60 percent of rent-to-own customers have at least a high school diploma, and almost 56 percent of renters have annual household incomes between $24,000 and $49,999.[61]

The meteoric rise of the rent-to-own industry leader, Rent-A-Center (RAC), highlights the growing industry. From 1993 until 2000, RAC went from controlling 27 stores to over 2,000 in all fifty states, Washington D.C., and Puerto Rico.[62] Annual RAC (traded as RCII) stock prices during this period increased each year. The company reported net earnings of $51.5 million in 2003.[63] As Robert Manning points out, these companies are "growing so large and so quickly that major manufacturers are eagerly courting them to forge strategic alliances. In spring 2000, for example, Gateway negotiated and exclusive rental-supply agreement with Rent-Way and its 1,100 stores for low-cost Internet-equipped computers."[64]

And to Spread the Risk, Investors Buy Asset-Backed Securities

At the start of this chapter we discussed how bank deregulation has affected the lending practices of both "traditional" and "fringe" banking. An important component of these changing practices has been the development of new ways for lenders to spread risk and thus be able to lend more and more. Credit securitization refers to a complex process of packaging, underwriting, and selling loans and other receivables as securities.[65] These securities are referred to as asset-backed securities (ABS), a general term that encompasses conventional home mortgages (i.e., mortgage-backed securities) and credit card loans (i.e., credit card asset-backed securities). In 2002, the ABS market was comprised of $6.6 trillion in tradable securities (see Appendix Figure 5.6).

Approximately 70 percent of this market was mortgage-backed securities issued primarily by government-sponsored secondary market lenders such as Fannie Mae, Ginnie Mae, and Freddie Mac. The remaining 30 percent of the securitized asset market is backed by assets including home equity loans, vehicle loans, and credit cards. Credit card ABS comprise approximately $400 billion of this market.[66]

While the process of securitizing conventional mortgages has been around since the 1960s, it was not until the mid-1980s that credit card loans began to be bundled and sold. Banc One Corporation initiated the first of a credit card asset backed security, a $50 million "Certificates for Amortizing Revolving Debts (CARDS)" issue, that laid the foundation for subsequent securitizations.[67] Since its introduction this process has become the primary way for the credit card industry to provide unsecured loans to consumers.[68] This process allows credit card issuers to spread the risk of lending money, thereby making it more attractive to do so.

The basic process of securitizing credit card loans works as follows: A card issuer—let's call them BigBank—provides credit-card loans to fifty customers, each of whom maintains a card balance of $1,000. BigBank then may decide to securitize these customers' receivables by placing them into a $50,000 "package." This package is then sold to a trust created for the exclusive purpose of purchasing loans from BigBank. Once the package is in the trust, securities (i.e., bonds) are created that are backed by the $50,000 and are sold to investors who then receive the payments that the customers are making on those loans. The price at which the security is traded is determined by the characteristics of the receivables that are pledged.

In 1989 the amount of consumer credit outstanding, as measured by pools of revolving securitized assets, was less than $18 billion. By 2003 it was nearly $400 billion.[69] The majority of credit card asset-backed securities are purchased by institutional investors (Manning 2003 testimony). As Robert Manning (2003) suggests, this practice can lead to perverse results. For example, when institutional investors such as pension funds purchase credit card asset-backed securities, they are basically attempting to finance workers' future retirement by profiting on workers' current consumer debt.

Are Credit Cards and Pawn Shops Substitutes for Getting Paid?

The American consumer is offered ever-diversifying ways to borrow money against their future earnings. The percentage growth in mortgage and consumer credit debt has been impressive. The annual percentage growth in home mortgage debt ranged between 5 and 15 percent from 1980 to 2003, and annual growth in consumer debt was between 5 and 18 percent in all but six years during this period (see Appendix Figure 5.7). At the same time real consumer purchasing power stagnates, the savings rate declines, and wages and incomes go flat for most Americans, suddenly all this credit becomes available to keep the consumer economy afloat (see Figure 5.6).

We are not suggesting that this state of affairs is a part of a master plan devised by corporate America or politicians in Washington D.C. Nor did thousands of business owners simultaneously sit down one day and say,

Figure 5.6

Median Before-Tax Family Income and Average Credit-Card Debt per Household (2001 Dollars)

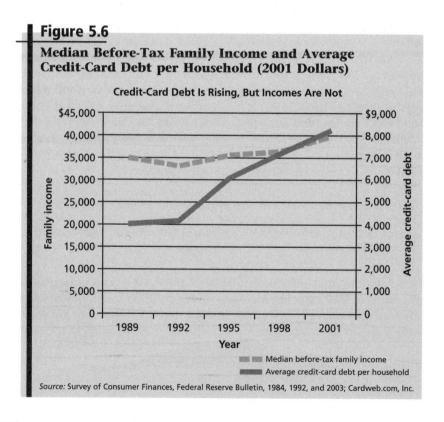

Credit-Card Debt Is Rising, But Incomes Are Not

Legend: Median before-tax family income; Average credit-card debt per household

Source: Survey of Consumer Finances, Federal Reserve Bulletin, 1984, 1992, and 2003; Cardweb.com, Inc.

"Hey, I've got an idea: Let's stop increasing the wages for our workers and then tell our banking buddies to make it easier for them to borrow money to buy things. That way, they'll never even notice the missing wages. Brilliant!" Instead, the confluence of the circumstances we've described over the past thirty-five years has led to the American middle class being given more and more credit in order to keep spending, thus maintaining the illusion of economic prosperity.

Some authors, such as John de Graaf and his coauthors in *Affluenza: The All Consuming Epidemic* and Juliet Schor in *The Overspent American: Upscaling, Downshifting, and the New Consumer*, argue that the rampant consumerism of American culture is to blame for this outcome. Americans are in debt, they argue, because they can't stop buying things that they really don't need. But this problem is not caused simply by individual weakness or frivolity. Marketers and companies spend billions of dollars to *create* demand for products. The perpetual bombardment of glitz and glamour provided by television and the increasing commercialization of every aspect of our daily lives produce tremendous pressures to consume.[70] As Alan Wolfe writes, this is why "so many of the middle-class Americans to whom we talked think that wearing school uniforms is a good idea— anything that detracts from the pressure of peers to buy more things would be welcome." While discussing these pressures Denise Lott of Rancho Barnardo, California, said, "The values are so skewed. I think that it is very difficult to combat that. You know how kids are. They want what other kids have. They want expensive sneakers and jackets. They have to have these things."[71]

Rich Moroni, a onetime debt collector who switched careers to become a credit counselor, articulates how individual choices interact with structural issues to create problematic consumer spending:

> The bottom line for most people is they just simply don't think about what kind of money they make and what kind of lifestyle they're living. And they do want to be richer. They want to look richer than they are. If you have five credit cards, that actually makes it very easy to look richer than you are. And then add merchandisers and advertisers to that, and it's a formula for disaster for a lot of people.[72]

Other authors argue that the main culprit in the rise of consumer debt is not frivolous purchases but increased housing costs.[73] Regardless of what the American middle class is buying, the key to keeping the economy afloat is their spending. Workers who are in debt work more hours as they fall into the cycle of "work and spend."[74] This cycle is unnecessary and detrimental to the future of the American middle class.

Most of the workplace changes that would enable the middle class to benefit from the productivity gains they've produced are in the hands of investors and financial elites. Yet practical changes could help workers break out of this destructive work and spend cycle. Workers can work shorter hours as productivity rises without sacrificing their own welfare; they could take longer vacations, have more leisure time, take care of infants and sick relatives, travel, plant gardens, join civic clubs of various kinds, become more politically active, exercise, or get more sleep.[75]

The cycle of work and spend may be fanned by consumer tastes, but it is fueled by an economic system that will indenture its consumers, loaning money, stripping assets and income in interest payments and new loans, and issuing payday loans so that hard-earned paychecks are "spoken for" by the time they arrive. This system does everything it can to avoid simply paying people more money.

From Washington to Wall Street: Marketing the Illusion

Nothing is more important in the face of a war than cutting taxes.
—House majority leader Tom DeLay, March 12, 2003

The private sector is not solely to blame for the economic distress of the middle class. The public sector persists in marketing the misleading illusion that American prosperity is tied to the affluence of the wealthy, and that government policies that improve the economic prospects of the wealthy will trickle down to the middle class. Neoconservative politics and supply-side economics, manifested through a combination of tax cuts, deregulation, corporate tax avoidance, and a shift of tax burdens onto earned income and away from unearned income, have fundamentally shaped the economic realities of the middle class. The increased presence of corporate lobbyists in Washington has contributed to policies that benefit investors by emphasizing short-term economic growth. But the "supply-side miracle" has yet to materialize for the middle class: instead of improving the state of the post-industrial peasant, government has only added to their plight.

The Neoconservative Persuasion

The reelection of George W. Bush in 2004 marked an important victory for neoconservatives. During his first term, Bush pushed through a major tax cut ostensibly to help the middle class that primarily benefited the wealthy, sought greater deregulation in multiple arenas, froze or cut funding for many government social programs, and dramatically increased spending on homeland security and defense. This combination of economic, social, and foreign policy reflects the neoconservative outlook of the administration.

Economist and op-ed writer Paul Krugman and other critics challenge that the Bush administration, with intellectual and rhetorical guidance from think tanks like the Heritage Foundation, are engaging in a "starve the beast" strategy that seeks to "slash government programs that help the poor and middle class, and use that savings to cut taxes for the rich."[1] Neoconservatives refute this characterization; it is, as William Kristol writes, "not a movement, as its conspiratorial critics would have it . . . [it is] a 'persuasion,' one that manifests itself over time, but erratically, and one whose meaning we clearly glimpse only in retrospect."[2] One uniting theme of neoconservative thought is a focus on economic growth, especially cutting taxes.

Two of the most prominent and influential neoconservative think tanks, the Heritage Foundation and the American Enterprise Institute, have developed a cottage industry for promoting tax cuts. Of course, not all tax cuts are equal. Members of these think tanks can and do criticize specific legislation promoted by the administration or Congress. On the 2001 tax rebates, Brian Reidl of the Heritage Foundation wrote:

> Washington borrowed billions from investors and then mailed that money to families in the form of $600 checks. This simple transfer of existing income had a predictable effect: consumer spending increased and investment spending decreased by a corresponding amount. No new wealth was created because the tax rebate was unrelated to productive behavior—no one had to work, save, or invest more in order to receive a rebate.[3]

Reidl argues that supply-side tax cuts, reducing marginal rates on business and workers, are effective because they "maximize long-run economic growth, which in turn raises income across the board."[4]

One aspect of neoconservative economic policy represents an important break from their conservative predecessors:

> Neocons have abandoned the adherence to balanced budgets that had long been a cornerstone of conservative policy. To conservatives, the budget must be balanced, and the policies that government pursues are limited by the need to be fiscally responsible, thus defined. Neocons elevated policy over budgets. As Irving Kristol puts it, "We should figure out what we want before we calculate what we can afford, not the reverse, which is the normal conservative predisposition."[5]

Indeed, the concern for balanced budgets that weighed so heavily on the minds of Republicans and Democrats during the 1990s has been thoroughly abandoned. According to Stelzer,   Now ?

> neoconservatives live quite comfortably with budget deficits, some because they believe that appropriate tax policies will shrink the deficits to manageable

proportions, others because they believe deficits to be largely irrelevant to an economy's performance, and still others because they believe deficits prevent the adoption of expensive additions to an already-generous welfare state.[6]

The Triumph of Supply-Side Economics

As we saw in Chapter 3, the supply-side economic policies introduced by the Reagan administration did not result in boom times. Despite this, a national assumption that supply-side economics was the best method persisted. The possibility that tax cuts for the wealthy would benefit the middle class was not only too good to be true, it was irresistible as a political strategy: the middle class simply had to wait for the results, for prosperity was just around the corner. When the new effects didn't materialize for most of the middle class, the new solution was logical and direct: tax cuts were obviously not deep enough and not pervasive enough, so we needed more of the same thing.

The Effects of Tax Cuts

The results of the supply-side tax cuts and the fiscal policies that followed in the 1980s and early 1990s added further problems to the plight of the middle class. Federal tax rates shifted radically in the direction of providing substantial tax breaks for the already wealthy (see Appendix Figure 6.1). But instead of watching the money roll in, the federal government ran record deficits and accumulated unprecedented levels of public debt. Tax receipts, never high as a percentage of GDP by international standards, dipped to a level just above Mexico's. Corporations in particular received huge tax breaks and in Washington the number of permanent lobbyists, most of them representing corporate interests, increased substantially.

The middle class saw very little of the Reagan tax cuts, and the effective tax rate change for virtually all American taxpayers below the top 10 percent of the income distribution was close to zero (see Appendix Figure 6.2). By contrast, wealthy households in the United States saw big drops in their effective taxation. Kevin Phillips describes the net effect of these tax cuts and other changes that came with them as a "capitalist heyday," comparable to the 1890s and the 1920s.[7]

Moreover, the so-called "supply-side miracle"—the increase in tax revenues that would follow from lowering tax rates—never materialized. What did materialize was a sea of government "red ink" (see Figure 6.1 and Appendix Figure 6.3). The federal debt, about $930 billion in 1980, ballooned to $2 trillion by mid-decade and $4 trillion by the early 1990s.[8]

Of course, plenty of evidence suggests that the United States was not on the side of the Laffer curve at which reducing tax rates would increase tax revenues, producing a situation in which tax cuts pay for themselves. Some of this evidence came from international comparisons, since the United States collects the lowest percentage of taxes as a percentage of total GDP of any industrialized country (see Appendix Figure 6.4).

The Federal government's retreat from taxing the rich and its inability to curb budget deficits had another insidious effect on wealth distribution. Saddled with a tight money supply, the United States began financing its government debt with investment income from wealthy Americans and foreign nationals, whose appetite for Treasury Bonds selling at favorable interest rates seemed insatiable. The financial payouts from the bonds also went to the Americans who had treasury bills in their investment portfolios, generally the very wealthy. As Kevin Phillips states:

Figure 6.1

Annual Public Debt, 1950–2010

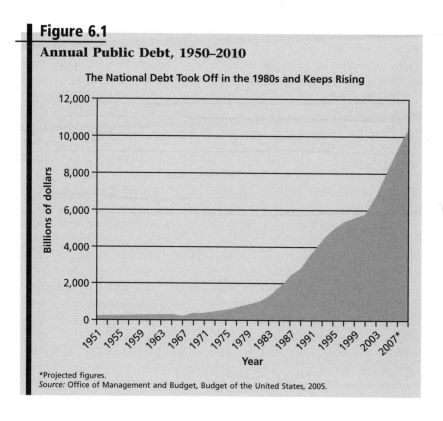

The National Debt Took Off in the 1980s and Keeps Rising

Billions of dollars (y-axis: 0, 2,000, 4,000, 6,000, 8,000, 10,000, 12,000)

Year (x-axis: 1951, 1955, 1959, 1963, 1967, 1971, 1975, 1979, 1983, 1987, 1991, 1995, 1999, 2003, 2007*)

*Projected figures.
Source: Office of Management and Budget, Budget of the United States, 2005.

The underlying problem was the Reagan Administration's need to borrow huge sums of money at high interest rates to fund the 1981 tax cuts, the defense buildup, and 1981–1982 recession spending. To avert feared inflationary effects, the Federal Reserve Board in 1981 and 1982 raised U.S. interest rates to record high levels. With U.S. Bonds paying 15 percent while equivalent instruments in Germany and Japan were paying 5 percent or 6 percent, capital poured into the United States. As foreigners bought dollars to invest in U.S. debt, the dollar soared against other currencies.[9]

This investment boom in U.S. debt kept the government afloat, but it redistributed wealth to those who were already wealthy. The strong dollar threatened to, and eventually did, ruin the country's international trade position. The results of this for the manufacturing industry were especially devastating; as U.S. markets were flooded by inexpensive imports in industries like electronics and automobiles, factories that provided steady employment and middle-class jobs were forced to lay off workers or shut down entirely.

The fervor for cutting taxes and the belief that such cuts would raise government revenues and benefit the middle class didn't subside, in spite of the wealth of evidence that the effects were slanted steeply in the direction of those already well off. Tax cutting by itself seemed to gain an unstoppable momentum, and states followed the federal government in cutting their own taxes. As each new piece of evidence suggesting that middle-class incomes were stagnant and tax benefits were few arose, the simple response by most politicians of both parties was that the benefits were "forthcoming."

The 1980s ushered in a long-term decline in the percentage of tax revenues taken from corporations (on corporate profits, generally a progressive form of taxation), and a gradual but steady increase in payroll taxes and individual income taxes as a percentage of Federal Revenues (see Figure 6.2). Further, a greater share of the federal tax burden was extracted using the regressive payroll tax to fund social security, a tax capped at $87,000 of personal income. Taxation at the federal level thus shifted toward earned income and away from unearned income.

Evidence shows that corporate taxation was declining and that corporate tax avoidance was rising: corporate tax loopholes grew from $8.3 billion to $119.9 billion annually from 1970 to 1986 (see Appendix Figure 6.5). The overall effective tax rate for the largest corporations in the United States dropped to 11.8 percent in 1982 before climbing back to 15 percent in 1984. This rate is far below the effective marginal income tax rate for high income earners, even with cuts in these top tax rates figured into the equation. Corporate taxes as a percentage of Federal Revenues declined to their lowest points since 1960 as corporate income tax receipts accounted for just 8.4 percent of all federal revenues in 2000. The long-term trend was unprecedented in any of the OECD (industrialized) countries. The effective tax rate for 275 major corporations between 1980 and 1984 aver-

Box 6.1

How to Avoid Paying Taxes

If you want to avoid paying taxes, the key is to find ways to do it legally. The good news is that, if you are rich and can afford it, you can seek the advice of people like Jonathan Blattmachr, a lawyer specializing in trusts and estates:

> The likes of Bill Gates, the Gettys, and the Rockefellers seek Blattmachr's counsel on how to make taxes shrink—and sometimes even vanish. His roster of clients reads like the Forbes 400 list, supplemented by the names of people whose vast wealth is little known because they avoid controlling interests in companies whose shares trade on Wall Street. . . . What the wealthy pay him for are the secret routes he has charted through the maze of the tax code. Over the years Blattmachr has found dozens of ways to navigate huge sums of money around government's many levies. He knows how to make a man who appears as a Midas before his bankers look like a pauper to the taxman . . . Once, Blattmachr devised a way that Bill Gates, the richest man in America, could reap $200 million in profits in Microsoft stock without paying the $56 million of capital gains taxes that federal law required at the time."[10]

For the powerful and wealthy, advisors like Blattmachr and corporate lobbyists are pushing beneficial loopholes; for the rest of us, increased tax burdens. What makes matters worse is that:

> The IRS budget has been restrained so severely that only one in five of the tax cheats it identifies is pursued to make him pay. The other four pay nothing. Tax law enforcement became so weak that businessman were quoted on the front page of the *New York Times* in the year 2000 boasting about how they neither paid taxes nor withheld them from their employees' paychecks. More than two years later, not one of them had been indicted or even forced through civil court action to pay up. Not only did more than 1,500 people, caught red-handed hiding money offshore when their banker turned over records of their crimes, escape prosecution, but most were not even asked to pay the taxes they had evaded.[11]

aged 15 percent (see Appendix Table 6.1). Since 1980, corporate income taxes as a percentage of GDP have been considerably lower in the U.S. than all other OECD countries (see Appendix Table 6.6).[12]

of course

Despite the comparatively low corporate taxation rates in the United States, many companies avoid paying any taxes at all. In one popular strategy called corporate inversion, a company creates a subsidiary stationed in an offshore location like Bermuda or Barbados, then transforms the subsidiary into the parent company. What would have originally been profits in the United States can then be drained out of the country as tax-deductible payments to the new parent company (see Appendix Figure

Figure 6.2

Composition of Federal Government Receipts by Source and Decade

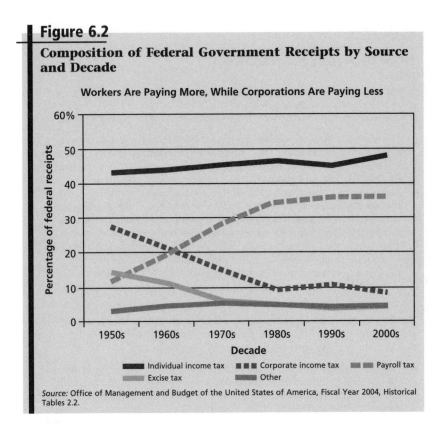

Workers Are Paying More, While Corporations Are Paying Less

Source: Office of Management and Budget of the United States of America, Fiscal Year 2004, Historical Tables 2.2.

6.7). As David Cay Johnston writes, "The tax savings from ostensibly moving a corporation's headquarters offshore are immense. Tyco estimated that it saved an average of $450 million each year after 1997, when it arranged to make Bermuda its tax headquarters while keeping its executive offices in the United States."[13] In the case of Tyco, not all the money ended up benefiting employees and shareholders: Tyco CEO Dennis Kozlowski and ex-Chief Financial Officer Mark Schwartz were convicted of stealing hundreds of millions of dollars from the company.

There were also changes in federal budget priorities (see Figure 6.3). The defense buildup from 1980 to 1990 was accompanied by cuts in the percentage of the federal budget devoted to education and social services (never a large percentage of the budget anyway) and income security. The amount of the federal budget devoted to servicing debt grew considerably while the amount spent on physical resources like national infrastructure declined. In the 1990s, as a result of economic expansion, these distributions shifted back toward the direction they were headed between 1970

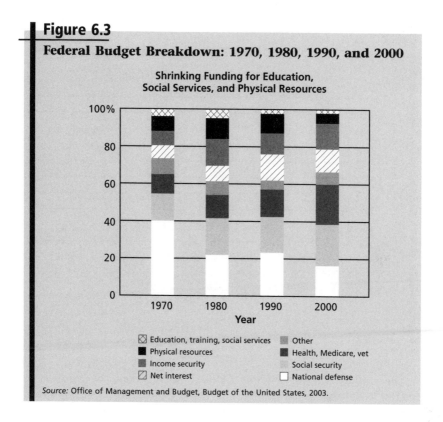

Figure 6.3

Federal Budget Breakdown: 1970, 1980, 1990, and 2000

Shrinking Funding for Education,
Social Services, and Physical Resources

Legend:
- Education, training, social services
- Physical resources
- Income security
- Net interest
- Other
- Health, Medicare, vet
- Social security
- National defense

Source: Office of Management and Budget, Budget of the United States, 2003.

and 1980, but the physical resources budget continued to decline and spending on social security rose again.

There was a largely unmeasured change in Washington as well, one that did not bode well for the prospects of those whose relative prosperity depends on earnings from a middle-class job: the rise of a permanent lobbying class in Washington (see Figure 6.4 on page 112).

The Lobbyists' Revolving Door

Lobbyists relentlessly petition Washington for specific tax and regulatory breaks for corporations. In the 1980s, the door between lobbyists, corporations, and government officials was opened wider than at any time in recent memory as the Reagan administration granted unprecedented government access to corporate representatives.

Figure 6.4

Number of Political Action Committees (PACs), 1974–1998

Huge Presence of Corporate America in Washington, D.C.

Source: Harold W. Stanley and Richard G. Niemi, eds. (2005), *Vital Statistics on American Politics, 2005–2006.*

The case of Edward C. (Pete) Aldridge Jr. illustrates the conflicts of interest that emerge as a result of these close connections between government and industry:

C. Wright Mills

> For years, the revolving door between the Pentagon and military contractors has spun without much notice in Washington. But the multiple roles played by top Pentagon and government officials, like Mr. Aldridge, who have joined the ranks of military contractors as executives, board members and lobbyists, are now coming under closer scrutiny after a top Air Force official negotiated a lucrative job contract with the Boeing Company while still overseeing Boeing business. This is not the first time Mr. Aldridge's actions have raised eyebrows. In 2005, in the month before he left the Pentagon for Lockheed's board, Mr. Aldridge approved a $3 billion contract to build 20 Lockheed F/A-22s, after having long criticized the program as overpriced and having threatened to cancel it.[14]

Despite the Clinton administration's attention to balancing the budget in the 1990s, and the need to continue cutting programs that helped the lower and middle classes, corporations still were able to finagle financial assistance. Jim Hightower describes one such subsidy:

> The Puerto Rican subsidy . . . encourages U.S. firms to move our jobs to the Caribbean by giving cash to companies for each Puerto Rican job they create. Mucho cash—it averages $27,000 per year for every Puerto Rican hired,

which is two to three times more than the worker is paid. Payment is not based on wages, but on the profits the firm makes. (I realize that this does not make sense, but I don't think it's intended to make sense.) Drug companies have found this particular goodie especially savory, and they have used it to move thousands of U.S. drug manufacturing jobs to the island— Johnson & Johnson has been given $50,000 for every job it moved to Puerto Rico under this program. Bristol Myers Squibb has received nearly $75,000, and Pfizer has been given $156,000. That is per worker, per year, costing us a total of a couple of billion bucks annually to subsidize our own job loss.[15]

The Reality for Everyone Else— Rising Taxes as a Percentage of Personal Income

While corporations and wealthy Americans saw their tax bills fall, average taxpayers (the median family income earner) saw theirs increase (see Appendix Figures 6.8 and 6.9). This increase was due to increases in Social Security payroll taxes and increases in state and local taxes, both generally regressive taxes (see Box 6.2).

Total taxes as a percentage of median family income in the United States have risen consistently since World War II, peaking at around 40 percent of family income in 1995 and declining slightly after that. That shift hides a much more serious shift in the sources of these taxes and the relatively progressive or regressive nature of the income source for federal, state, and local governments. Since 1955, the trend has been clear: Federal taxes on income, usually collected through a graduated income tax, have declined as a source of taxation on the nation's middle class. This decline has been more than offset by increases in payroll taxes (since 1955, from under 10 percent of total tax bills for median income earners to 20 percent) and sharp increases in state and local taxes as a percentage of total tax bills. Much of this state and local revenue is collected using sales and excise taxes that disproportionately extract income from the middle class and the poor.

In fact, state and local taxation usually is far more regressive in its effect than is taxation by the federal government. For example, the poor and middle class pay a larger percentage of their incomes to state and local governments in taxes than do the relatively well-off. State and local sales and excise taxes explain most of this disproportion: while income taxes are generally progressively administered, the weight of sales and excise taxes falls disproportionately on the poor and middle class (see Appendix Figure 6.10).[16]

Box 6.2

Regressive and Progressive Taxation

Regressive taxes, which take a higher percentage of income from people with low incomes, are more burdensome on low-income individuals than on high-income individuals and corporations. Examples of regressive taxes are the Social Security payroll tax, which is 12.4% on the first $87,000 of income and zero percent on any income over and above that. So, for example, someone who earns $87,000 a year owes $11,049 in Social Security payroll taxes, exactly 12.4% of her income, while another making $200,000 still pays just $11,049, in this case only 5.5% of her total income.

Sales and value-added taxes are levied against consumption and don't take into account the income or earnings of the consumer making the purchase. Sales taxes on food and other essentials take higher percentages of incomes from families and individuals with lower incomes because these people spend a greater percentage of their income on these items. The same is true of value-added taxes, which are paid by businesses that pass costs on to consumers, regardless of their ability to pay.

Progressive taxes, on the other hand, take a larger percentage of income from those with higher incomes. For example, U.S. federal income taxes are progressive, taxing incomes at different rates depending on the size of income. As of 2004, the United States had six income-tax brackets:

Income: $1–$7,300	Tax bracket: 10%
Income: $7,301–$29,700	Tax bracket: 15%
Income: $29,701–$71,950	Tax bracket: 25%
Income: $71,951–$150,150	Tax bracket: 28%
Income: $150,151–$326,450	Tax bracket: 33%
Income: $326,451 and above	Tax bracket: 35%

The complicating factor is that individuals owe the U.S. Treasury the listed percentage of income *for each dollar within each range*, so someone making $45,000 would pay 10 percent on the first $7,300, 15 percent on the next $22,399, and 25 percent on the remaining $15,301 of income ($730 + $3,360 + $3,825 = $7,915 in federal tax, before deductions).

Of course, the relative fairness of state and local taxes varies greatly. The ten most regressive state tax systems tax their poorest citizens several hundred times the percentage of income they tax their wealthiest citizens, and many do the same to the middle class as well. Of these ten states, three—Illinois, Michigan, and Pennsylvania—are in the "rust belt," one—South Dakota—is in the upper Midwest, one—Washington—is in the Pacific Northwest, and the remaining six—Florida, Texas, Tennessee, Louisiana, and Alabama—are in the South or Southeast. With the exception of California and Utah, the states with the most regressive sales taxes are all in the South, and almost all of these states collect sales taxes on groceries (see Appendix Figures 6.11 and 6.12).

By contrast, the six states with the most progressive income taxes— *best* California, New Mexico, Rhode Island, Vermont, Idaho, and Maine—tax the income of the poor relatively little and even allow tax credits to ✓ exceed the total amount of income tax owed (hence, they have negative effective tax rates). All of them have highly graduated tax rate systems (see Appendix Figure 6.13).

This evidence overwhelmingly indicates a significant, long-term change in the nature of taxation in this country. We have switched from a system that taxes people on the basis of their ability to pay to a system that taxes unearned income from capital stock relatively little and earned income from work significantly more. Further, we've shifted the relative tax burdens toward earned income below the eightieth percentile of the earnings distribution and shifted tax burdens toward regressive sales taxes, excise taxes, and payroll taxes. The result is a government that does less for those who are not already wealthy, extracting more taxes from the have-nots, who don't reflect powerful political constituencies whose economic welfare most politicians care about.

These policies flourished under the administrations of Ronald Reagan and George H. W. Bush, but Republicans have not been exclusively to blame for these trends. Bill Clinton thwarted Bush's reelection attempt in 1992 largely because of the faltering economy, which was in "jobless recovery" from the 1990–1991 recession. The budget deficit had risen to 4.2 percent of GDP, up from 2.8 percent in 1989; unemployment was at 7.3 percent.[17] James Carville's now famous rally cry for the Clinton campaign—"It's the economy, stupid!"—rang true with many Americans.

Clinton promised to ease the tax burden of the middle class and to make the rich "pay their fair share." However, this never really happened; instead, in 1996 Clinton and the Republican-controlled Congress turned their attention to cutting taxes on capital gains. Taking a page from the "voodoo economics" of Reagan, the Clinton administration and the Republican-controlled Congress argued that a capital gains tax cut—i.e., taxes on the increased value of shares and real estate—would increase government revenue because many investors would cash in to take advantage of the lower rate, leading to a short-term increase in government revenues. Despite the negative long-term effects of cutting capital gains taxes, the idea was popular with politicians beholden to the interests of Wall Street and campaign finance, and there was widespread public support for the cut. Middle-class Americans widely rallied with the wealthy to protect their common interests. As Stiglitz writes:

> Everybody had their few shares (though most of their shares were held in accounts in which the accumulations were, in any case, tax-free). They would do everything they could to protect these little pieces of capitalism against

the rapacious government. Ronald Reagan had had his ultimate victory. No matter that the capital gains tax cut saved the upper-income taxpayer $100 for every $5 that the middle-income taxpayer was spared.[18]

But Wait a Minute! Haven't the Bush Tax Cuts Done Better?

Of course one could argue that the effects of the Reagan-era tax cuts are past history. What about the tax cuts of the current Bush administration? Is it possible that the tax cuts of the past and current tax cuts have not been structured the same way and won't have the same effects?

While this outcome is possible, it is doubtful, at least according to the Institute on Taxation and Economic Policy (see Figure 6.5). As with the tax cuts of the past thirty years, the latest round of tax cuts seem to be heading toward the same distributional consequences as those of the Reagan era—big tax cuts for the wealthy and tax increases for everyone else.

Looking at the change in total federal taxes resulting from the tax cuts, by 2010 (given that there are no major changes) the top 1 percent of income earners will see their share of federal taxes drop 2.7 percent, while everyone else but the top 5 percent will see their share of federal taxes increase 3.8 percent (see Appendix Figure 6.14). Almost all of the 2003–2006 benefits from the tax cut accrue to the top 15 percent of all income earners, and the positive effects for all but the top 5 percent of income earners get smaller while the concentration of benefits in the top 1 percent of income earners gets larger.

On top of this, a large percentage of taxpayers will get under $100 in tax relief from the Bush Tax Cut Program, and the share that will get under $100 in tax relief will grow to an average of 88 percent of all taxpayers by 2006. Ironically, the states with the highest numbers of taxpayers getting refunds of under $100 are Alabama, Arkansas, Louisiana, Mississippi, and West Virginia—all states that went to George W. Bush in the 2000 and 2004 elections. The five states with the fewest taxpayers that fall into the under-$100 category are Connecticut, New Hampshire, New Jersey, Vermont, and Wyoming; of these, only Wyoming and New Hampshire delivered their electoral votes to Bush (see Appendix Figure 6.15).

The effects are not evenly distributed across families in different circumstances either. A large majority of taxpayers receiving less than $100 from the 2003 tax cut are single and the biggest beneficiaries are married parents. This outcome follows logically from the increase in income inequality between these groups generally (see Appendix Figure 6.16).[19]

The current administration has also brought back record-high budget deficits: a deficit of over $400 billion is projected for 2006.[20] Unlike the

Figure 6.5

Distributional Effects of the 2003 Tax Cut Plan in 2003–2006

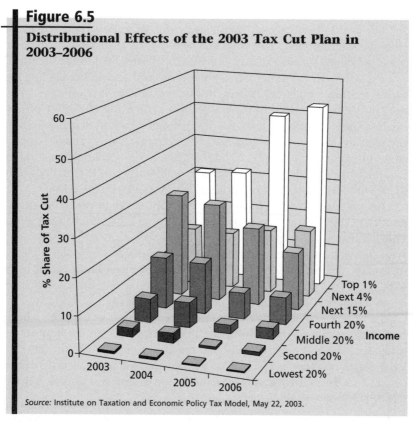

Source: Institute on Taxation and Economic Policy Tax Model, May 22, 2003.

Reagan administration, however, this administration is only beginning to tighten the money supply to drive up interest rates to pay for growing government debts. As of the writing of this book, June 2006, only the relative productivity of the economy has kept the budget outlook of the federal government from looking completely disastrous.

Persistent Inflation and Benefit Declines for the Middle Class

Affording the Middle-Class Lifestyle

In addition to these changes to federal, payroll, state, and local taxes, there are other, less obvious pressures on post-industrial peasants. Persistent inflation on the big-ticket commodities consumers buy, increased prices for important services like health care and education, and declining employer commitment to providing health care and stable retirement options increase the uncertainty and volatility of their economic situation.

Let's start with the basics. Most Americans want to own homes, and for many, the unprecedented decline in home mortgage interest rates since the late 1990s has made owning a home a reality. But the effect of low interest rates has masked a rise on the price of new and existing homes: the median price of a new house in real dollars has risen almost 40 percent in twenty years, from $110,000 to $150,000 in 1992 dollars, and the sale price of existing homes has risen as well, but less substantially, from $108,000 to $122,000 in 1992 dollars (see Appendix Figure 6.17).[21]

The real estate market expects average consumers to pay these astronomically higher prices with paychecks that have hardly changed a bit. The nominal dollar increases are much larger than that, and these are the "real" prices that people see in the real estate guides as they look for places to live. By this measure, the median sale price of new homes is close to $200,000 ($140,000 more than in 1980), and the median sale price of existing homes is $160,000 (see Appendix Figure 6.18).

The widely available streams of credit we discussed in Chapter 3 have made buying a house more affordable, in the sense that middle-class Americans can now borrow money to achieve this American dream. But this same dream becomes less affordable when it comes to the sale price of the house. This has four effects on potential home buyers, and not all of these effects are bad:

1. Loan interest rates are low, so the amount of interest on a home loan for more expensive houses won't be any higher than they were for much more modestly priced homes in the late 1970s and early 1980s. (This is a good thing.)

2. The equity accrued in the home will be larger over the life of the loan as long as housing prices remain stable or inflate. (Another good thing.)

3. Payments on these costly homes will take a larger percentage from paychecks that are not increasing in real dollars. (Not good.)

4. Many new homes are sold to buyers who use unconventional mortgages, with less money down and "balloon clauses" that allow interest rates to rise over the life of the loan. Further, the total value of the house depends on the continued rise in real estate prices that are fueled in part by low interest rates for home mortgages. As the fed raises interest rates the homebuyers market will slow down, homes will be more difficult to buy and sell, and balloon clauses in many unconventional mortgages will increase house payments. (Not good!)

Box 6.3

Greenspan Expresses Concerns Over Unconventional Mortgages

In a September 2005 address to the American Bankers Association Annual Convention, Alan Greenspan, Chair of the Federal Reserve, expressed concern over the rise in unconventional mortgages in which buyers pay no money down, pay interest rates that change over the life of the loan (Adjustable Rate Mortgages or ARMs), or buy houses using "interest-only" loans, with payments credited to the interest of the loan but not the principal. Unconventional mortgages allow buyers who barely qualify to purchase homes at inflated prices. Greenspan warned that a slump in price gains may lead to losses for both borrowers and lenders. The risk to the economy is magnified because consumers use about half the money they pull from their homes upon refinancing for consumption or re- *Brutal* payment of debts. Greenspan asserted that the abundance of interest-only loans and the introduction of "exotic" variable-rate mortgages "are developments that bear close scrutiny."[22]

Positive benefits of home ownership also depend on whether or not the home owner has borrowed against the house's equity. Bill and Sheryl did so, and they have almost no equity in their house at all, even though they've lived there for fifteen years. By the time they pay off their second mortgage and their regular mortgage, they'll be past retirement age and chances are their home won't be paid off even then. On top of this, they've been cannibalizing their savings to maintain their life style in the house they presently own, and they're one missed paycheck away from falling behind on the payments and heading toward bankruptcy.

We can see the same trend in the increased price of new cars. As we discussed in Chapter 5, more Americans are leasing new cars rather than buying them, partially because of stagnant real incomes. But there is another reason why leasing has become so prevalent: the increased cost of cars. The rise in the average sale price of imported cars is especially stark: in current dollars the prices have nearly doubled, and in real dollars the price has risen by almost one third during the 1990s. Domestic new car average prices have risen by about one third as well in both real and current dollars (see Appendix Figure 6.19). No doubt some of the increased price of imported cars involves increased luxury consumption by the relatively well off who buy BMWs and Mercedes-Benzes instead of Hondas and Toyotas. But the demand for imported cars has remained strong in the United States even in the face of world overcapacity in auto production and high prices.

The High Cost of College Education

The middle class relies on public institutions of higher education as places of opportunity for their children. Traditionally, these institutions provide a high-quality education at a relatively modest cost. The difference in cost between a public and private college education is considerable—conventionally, a private education costs about twice as much as a public education—and the differences in relative costs have risen steadily over the 1980s and 1990s.

What can Bill and Sheryl expect for their son Dillon, currently enrolled in college, and for their daughter Clara, just a few years away from starting? Let's start by looking at real returns to education over time (see Figure 6.6). Without a doubt, education pays dividends in terms of workplace earnings: the median income for men with at least a bachelor's degree has always been around $50,000 in real terms for men, and the median earnings growth for women graduates has also been substantial, from just under $25,000 in 1965 to $38,000 in 2002. (For women, these earnings gains are in real dollars that result from a variety of factors including declines in labor market discrimination and the opening up of professional schools.[23])

However, trends for males ominously reveal real declines in the value of education at levels below those who receive college degrees. In fact, almost all the rising earnings gap between college-educated and non-college-educated men since the early 1970s results from declines in the real value of education below the college level, not increases in the value of a college education. This trend does not occur for women; instead, the gap between the earnings of the college educated and non-college educated woman is rising because returns to a college education are growing.

These figures hide another trend that is decreasing the value of college education, not to mention the value of graduate and professional degrees: growing earnings inequality within the traditional professions college graduates aspire to enter.[24] As Michael Mandel and others have pointed out, a college education has become increasingly like a lottery ticket: It is better to be in the lottery than not to have a ticket, but having a ticket does not guarantee winning.[25]

The same trend that has affected housing and transportation costs has also affected the costs of public higher education (see Figure 6.7).

Average costs for public four-year colleges and universities have risen at a rate several times the rate of inflation, from around $4,000 per year to around $10,000 per year.[26] As we saw in Chapter 3, one mechanism for students to pay these increased costs has been for them to take on

Figure 6.6a

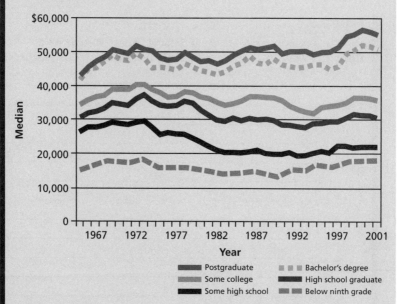

Male Median Earnings by Education Level, 1965–2001 (2001 Dollars)

Figure 6.6b

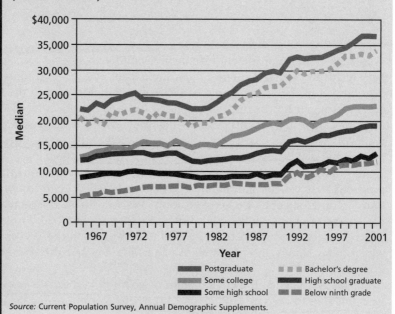

Female Median Earnings by Education Level, 1965–2001 (2001 Dollars)

Source: Current Population Survey, Annual Demographic Supplements.

Figure 6.7

Public Four-Year College Tuition, Fees, Room and Board, 1985–2003 (Current and Constant 1992 Dollars)

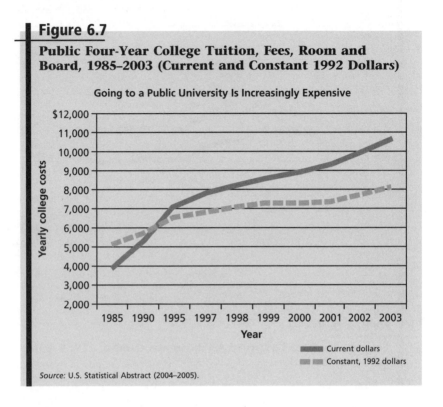

Going to a Public University Is Increasingly Expensive

Current dollars
Constant, 1992 dollars

Source: U.S. Statistical Abstract (2004–2005).

ever-larger amounts of student loan debt. Even though student loans may have relatively favorable interest rates, these loans add to the cumulative debt burden of the young would-be post-industrial peasant, and the federal government has increasingly replaced loans as the preferred mechanism for supporting students pursuing higher education (see Appendix Figure 6.20). As with the other trends we've examined in this book, elites are loaning the middle class money rather than giving it to them.

Another trend tied to the decline of state and local investments in programs that benefit the middle class is the lessened contribution of state funding of public higher education. We see this in the increased percentage of public higher education costs that are funded by tuition, which has risen from 13 percent in 1980 to 19 percent in the 1990s, and which today shows only slight signs of turning downward (see Appendix Figure 6.21).

For many students, the combination of going to classes and working part-time jobs to keep up with credit-card payments can prove too much to handle. In 1998, an Indiana University administrator claimed, "We lose more students to credit-card debt than academic failure."[27] For those that don't drop out, the seeds of post-industrial peonage are already sown by the time they leave college and enter the work force. Graduates with high debt levels have trouble finding jobs because employers review credit reports. One interviewee was asked by a major Wall Street banking firm, "How can we feel comfortable about you managing large sums of money when you have had such difficulty handing your own credit-card debts?"[28]

Worse still, the psychological stress resulting from severe debt can lead to emotional crisis and suicide (see Box 6.4). The problems associated with college affordability and the temptations of debt sometimes have tragic results.

The middle class thus pay a higher share of their income in taxes to state and local governments and a higher percentage of their income to the federal government in payroll taxes, yet they receive little if any relief from the much-ballyhooed tax cuts of the past twenty years. Moreover, middle-class Americans have seen subsidies for state activities like public higher education that benefit them cut, and the costs of a route to upward mobility increase.

Vanishing Benefits and the Costs of Working

Nearly eight out of ten Americans worry a fair amount or a great deal about the availability and affordability of healthcare.[29] And no wonder: especially in the past fifteen years, employers have reduced or eliminated their commitments to providing healthcare coverage for their employees. According to the Department of Labor, the percentage of the civilian workforce covered by employer-provided health plans dropped from 63 percent in 1992–1993 to 45 percent in 2002.[30] Almost all these plans require employee contributions for single and family coverage, and those contributions have risen almost 75 percent in the past decade, from an average of $60.24 per month to $228.98 per month. Meanwhile, the cost of healthcare is rising much more quickly than the rate of inflation, and the number of Americans without any health-insurance coverage or who rely on Medicare (for retirees) or Medicaid (for those with low-incomes who can't afford any other type of medical coverage) has grown considerably (see Appendix Figures 6.22, 6.23, and 6.24). For a large percentage of the middle class and most of the poor, our advice is, "Don't get sick."

For the growing number of two-income and single-parent families, another concern is the cost and availability of quality daycare. The average weekly price of daycare rose in real dollar terms by almost 50 percent from 1985 to 2000, from $55 a week to $83 (see Appendix Figure 6.25).

Box 6.4

Debt Temptations Have Very Human Costs

My son, Sean Moyer, committed suicide on February 7, 1998. He was 22 years old, a junior at the University of Oklahoma, and $10,000 in debt to credit card companies. . . . He was a national merit finalists and earned a full-ride scholarship to the University of Texas at Dallas. He was so bright about many things but so stupid when it came to managing money—he just couldn't do it. I remember the day his father and I took him off to college. We were so full of excitement about his future. The excitement about living on campus, being in the big city, his classes, and the opportunities he would have. I also remember the credit card companies having booths at the union trying to get Sean and other freshmen to sign up. They offered T-shirts and other things just for opening an account. . . . Sean got his first card soon after he started college. While attending UT he worked as a gift wrapper and sales person at Marshall Fields. He was making minimum wage. His meager salary didn't bother the credit card companies. By the time he died, he had 12 credit cards including 1 MasterCard, 2 Visas, Neiman-Marcus, Saks 5th Avenue, Macy's, Marshall Fields, Conoco, and Discover. How these companies can justify giving a credit card to a person making $5.15 an hour is beyond me. . . . Sean tried to pay off his debts. He went through credit counseling while in Dallas but he fell further and further behind. When he was 21 he realized he couldn't afford Dallas and moved back home to attend the University of Oklahoma. He worked two jobs while at OU. Still he couldn't make ends meet.

A week before Sean killed himself Sean and I had a long talk about his debts and his future. He told me he had no idea how to get out of his financial mess and didn't see much of a future for himself. He had wanted to go to law school but didn't think he could get a loan to pay tuition because he owed so much on his cards. His father and I were appalled that he had gotten so much in debt but we also didn't have an extra $10,000 to pay his bills. He thought he was a failure at 22. I will never know the exact reason Sean killed himself . . . but I have no doubt that credit card debt played a significant part in his decision.

My daughter, Mitzi Pool, was a first-year student at the University of Oklahoma in 1997. She had a small scholarship and student loans to get herself through college. She had grown up most of her life in a single-parent environment and missed out on a lot of the finer things in life. . . . She took a 12–14 hour per week part-time job to pay her car insurance and any spending money. She had applied, received, and maxed out 3 credit cards within the short three and one-half months of her college life. . . . On December 1, 1997 at 7:30 p.m., she called me crying and upset. She had lost her part-time job and did not know what she was going to do until school was out at the semester break. I tried to assure her that when she came home for the weekend we would sit down and go over her bills and work some plan out. I was not aware of the credit cards she had gained. This was my last conversation with my daughter. With her checkbook and bills spread out on her bed, my lovely daughter committed suicide that night. No letter, no explanation. The $2,500 line of credit card debt does not sound like much to you and me, but for an 18 year old trying to be an adult too fast, $2,500 is devastating.[31]

While the upward trend is evident, the actual "average cost" masks significant variation in the amount families spend on childcare. National statistics on average costs include families using childcare a few hours a week as well as those using it full-time.[32] For families with two working parents, full-time daycare can easily cost between $6,000 and $10,000 a year *per child*. To put this in perspective:

> Day care for the first four years of a child's life is almost twice as expensive as four years of tuition at the University of Washington. . . . In King County, the median cost for full-time infant care at a day care center was $805 a month in 2000, according to a state survey. For toddlers, the monthly cost was $660; for preschoolers $565. That adds up to about $31,500, compared with about $16,700 for four years of tuition for a UW undergrad.[33]

The combined costs of healthcare and childcare, all taken from average paychecks that haven't increased, have taken a big bite out of the budget of the average middle-class consumer.

Even retirement pensions, which employees used to expect to receive after devoting long years of service to a company, are being attacked by employers and economic elites. The number of workers with guaranteed pensions has not grown in proportion to the workforce (see Appendix Figure 6.25). Increasingly, companies are setting up 401(k) plans for their employees, or have "optional" 401(k) plans that employees may contribute to out of their earnings. These plans often have vesting requirements and don't allow workers to determine where the money will be invested. For 32 percent of the workforce, funds are invested only in the employer's stock.[34] Combined with declines in the U.S. savings rate and in defined pension coverage in plans that guarantee a payout at retirement, this means that Americans' retirement depends increasingly on Social Security or the whims of an undiversified "casino economy" stock portfolio that they do not control (see Box 6.5).

Today, uncertainty surrounds even Social Security, a public benefit that working Americans have almost taken for granted since the 1930s. In 1935 President Roosevelt signed the Social Security Act, establishing two national social insurance programs to address the risks of old age and unemployment. Through a series of amendments in most decades since its creation, changes have expanded and redefined this program. For generations, working Americans have planned on receiving social security payments once they retire. Although for many these payments alone are not enough to provide a comfortable retirement, especially in the face of rising healthcare and prescription costs, the payments still provide much needed income.

Political debates about the potential—and in the minds of many, the "inevitable"—insolvency of the Social Security program have driven recent discussions of the program. Estimates of its fiscal health vary widely depending on what assumptions—for example, the rate of economic growth or demographic changes—are made. In 2001, the President's Commission on

Box 6.5

Retirement and the Collapse of Enron

Before "Enron" became synonymous with scandal, failure, and bankruptcy, it was the poster child of innovation and corporate success. The Texas-based company began with the merging of InterNorth and the Houston Natural Gas Company in 1985, and became the largest natural-gas pipeline company in the United States. By the late 1990s the company expanded into an energy trading company, buying and selling gas, electricity, metals, paper, financial contracts, and other commodities. Many viewed the company's meteoric rise and expansion—revenues grew from $4.6 billion in 1990 to $101 billion in 2000—as a testament to the new face of the post-industrial economy: diversified, complex, and aggressive.

However, much of Enron's success was fabricated through accounting practices that hid debts and artificially inflated profits. As a result in December 2001, after filing for bankruptcy, Enron faced criminal investigation by the Justice Department. The collapse of Enron left over 4,000 employees, many of whom lost their entire life savings, out of work. Like many other companies, Enron had encouraged employees to invest in company stock as a part of their 401(k) plan and matched employee contributions with Enron stock. In the fall 2001, as Enron stock began to plummet, the company's retirement plan was in the process of being transferred to a different administrator and was in "lockdown"—meaning that participants could not change or sell their Enron stock during that period.[35]

One of those ex-employees is Robert Smoot of League City, Texas.

> An electrical engineer, Smoot was out of work and hadn't had a job interview since January. In addition, he and the others laid off in December had received just $4,500 in severance pay, rather than the sort of severance to which they would normally be entitled, larger sums based on how long they had worked at Enron. For him, that would be worth several months' salary—if the bankruptcy company ever paid it. Instead Smoot was spending down his savings. "We're doing okay right now, but that money's going to run out," he said. "I'm angry at what happened—treating the people laid off like trash."
>
> The dramatic collapse of Enron took people like Robert Smoot completely by surprise. But most people were surprised. There were innocent victims like Smoot, who lost not only his job but also thousands of dollars in worthless stock options and in the Enron stock he'd bought with his 401(k) retirement savings plan. There were public pension funds, which had seen their Enron investments plunge to miniscule value. . . .[36]

Social Security reported that payments from the program will begin to exceed revenue in 2016, and the trust fund will go broke in 2038; the Board of Trustees of Social Security put the date at 2041[37]; and the non-partisan Congressional Budget Office stated that payments will exceed revenues in 2020, and in 2053 the program will no longer be able to pay

Box 6.6

Cut Pensions, Make Profits

Robert S. Miller is a CEO turnaround artist with a plan. He turns around Rust Belt companies by jettisoning their pension plans. As CEO of Bethlehem Steel in 2002, Mr. Miller shut down the pension plan, leaving a federal government program to meet the company's $3.7 million in unfunded pension obligations to retirees. This turned a down-and-out company into a prime acquisition target. Two years later, as chief executive of Federal-Mogul, an auto parts manufacturer in Southfield, Michigan, Mr. Miller worked to wind up the pension plan for 37,000 employees in England. But the British government feared that the default would swamp the new pension insurance fund they had created. Now Mr. Miller is at Delphi, an auto parts maker that was spun off by General Motors in 1999. The same financial alchemy has been performed at Polaroid, U.S. Airways, and textile companies like Cone Mills and WestPoint Stevens.

One reason this is happening is because the U.S. government insurer of pensions, The Pension Benefit Guaranty Corporation, has become an increasingly popular option for private capital funds and investors to turn bankrupt companies into quick profit makers. The key is to shift responsibility for pensions that weigh heavily as bank loans on a company's balance sheet, to the pension corporation.

There are no exact estimates of the number of companies that are shedding pensions and placing pension obligations with the Pension Guaranty Insurance Corporation, but Lynn M. LoPucki, a professor of law at the University of California at Los Angeles, has tracked corporate pension plans since 1980 and says there is a clear upward trend in corporate attempts to stop funding pensions altogether.[38]

the full benefits.[39] The stability of Social Security is obviously in jeopardy. One out of two Americans thinks that when he or she retires, Social Security will pay no benefits. There is even less confidence in the president's plan to create personal retirement accounts and a reduction in guaranteed benefits. In June 2005, only 34 percent of Americans approved of the way President Bush was handling social security, while 62 percent of Americans disapproved.[40]

As we've shown in this chapter, the benefits middle-class Americans have come to depend on have been placed out of reach. But there is mounting evidence that the post-industrial peasant is running out of patience, and that the combination of private and public policies that have fueled economic stagnation have hardened and coarsened American public life.

The Consequences of Post-Industrial Peonage

Exploitation without rebellion seems to me far more ordinary state of affairs than revolutionary war.

—James C. Scott

Don't talk about the majority of bums who live in tin huts. They shouldn't even vote. . . . Anyone who goes on welfare should lose their right to vote. They are parasites.

—Michael Savage, AM Talk Show Host, April 18, 2002

Well, what if you said something like, "If this happens in the United States and we determine that it is the result of extremist, fundamentalist Muslims, you know, you could take out their holy sites"?

—Rep. Tom Tancredo (Colorado) on a Florida Radio Talk Show

A religious war is like children fighting over who has the strongest imaginary friend.

—Vegard Skjefstad

Our analysis thus far has highlighted the plight of the middle class and the creation of the post-industrial peasant—a class of people whose indebtedness and economic instability at the hands of elites has rendered them politically powerless, living from one paycheck to the next, one misstep away from economic disaster.

The deterioration of the middle class has not affected only its own members; changes in the economic standing and plight of the middle class have had broad implications for the overall coarsening of American life. The middle class was the bedrock on which an advanced consumer economy was built. The rules of the middle-class game defined not only how to economically get ahead, but in a broader sense what many people defined as right and wrong.

Several authors have analyzed the sociological impact of changes to the middle class.[1] We focus on four important economic and social consequences.

1. The record number of bankruptcies and overall tightness of the middle-class budget leave most consumers with little to fall back on when job losses, health crises, divorces, or general misfortunes strike.

2. The cultural contradictions of American politics have become increasingly visible as the unbridled commitment to free market capitalism tugs at the fabric of the social order that most members of the middle class rely on.

3. The result of these problems and contradictions is declining confidence in public institutions and the fraying of community ties that were once major components of middle-class life.

4. A hardening of public discourse and a general politics of displacement encourage an "us vs. them" mentality, combined with a form of identity politics that divides Americans.

These trends make it unlikely that middle-class Americans will recognize important economic commonalities and act on them.

To contextualize our discussion of these four consequences, we build this chapter around ideas raised by James Scott in his groundbreaking 1976 book *The Moral Economy of the Peasant*[2] and explore how issues of subsistence and reciprocity may be applicable to the plight of the post-industrial peasant. Scott's analysis raises important questions about the possibility of maintaining strong communities and reciprocity norms for the indebted middle class. Understanding these factors sheds light on why the middle class has not yet collectively fought to break free of the system that is controlling them.

Subsistence, Reciprocity, and Community

In *The Moral Economy of the Peasant*, James Scott attempts to explain the seemingly strange and irrational practices of subsistence peasants in modern Southeast Asia. Obviously, many aspects of this society are not comparable to twenty-first century middle-class America, but Scott's analysis presents some key aspects of peasant life relevant for our topic.

The peasant world, both in our feudal past and in some modern societies, is ordered around subsistence and securing subsistence, with all other concerns subordinate to these. As a result, peasants prefer arrangements with landlords that guarantee subsistence over those that provide a potential for higher profit but that put subsistence at risk. The village exists as a form of communal insurance that guarantees a minimal level of subsistence. Yet subsistence is far from "communal equality," and rights to subsistence come at considerable social penalties and costs. Because subsistence is a fundamental social right, social relationships are evaluated on their conformity to the *norm of reciprocity*: people should help those who help them, and the help provided should be in rough proportion to the favors received.

That there is a norm of reciprocity within the community does not mean that all is cheerful as a result of it. Instead, it means that some minimal level of subsistence can be expected from the village community. Scott says of these norms:

> They imply only that all are entitled to a *living* out of the resources within the village, and that living is attained often at the cost of a loss of status and autonomy. They work, moreover, in large measure through the abrasive force of gossip and envy and the knowledge that the abandoned poor are likely to be a real and present danger to better-off villagers.[3]

Land tenure arrangements are evaluated based on the evaluation of the subsistence needs of the peasant as primary. Very exploitative arrangements that guarantee subsistence are often preferred to systems that on the surface appear less exploitative. Thus systems that extract rents or crops in proportion to peasants' income are often viewed as more acceptable than "fixed" payments that do not vary with peasant income. As Scott states further, "claims on peasant incomes by landlords, moneylenders, or the state were never legitimate when they infringed on what was judged to be the *minimal culturally defined subsistence level* . . . the appeal in almost every case to the past—to traditional practices—and the revolts . . . are best seen as defensive reactions."[4]

Does this sound familiar? Do the defensive reactions (including appeals to tradition) by peasants whose subsistence is threatened allude to the political alienation and anger expressed by the American middle class struggling to get by? Are there signs that the post-industrial peasants are responding in similar ways as they find the old middle-class rules becoming increasingly irrelevant?

Let's further compare the situation of peasants in these systems and our post-industrial peasant:

1. For peasants in feudal and postwar Southern economies, the central concern was *access to land* to grow food; for post-industrial peasants, it is *access to income* to secure the American dream.

2. Agrarian peasants were guided by a *subsistence ethic*; post-industrial peasants are struggling to make sense of an ethic that runs counter to the principles presumed to guide American society, an ethic that idealizes the get-rich-quick schemes of the few in place of the hard work of the many (see Table 2.1).

Further, the new economic arrangements of the post-industrial economy have replaced rising earned income with rising borrowed income, increasing the dependency of the post-industrial peasant on a landlord class of employers and creditors. The political responses to the post-industrial peasant's plight reflect responses to violations of the "norms of middle class subsistence." For the post-industrial peasant, "subsistence" includes some necessities that "were luxuries only yesterday. A second car, and child care, for example, are now necessities for millions of households with two earners commuting to jobs."[5]

Most members of the middle class remember the old rules for getting ahead, which can be summarized by one simple idea: *If I work hard, things will work out fine.* The middle-class ethic was built on the concept of self-sufficiency: good, responsible people take care of themselves. They work. They marry and stay together. They raise children. They contribute to the economy as workers and consumers. They pay their bills.

Granted, there were exceptions to this ethic. For example, one of the biggest tax breaks in the federal tax code is the mortgage interest deduction. While this allows millions of Americans to buy houses that they might not otherwise be able to afford, it is a subsidy to the housing industry and a substantial benefit for homeowners. Until very recently, the Social Security system was paying out far more money in benefits to recipients than they and their employers ever contributed. Likewise, the interest payments for most of the student loans that so many rely on to pay for college expenses are subsidized by the Federal government. Adding up the costs of these "benefits," it is difficult to say that most members of the middle class were standing *completely* on their own; still, the perception is important and generally true.

The standard set of middle-class rules is substantively different in many important ways from the rules governing the workings of subsistence peasants living in villages. But Scott's analysis and the similarities between the systems raise intriguing questions relevant to the current plight of the post-industrial peasant. First, is there a set of reciprocity norms for middle class life that have been violated by elites? Second, are there signs of activities of the backward-looking, frayed communities that seek safety first and accept exploitation in exchange for subsistence? And if so, what does this herald for the future of the American middle class?

As far as norms are concerned, it is clear that the middle-class understanding of how life works has changed. The job instability of the past twenty years flies in the face of the idea that good, steady work is rewarded with long-term commitments from employers. Moreover, wages from average jobs have not increased, but the expenses and taxes the middle class pay have either stayed the same or risen. Such middle-class markers as home and car ownership have become much more difficult to attain, and consumption is fueled by debt—the same mechanism that fueled dependency in the feudal and sharecropping systems of a prior age.

From the standpoint of control and independence, the middle class has surrendered much of its independence, or had its independence expropriated, by elites who have replaced earned income from jobs with credit and debt. This credit and debt allows employers to dictate the terms and conditions of employment to employees who must work harder, and who are in poor bargaining positions because of looming insolvency and bankruptcy. Further, this new landlord class now dominates political life through political action committees and privileged access to politicians who skew the tax system and government regulation to serve their interests. Post-industrial peasants, like their predecessors, suspect that something is wrong and that the system is rigged against them, but coherent political action to combat these trends seems to be beyond their reach.

"A Pox on Both Their Houses": Examples of Middle-Class Alienation from Politics and Community

Scott Clark and Robert Boyer, two harried members of the middle class recently interviewed by the *Washington Post*,[6] provide real-life examples of this political alienation. Scott, fifty-one, worked for the Viasystems Inc. circuit board factory in suburban Richmond, Virginia, from the mid-1970s until Lucent Technologies bought the company in 2001, closing the plant. Viasystems Inc., the only domestic producer of circuit boards in the United States, employed 2,350 people. After his plant closed, Scott started doing deliveries as a driver-for-hire, working thirteen-hour days delivering office mail for four different companies with no vacation or benefits. Scott doesn't have much patience for politicians:

> When Sen. John F. Kerry (Mass.), the Democratic presidential nominee, comes on the radio to talk about the economy, proclaiming, "I believe in building up our great middle class," Clark sneers, "Yeah, right." When President Bush's voice echoes through the cab a little later, Clark dubs him "a liar."

He's not the only one angry with politicians and pundits. Robert Boyer, one of Scott's ex-coworkers, fumes, "When these guys get on the boob tube and say there's jobs out there, you just gotta go out there and get them, it makes me want to go out there and grab them by the throat and say, 'Where? Where are the jobs at?'"

The cynicism that Scott and Robert have toward politics is understandable,⁷ but beyond expressing their displeasure by grumbling, they may not have the time to muster the energy for civic engagement in other venues. The ever increasing efforts they need to engage in to simply maintain the lifestyle that the middle class has expected in the United States has taken a serious toll on their ability to engage in the activities that maintain communities.

Some of the middle-class Americans interviewed by sociologist Alan Wolfe as part of the Middle Class Morality Project echoed these concerns.⁸ One respondent described community life by saying: "It's almost as if we set up our own islands. It's a street full of islands. And, you know, we would love to have a great relationship and great neighbors and that sort of thing, but it has just never evolved." Another said: "We don't know who those people are or how they spend their time. We pass them on the street. We talk across the fence, but socially we don't do things with our neighbors to speak of." Rachel Benjamin, a dentist from Brookline, Massachusetts, provides a concise explanation for why middle-class Americans feel so disconnected from one another: "People just have less time. . . . When you look at the number of hours people spend at work now, the whole issue of living in the suburbs has cut time off people's days. Having dual-career families cuts time out of the day."⁹

In addition to finding it extremely difficult to build and maintain supportive communities, members of the middle class see little support from politicians and other elites, believing that they don't understand the realities of everyday life. The economy may be humming along, but that means little to Scott Clark, who is forced to work long hours with little job security to make ends meet. If he or any of our protagonists found time to read the newspaper, they would have found fresh evidence of just how out of touch some of our elected officials are. Take the following examples,¹⁰ starting with this one from 1997:

> "I'm not a wealthy man," said House Speaker Newt Gingrich . . . explaining
> why, despite his $171,500 salary, he needed a loan from former Sen. Bob Dole
> to pay an Ethics Committee fine. "I'm a middle-class guy."

Gingrich's salary alone was a mere four times the median income in the United States.

The prior year, Fred Heineman, former Republican Congressman from North Carolina, said that

> his combined congressional salary and police pension (as an officer in New
> York City and the chief in Raleigh) of $183,500 made him lower middle class.
> "When I see someone who is making anywhere from $300,000 to $750,000,"
> Heineman was quoted as saying, "that's middle class."

What would Bill and Sheryl or David and Monica have to say about that?

Of course, not all politicians have such outlandish views on what middle-class Americans make. Still, each high-profile quote just confirms what many middle-class Americans already suspect: the decision makers are out of touch with the realities of middle-class life. This disconnect can and does lead to alienation and pent-up anger for many middle-class Americans. But before turning to these political and cultural outcomes, let's first look at an important economic consequence of the middle class squeeze.

Record Numbers of Bankruptcies

Elizabeth Warren Sullivan and Jay L. Westbrook's *The Fragile Middle Class: Americans in Debt* (2000) and Elizabeth Warren and Amelia Warrent Tyagi's *The Two-Income Trap: Why Middle Class Mothers and Fathers Are Going Broke* (2003) document how the middle-class family is more likely to end up in bankruptcy court now than at any other time in American history (see Figure 7.1).[11]

The Fragile Middle Class analyzes the myriad reasons why Americans have been filing up to 1 million bankruptcy claims per year, including job and income loss, sickness and injury, divorce, home ownership (mortgage payments that are too high), and too much credit. Of these, the effects of credit and home ownership are (or appear to be) voluntary, while the effects of job loss, sickness, and divorce are less so. The book concludes that the cause of this epidemic of bankruptcies is the lack of a viable back-up plan for people who suffer misfortunes. There is little financial "slack" in most late twentieth- and early twenty-first-century middle-class budgets, so slight changes in economic circumstances often lead to financial disaster.

Figure 7.1

**U.S. Personal Bankruptcy Filings, 1985–2004
(in Thousands of Dollars)**

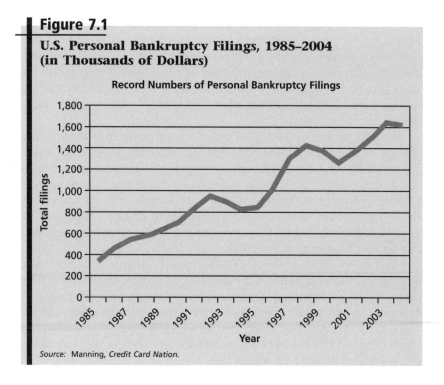

Record Numbers of Personal Bankruptcy Filings

Source: Manning, *Credit Card Nation.*

The Two-Income Trap makes a similar argument, claiming that one reason the American middle class is having so much trouble is because two incomes are now needed to cover what one income used to pay for, and that unregulated credit markets have allowed Americans to pile up huge amounts of debt. As our Chapter 3 shows, debt now equals 100 percent of most family income, if not more.

The Two-Income Trap also suggests that there is now no reliable public or private "safety net" for members of the middle class. While the public safety net that exists for the middle class, unemployment insurance and Social Security, can offer modest protection for some, the majority of middle-class families don't qualify for these limited public programs. Whom can these people call on for assistance as they struggle to stay afloat? Historically, housewives and stay-at-home moms have provided a private safety net; because the financial situation of the household was not predicated on their paid labor, in hard times they could enter the workforce and bring in extra income. This private safety net is disappearing because more and more families are now two-earner families to begin with; there is no "reserve worker" to step up when things get tight.

Warren and Tyagi argue that most of the money that the second earner is bringing in goes toward buying suburban houses in neighborhoods with good schools, and that the premium on these houses drives the costs of home ownership upward. They also rail against changed provisions in bankruptcy laws that claim bankruptcy is an "automatic way out for irresponsible spenders" and other "freeloaders" who are abusing the financial system.

Of course, as Warren and Tyagi point out, the problem is further exacerbated by the high divorce rate and the growing presence of single-parent families in the United States. These families have few prospects in an economic poker game that requires two incomes just to ante up. And many of the problems associated with time, money, and affordability of the lifestyle of the middle class are unreachable by single parents, let alone married and cohabiting parents attempting to get by on two incomes that don't grow and jobs that don't last.

Thus, post-industrial peonage often ends in financial insolvency and bankruptcy. Granted, much of the spending associated with accumulating debt is voluntary, but the banking industry and others have spent millions of dollars peddling their wares—money available through credit and the "good life" it brings—to virtually anyone who will listen, and some of this plight is caused by unstable jobs and healthcare expenses that aren't covered. Is this really the best we can do?

Box 7.1

Recent Changes in Federal Bankruptcy Law

In 2005, after eight years of trying and three failed attempts the credit card industry finally got the bankruptcy changes they'd been lobbying for. The new bankruptcy law, which took effect on October 17, 2005, prohibits some people from filing for bankruptcy at all, makes it more difficult for consumers to arrange manageable payment plans, and has fewer protections from collection efforts than the bankruptcy laws in effect since 1978.[12]

One change the new bankruptcy law puts into effect bars those with above-average income from filing for Chapter 7 bankruptcy, in which debts can be wiped out entirely. Those who pass a "means test" that suggests they have at least $100 a month left after paying certain debts and expenses will have to file a five-year repayment plan under more restrictive Chapter 13 bankruptcy laws. People who file for Chapter 7 will also be required to get professional credit counseling. These changes will make it more difficult for the middle class to file for bankruptcy when faced with unexpected job losses or medical expenses.

The Cultural Contradictions of American Politics

In a perceptive but often overlooked book, *Beyond Left and Right: The Future of Radical Politics* (1994),[13] Anthony Giddens persuasively argues that the conservative movement (or "neoliberal" movement, in his terminology) is driven by a fundamental contradiction. The movement's support of unbridled free markets and global capitalism is supposed to be founded on a bedrock of traditional family values, but these same traditional family values, and the cultural and community traditions they foster, are the very things that unbridled free markets attack. Markets and their activities are radically de-traditionalizing influences on the social fabric.

Giddens's solution to this problem is to recognize that the choice of some traditions is conscious and that dimensions of the traditional social order must be preserved. This is the "radical" conception of traditionalism that attempts to shield some of what we value in terms of families and communities from the unbridled influence of markets.

The present neoconservative movement in the United States pays lip service to traditional family values, but only as long as they don't cost anyone money or productivity. Many champion traditional family values—usually the values of the 1950s, complete with subordinate women in nuclear families, neighborhood segregated schools, and one-earner households—as the ideal that will lead society to happiness once and for all. Yet the conservative movement does precious little to make their dreams a reality. The very trends we discuss are (in part) the product of changes the conservative movement has championed, regardless of whether specific political decisions or policies were responsible for bringing them about.

In a speech for the American Enterprise Institute, Charles Kessler offers a sympathetic critique of the conservative movement:[14]

> American conservatives have always been more confident of what they were against than what they were *for*. Sparked by their opposition to President Clinton's health care plan, for example, right-wing Republicans won an enormous electoral victory, capturing the House of Representatives and the Senate in 1994. Hopeful that American liberalism, like Soviet Communism, was historically doomed and needed only a final shove to topple it into the grave, Republicans led by Newt Gingrich (the first Republican Speaker of the House in forty years) tried to convert the public's rejection of ClintonCare into approval of the Contract With America, the initial installment of what they promised would be a positive agenda for conservative governance.

But, as Kessler points out, a clear assertion of conservative principles was not forthcoming.

The neoconservative movement has been successful in promulgating the idea that people who play by the rules should be rewarded for doing so, and that those who don't play by the rules deserve no rewards. Their policies thus fuel resentment while making the goals of the old rules unattainable; they've shown almost no inclination to act on their broad portrayals except through the politics of cultural resentment. Their policies imply that if only more repression was directed at those who don't follow the rules, such as minorities, the poor, gays and lesbians, and the urban underclass, then those who do play by the rules would succeed. At the same time, those bigwigs who don't play by the rules at all—who stuff their pockets full of stolen Monopoly money—are completely ignored in the neoconservative mindset.[15]

So a significant portion of the middle class believes that if they vote for the right people, they will benefit from tax cuts and those who don't play by the rules will be punished. But with each round of elections, the tax cuts benefit instead those already well off, more taxes are excised from the middle class, wages remain flat, and the values the neoconservative movement claims to champion become more untenable:

> On the one hand, neoliberalism is hostile to tradition—and is indeed one of the main forces sweeping away tradition everywhere, as a result of the promotion of market forces and an aggressive individualism. On the other, it depends upon the persistence of tradition for its legitimacy and its attachment to conservatism—in the areas of the nation, religion, gender, and the family. Having no proper theoretical rationale, its defense of tradition in these areas takes the form of fundamentalism. . . . [In the arena of family values,] the expansion of market society . . . is a prime force promoting those very disintegrative forces affecting family life which neoliberalism, wearing its fundamentalist hat, diagnoses and so vigorously opposes. This is an unstable mix indeed.[16]

This may be a transient formula for electoral victory, or a formula for fomenting cultural resentment and hatred. But it is certainly *not* a formula for reinvigorating the middle class.

Of course, conservatives and neoliberals are not exclusively to blame for the plight of the middle class. The American left has shown little or no connection to the values of the middle class and in some cases openly despises them. Worse still, the Democratic Party, as the world's second most enthusiastic capitalist party,[17] has ignored the economic interests and cultural concerns of the middle class. In their 2000 study of "America's forgotten majority"—the white working class Americans who make up about 55 percent of the voting population, the majority of whom face the same economic realities as those we label middle class—Ruy Teixeira and Joel Rogers write:

> the changes that these voters really want—and that aren't being offered in sufficient quantities by either of the major parties at present—are improvements in basic aspects of their lives. They have a multitude of difficulties and concerns that the "new economy" . . . is highly unlikely to solve on its own. The health insurance situation is becoming more, not less, precarious. Providing for a secure retirement is becoming more, not less, difficult. Getting the right education and training is becoming more challenging, even as it becomes more important. Resolving the tensions between work and family life is becoming more daunting with every passing year. Competing in a global economy is making it harder, not easier, to ensure one's family a decent standard of living.[18]

Thus is the post-industrial peasant resentful of both political parties and their records of the past twenty-five years. In this context, it's no wonder that Scott Clark and Robert Boyer are mad.

The Fraying of Community

The plight of the post-industrial peasant has consequences for the fraying of community life. In 1985, Robert N. Bellah, Richard Madsen, William M. Sullivan, Ann Swidler, and Steven M. Tipton's *Habits of the Heart: Individualism and Commitment in American Life* was a bellwether of the fraying of community that resulted from the precarious state of the middle class. This research project involved focus groups and surveys among representative samples of Americans, all of whom were asked to discuss their aspirations for life and their conceptions of goodness. What came through in their interviews was that most aspirations were individual and intimate; national life and community life were rarely if ever mentioned:

> In our interviews it became clear that for most of those to whom we spoke, the touchstones of truth and goodness lie in individual experience and intimate relationships. Both the social situations of middle-class life and the vocabularies of everyday language predispose toward private sources of meaning. We also found strong identification with the United States as a national community. Yet, though the nation was viewed as good, "government" and "politics" often had negative connotations. Americans, it would seem, are genuinely ambivalent about public life, and this ambivalence makes it difficult to address the problems confronting us as a whole.[19]

Using National Election Studies data, Teixeira and Rogers show the dramatic decrease in the public's trust of government from 1964 through the mid-1990s. In 1964, nearly 80 percent of respondents said they trusted the government in Washington to do the right thing "most or all of the time"; by 1980, just above 25 percent agreed; and in 1996, slightly less than 30 percent.

Our discussions have suggested some good reasons for this decline, both before and after 1985. The deindustrialization of the 1980s and corporate downsizing of the 1990s tore the fabric of the middle class, and little evidence suggests that government at any level has done much to stop these activities; indeed, the government has not indicated that it intends to do anything about the current crisis of exporting white-collar service jobs to India and other English-speaking parts of the developing world (see Box 1.5). Small wonder the middle class doesn't trust governments and public life; what has it done for them lately?

In addition to doing little to preserve the jobs that provide the earnings that make middle-class life possible, federal and state governments radically altered their fiscal and taxation policies in favor of the wealthy and those with unearned income (see Chapter 6). The real, and unresolved, issue for political sociologists and other observers is how helping the poor came to be defined as a social experiment that failed, while the massive government aided redistribution of wealth to the rich was labeled unleashing free market capitalism.

In 2000, Robert Putnam published his groundbreaking *Bowling Alone: The Collapse and Revival of American Community*,[20] which discusses what Putnam considers to be an alarming decline in *social* capital, the interactive activities that make communities and neighborhoods better places to live. Putnam documents declines in civic participation of all kinds from voting to church attendance to membership in local civic organizations. Along with this, he documents declines in mutual trust, honesty, and reciprocity across the twentieth century, trends that seem especially pronounced in the 1980s and 1990s.

Putnam blames television, increased working hours, and nonstandard working hours for these trends. But could they be due instead to changes in the economic life of the middle class? As Scott points out in *The Moral Economy of the Peasant*, people who are barely getting by are generous only because they have to be. This stinginess results in less participation in the activities and groups that once formed the fabric of American community life.

People are more likely to volunteer, get involved in their communities, and make a difference in the lives of children, the elderly, the poor, and others if they have a stable economic base. Increasingly, post-industrial peasants do not have that base, so volunteerism and a sense of community suffer as Putnam describes. They spend more time commuting to work, more hours at work, and more hours as a family working, all for earnings that don't increase in value.

This situation is especially ironic considering the political messages of the past twenty years. In George H. W. Bush's 1988 presidential campaign, Americans were told to look toward a "thousand points of light," to develop a new public spirit, civic awareness, and sense of volunteerism and community. While Bush's appeal may have been sincere, the economic policies he embraced were eroding the soil from which such civic spirit must grow. Our "thousand points of light" requires electricity to work, and stable jobs with reasonable working hours, good wages, health care benefits, and some prospects for retirement are the power plant.

Political Alienation and Anger: Hardening of Public Discourse and the Politics of Displacement

Imagine that you are a new arrival in a strange land called the United States of America. You've been told that this is "the world's greatest democracy," a country where each person has the right to speak his or her own mind and to participate fully in the political process. This political process, in turn, creates the laws and policies that shape and govern the nation. You imagine that people all across this land must be continuously engaged in reflection and debate on important issues. Surely, in this land of democracy and opportunity people will be actively engaged in the political process; they will yearn for greater understanding of the problems they collectively face; they will revel in new knowledge and strive to share this knowledge with others with the hopes of creating a better society for all. So to learn more about this process you start by looking at the Declaration of Independence and the Constitution; clearly these are bedrock documents. But you decide that they are pretty old and stuffy and probably won't tell you a lot about what people here and now care about. To really get a sense of the political discourse, you turn to the mass media: cable television and the popular press.

Spend a few minutes watching MSNBC or FOXNews and the coarsening of American politics quickly becomes apparent. Political "debate" and "commentary" shows, like Crossfire, Hardball, Hannity and Colmes, and The O'Reilly Factor, provide simplistic, caustic, and often highly partisan glimpses of complex issues. This is not political discourse; it is simply a form of political theater. It is stylized name-calling that gives the illusion of reasoned debate. As comedian Jon Stewart said during an appearance on Crossfire, calling their show a "debate show" is "like saying pro wrestling is a show about athletic competition."[21]

In the realm of popular press, there seems to be no end to new non-fiction works about current events and politics. Unfortunately we once again find evidence of a polarized and coarse debate, pitting "us" against "them." Take for example, the opening lines of syndicated columnist and bestselling author Ann Coulter's book *Treason: Liberal Treachery from the Cold War to the War on Terrorism*:

> Liberals have a preternatural gift for striking a position on the side of trea-son. You could be talking about Scrabble and they would instantly leap to the anti-American position. Everyone says liberals love America, too. No they don't. Whenever the nation is under attack, from within or without, liberals side with the enemy. This is their essence.[22]

Clearly these are not the opening lines of a book that will attempt to find common ground.

Of course, controversial and antagonist writing is not limited to con-servative authors. James Hightower begins his *Thieves in High Places: They've Stolen Our Country—and it's Time to Take it Back* with the following:

> **klep-to-crat na-tion** (klep'te krat ná' shen), *n.* **1.** a body of people ruled by thieves **2.** a government characterized by the practice of transferring money and power from the many to the few **3.** a ruling class of moneyed elites that usurps liberty, justice, sovereignty, and other democratic rights from the people **4.** the USA in 2003[23]

The quotes from Coulter and Hightower represent a tendency to use name-calling and boundary making to make a political point. This tendency is most prevalent on the AM dial: the most popular form of talk radio has been the vitriolic ranting of Rush Limbaugh and the series of Rush-like commentators who have joined his ranks. In 1980, there were about seventy-five commercial talk stations in the United States, and in 2003 there were about 1,300.

> From the advent of Limbaugh in the late 1980s to today . . . nearly all of that talk radio programming has been of the right-wing variety. Limbaugh's suc-cess spawned an entire industry of Rush-wannabees and Rush clones, even shifting long-time non-political talk hosts into making right-wing proclama-tions in order to retain market share. The industry discovered right-wing talk radio, found it profitable, and thought that conservative talk was the only kind of talk that could work on the AM dial.[24]

Okay, you might say, these shows and books may be a bit caustic, but they're just entertainment. The tone is different within the hallowed halls of Congress, right? Unfortunately, we also witness this coarseness in pub-lic debate by our elected public officials.

Pointing out this changing tone of debate in Washington, Paul Krug-man notes that Senator Phil Gramm "declared that a proposal to impose a one-time capital gains levy on people who renounce U.S. citizenship in order to avoid paying taxes was 'right out of Nazi Germany.'" This

Box 7.2

The Waxing and Waning of Militia Movements

The Anti-Defamation League, a leading monitor of militia and hate group activity, believes that there are currently active militias in twenty-eight states. The recent activity and growth of militia movements represent a growth in the expression of political alienation and fragmentation in the United States. The present incarnation of the militia movement, which arose in the mid-1990s in the wake of deadly standoffs at Ruby Ridge, Idaho, and Waco, Texas, increased in popularity because of the media exposure given to those tragedies. Militias also garnered great publicity following the Oklahoma City bombing in 1995, though there is considerable debate about direct connections between militias and the perpetrators of that act.

Militia movements tend to develop around conspiracy theories suggesting that the United States is subordinating itself to a "one-world government," and that changes by the federal government, especially after the terrorist attacks of September 11, 2001, are further evidence of a conspiracy to subordinate whites and Christians to others, especially immigrants, Jews, and African Americans. Like many on the political far right and far left, these militia members view the "Global War on Terrorism" as directed at themselves, not foreign terrorists like Osama bin Laden, and consider antiterrorism measures such as the Patriot Act merely prelude to mass gun confiscation and martial law.

One West Virginia militia member, upon learning of a scheduled Marine Corps urban training exercise in Morgantown, West Virginia, in the spring of 2004, posted to a militia message board: "This is training for door to door searches of civilian homes. I can't help but think this is training for gun confiscation. I am not too happy about it happening in my home town, but I have no control. If this is training for Iraq, then what is the war in Iraq training for? Large scale gun confiscation."

Such attitudes, especially a sense that time is running out, are common. Jack Keck of the South Carolina Minutemen wrote in February 2004 "the time is at hand for what can and must be done. Big brother is stripping us of our rights daily and we all know what is coming and what we must do."

Similarly, James Michael of New Hampshire announced in January 2004 that "my friends and I have formed a cell. After many months of working together on other causes, we have desided [sic] to begin our own group here in Wakefield, New Hampshire republic. We have searched our hearts and prayed, and have decided we can wait no more . . . We are small in number now, but I think others will join with a [sic] organized unit to join ranks with."[25]

Of course, while we're all worrying about our guns, we aren't paying attention to our money.

comparison was denounced by others, including the ranking Republican on the Senate Finance Committee, Charles Grassley. Yet, as Krugman notes, a few weeks prior Grassley had also used a Hitler analogy to get his political point across: "I am sure voters will get their fill of statistics claiming that the Bush tax cut hands out 40 percent of its benefits to the top 1 percent of taxpayers. That is not merely misleading, it is outright false. Some folks must be under the impression that as long as something is repeated often enough, it will become true. That was how Adolf Hitler got to the top."[26]

The tone in Washington doesn't show signs of changing. The Bush administration's strident unilateralism after the attacks of September 11, 2001, and during the buildup to the war in Iraq told the world and Americans who disagreed with this course of action "You are either with us or against us." The message that this sends is once again clear: it is "us" vs. "them"—there is no middle ground.

Several commentators have discussed the growth of alienation and cynicism in the American electorate.[27] Kevin Phillips's *Boiling Point: Republicans, Democrats, and the End of Middle Class Prosperity* documents how during the 1980s Washington turned to a "soak the middle class" strategy to fuel the latest capitalist heyday, mirroring the capitalist heydays of the 1920s and 1890s. The combination of government debt, changed government funding priorities, and the growth of "one world" economic ideologies placed the middle class in a position in which prosperity was sacrificed for a "rentier class" of capitalists that don't make anything and don't employ anyone, and do little but look to Washington for additional tax and deregulation favors.

Thomas Byrne Edsall and Mary D. Edsall's *Chain Reaction* (1992) highlights a process all too familiar in American politics: the association of government action with high taxes in the name of race and civil rights, and the ability of conservative politicians to exploit this association to garner votes and political power. The Edsalls blame the Democratic Party for abandoning, or appearing to abandon, their original working-class constituency to garner votes from minority groups. The resulting misgivings about trends in government programs and the economic instability of the 1970s provided a window of opportunity for the Republican Party to regain electoral stamina by drawing connections between high taxes and "social experiments" that did little for the average voter, or worse, provided minorities with superordinate sets of "rights" (through affirmative action and zealous civil rights enforcement) that could be used against whites in the workplace and public institutions.

Why would the embattled middle class latch onto the "race, rights, and taxes" framework as a viable political action strategy? Our research provides several possible reasons:

1. The tax system is biased against the middle class and to some extent, the poor, and taxes have shifted from progressive sources (income taxes) to regressive sources (payroll taxes and state and local sales

taxes). The lion's share of the taxes that pay for the welfare state are extracted from the people just above welfare recipients—a formula for resentment and hatred.

2. Our embattled member of the middle class has no reason to choose another political course of action, given that the Democratic Party seems unable to articulate a coherent politics of the middle class that can compete with the right's focus on social pathology, high taxes, and "violating the rules."

3. The middle class is faced with two sets of "middle-class rule viola- tors," one visible—the poor and minority groups, as portrayed by conservatives and media—and one that is beyond their control—the wealthy, who have paid themselves handsomely from the productiv- ity gains the middle class have helped produce. It is far easier for the middle class to express their resentment over the workings of the sys- tem by insisting on control over the visible, subordinate group.

And Please! Let's Fight about *Anything* but Money . . .

Philosopher Jean Bethke Elshtain in her important book *Democracy on Trial* (1995) suggests that much of what we call public life and public discourse has been coarsened and hardened by identity politics—the belief that there is no public sphere and that all arguments come down to the affirmation of personal identities. She faults academics, activists, and others for turn- ing the pursuit of individual rights into an unbridled war of "us vs. them," in which group boundaries are created through nonnegotiable and un- changeable personal identities that reflect the sum total of all that is nec- essary to wage war in the political arena.

In political life, battles over personal identities and ensuing culture wars eliminate common obligations and public spheres of political discourse about shared problems. Elshtain refers to this predicament as the "politics of displacement":

> The central characteristic of the politics of displacement is that private iden- tity takes precedence over public ends or purposes; indeed one's private iden- tity becomes who and what one is *in public*, and public life is about con- firming that identity. The citizen gives way before the aggrieved member of a self-defined or contained group. Because the group is aggrieved—the word of choice in most polemics is enraged—the civility inherent in those rule- governed activities that allow a pluralist society to persist falters.[28]

Elshtain blames feminists, environmentalists, gays and lesbians, and representatives of racial minority groups for engaging in the "politics of displacement." But it is time to ask some other, harder questions about the "politics of displacement" as a consequence of the plight of the middle class. For example, what are we to make of the millions of listeners of hate radio and other talk radio media that do little except ridicule those who aren't like "the rest of us"? What are we to make of negative campaign ads and the growing obsession with the "other" that this form of communication implies? These forms of public discourse involve the same dynamic now pervading middle-class life in the United States. Post-industrial peasants, the people who play by the rules, are the "us," and those who don't play by the rules are "them." Our virtues are defined by their vices.

More insidiously, the politics of displacement is routinely played out in our legislative bodies any time proposals for tangible improvements to middle-class life reach the limelight. Want to talk about healthcare for all? Sidetrack the discussion by bringing up abortion and stem cell research that "they" want. Want to talk about family-friendly social policies like family leave and childcare subsidies? Rant instead about gay marriage, cohabiting partners, and how these benefits shouldn't apply to them. Want to discuss why American corporations export jobs overseas and hire illegal immigrants here at home? Sidetrack the discussion by mentioning how much unemployment an increase in the minimum wage would bring. Want to discuss improvements to the public schools? Propose that school prayer and vouchers that aren't large enough to pay for real school choice are the answer.

The list goes on, but the important point is that a politics of displacement operates at multiple levels of the American political system, diverting attention from the economic problems of the middle class. These diversionary tactics have become more pervasive as the problems of the middle class have worsened, and the media outlets that convey these messages portray the topics of these tactics as the real issues.

Of course, stem cell research, abortion, gay marriage, and school vouchers are important issues that deserve public debate, important both for those directly affected and for the country as a whole. But by allowing our political discourse to focus solely on these issues, politicians divert the collective attention of the middle class from the issues that can unite us. The rules of middle-class life have been violated, but the middle class has not yet found the political will to demand better. We might be the policy wonks that Robert Boyer complains about, but we are willing to bet our upper middle-class salaries that engaging in the politics of displacement will *not* create a better economic life for Robert and his compatriots.

The alienation and anger resulting from the violations of the norms of middle-class life is pervasive. Rising bankruptcies, the growing cultural contradictions of American politics, the fraying and straining of communities, and the growing politics of displacement are cultural manifestations of the economic plight of the post-industrial peasant. Identifying these manifestations helps explain why significant portions of the middle class have apparently resigned themselves to peonage.

Will this continue? Is there any hope for change in this situation? In our final chapter, we offer a manifesto for the middle class that provides some individual and collective possibilities for change.

What Can We Do? A Manifesto
for the Middle Class

Most people want to live in a capitalist economy, not a capitalist society.
—Juliet Schor[1]

A world of difference separates an economy that loans money to consumers and one that pays them. In the first case, consumers earn adequate wages, pay cash, and use credit reasonably, planning their futures and prepared for the uncertainties of the present. In the second, consumers borrow because they can't save cash and have inescapable debts, stifling their financial growth and forbidding planning for the future. On the surface, consumers in these different economies may seem the same because they spend money on the same goods and services. But in one case the consumer is in control, and in the other financial institutions and investors in consumer debt hold the reins.

The dilemma of the middle class is not easily solved, but since prosperous economies depend on the middle class as consumers, some changes are essential. We know that there are no magic beans we can plant in the post-industrial peasants' garden to grow a beanstalk that reaches to wealthy elites and their pots of gold. Entrenched and powerful interests, global economic trends, advancing technology, long-held cultural beliefs, corporate actions, and governmental policies come together to shape the distribution of rewards in our economy and society. Challenging and transforming these institutions and trends will take time, but reestablishing the security and stability of the American middle class is within our reach.

Clearly, doing so requires concerted collective action, but that doesn't mean that we should not also address our own particular situations and individual needs.

Individual Responses: Avoiding the Trap of Post-Industrial Peonage

The social, economic, and political structures that have produced the post-industrial peasant are too big to be combated effectively by individuals. This does not mean, however, that there is nothing that you can do to reduce your chances of becoming one. Not all of the measures necessary to avoid peonage are easy. Worse, not all of them are in your control—sudden joblessness or illness may be inevitable. For the decisions in your control, we offer a few practical suggestions guided by the premise that middle-class aspirations and the American Dream are perfectly legitimate desires in our society.

Credit Is a Good Servant but a Bad Master

The post-industrial, deregulated American economy provides seemingly infinite ways to accumulate debts. Since the early 1980s, the most popular way of doing so has been through credit cards.

The array of interest rates and fees built into credit cards is bewildering. Many have annual fees; some accumulate interest from the date of purchase; some calculate interest based on the amount owed, using recondite formulas; some offer low interest rates at the start that balloon to much higher rates after six months or a year; many include "universal default" clauses that allow companies to automatically raise interest rates, even if payments are made on time, if other loans default or if the lender determines the cardholder has too much overall debt. Still, nobody can deny that credit cards are convenient and an almost necessary part of American economic life.

Here are three suggestions on how to protect yourself from sinking into the credit quagmire:

1. *Get a credit card that is also a debit card*. Debit cards allow you to deduct charges automatically from a checking account. The advantage is that, in effect, you are writing a check for purchases using funds you already have rather than slowly accumulating debts that you have to pay off later. If you use the debit side of your credit card for some of your purchases, you avoid accumulating interest charges and you pay for purchases out of your current funds. You'll have less money at the end of the month, but fewer debts—and you won't

have to carry large amounts of cash or go through the hassle of writing checks for your purchases. One drawback to debit cards is that they generally do not have the same legal protections against fraud and theft that credit cards offer; however, this situation is changing so that fraud protection will soon apply to the debit portion of debit/credit cards.

2. *Be a ruthless credit card shopper.* Look for and keep cards with no annual fees and low interest rates—they're out there, but it takes some effort to find them. Don't assume that your local bank, or a nationally visible bank that issues hundreds of thousands of credit cards, has the best deal. Read the fine print on credit agreements, and don't be sweet-talked into low short-term interest rates in exchange for higher long-term ones.

   As we mentioned earlier, every American receives around seventy-five credit card offers a year. Those credit card companies must really want our business! Why not shop for the best deal? They're only taking our money, after all.

3. *Develop a "weight-loss clinic" philosophy toward credit card debt: If you don't put it there in the first place, you don't have to go on a "diet" to take it off.* Granted, this is easier said than done. But consumers who use credit cards that are also debit cards and who comparison shop for the best interest rates and low annual fees can also keep track of how much they charge and put themselves on a payment program that pays down their debts rather than builds them.

   Be particularly wary of minimum payments that do little else but allow interest to accumulate on your purchases. The best practice with credit cards is to pay your balance off completely every month. Barring this, the best practice is to make payments so that the balance on the credit card shifts downward each month.

Credit is both an opportunity and a cost. The right decisions will keep credit from turning you into a post-industrial peasant whom employers can strong-arm into extra hours and whom credit sharks can milk for assets and cash.

Buy the Big-Ticket Items You Want, and Don't Lease or Rent Them

On its surface, leasing or renting a household item such as a couch, stereo, or microwave oven might seem a good idea, but as we've discussed the costs of doing so often become overwhelming. Whether you buy or lease a car, for example, depends a good deal on your personal circumstances and tastes. When seeking a deal that's right for you, keep the following in mind:

1. *Renting to own is always a bad deal.* Regardless of what you want to buy, it is always better to buy that item using cash, a credit card, or available credit from stores than it is to rent the item in anticipation of owning it. The interest rates on most rent-to-own deals are several hundred percent a year. Many stores offer much better six- to twelve-month "same as cash" no-interest deals; consider setting up a payment plan that pays off your purchase in the "same as cash" window before interest starts to accumulate.

2. *Don't lease cars; buy them instead.* If you have a good job, not much in savings, and a very old car that's suddenly broken down, leasing a car might be a viable short-term strategy to keep you moving until you decide what you want to do for your next car. Outside of this one circumstance, buying cars is a better deal because you get to keep the car longer and, provided you keep up the car's maintenance, the time you drive the car after it is paid off drastically reduces your overall costs. When you lease a car, you never free yourself from a cycle of payments: you first make lease payments during the terms of the lease, then either turn the car in and lease another one or buy the car you just leased and start paying a car loan that eventually leads to ownership of the car. In either case, you are paying for your car far longer than you would if you'd simply taken out a four-, five-, or even six-year loan to make the car payments.

    If you want a luxury or sports car, you can take advantage of the growing auto leasing market. Consider buying a car someone else leased for two years. The original lessee has absorbed much of the depreciation in the car you'll want to buy, the car has usually been well-maintained (otherwise, the original lessee would owe the car dealership a lot in closing costs for the lease), and the price is often one-half to two-thirds the cost of a comparable new car. Moreover, as our leasing inventory of popular cars makes clear (see Appendix Table 5.1), people tend to lease popular luxury cars that people want to have. You should be able to find a good deal on an almost-new car.

Saving Money Is a Habit that Starts Small

Regardless of their economic circumstances, most people don't make a habit of saving money. As we showed in Chapter 3, the U.S. savings rate is low for several reasons, but the number of people with no savings at all is alarming. Our advice here is simple:

1. *Start saving early, and start small.* Considering the evidence we've pre-sented on flat wages, high taxes, higher prices, and job instability, it's clear that people don't have a lot of money to save. But saving a lit-tle money is better than not saving any at all. Financial analysts will tell you that people who end up with big nest eggs when they retire often started by saving small amounts when they weren't making very much money.

    Putting 10 dollars a month in a money market account is a good place to start. Money market accounts generally pay higher interest rates than passbook savings accounts (which pay as low as 0 percent interest) yet still provide liquidity (that is, you have access to this money without having to pay penalties). As your nest egg grows, look into putting some of your savings into short-term certificates or other investment products, which pay higher interest rates but do not provide the same level of liquidity.

2. *Make saving a habit.* Doing so eventually makes saving relatively pain-less: once you start putting away a fixed amount of money at regular intervals, you start not to miss it. If you put money in an account regularly and pretend it isn't there, you eventually build up a reserve fund that will be there when you need it. This makes saving for the future easier as well.

Buy a House You Can Afford

No doubt, owning a house is far better than renting in the United States. Owning provides cumulative financial advantages over time and tax ad-vantages that accrue relatively early in the term of the mortgage. But this assumes that you buy a house you can afford to pay for, not one you can barely afford, and only if your economic circumstances remain the same or improve. As Warren and Tyagi point out in *The Two-Income Trap*, pur-chasing a house that requires two high and rising incomes to make the payments has "bankruptcy" written all over it.[2] Purchase a more modest home you can afford rather than an expensive, trendy home that the bank or mortgage company will foreclose on.

Obviously, we're making some assumptions here that for many are sim-ply not true. Real estate where you live might be unaffordable for mem-bers of the middle class regardless of the interest rates available on mort-gages. You might live in a part of the country where real estate prices go through boom and bust cycles—California and New England seem especially susceptible to this problem—in which case the type of house you can afford depends on what phase of the cycle the area is in. And in parts of the country where housing values are stagnant or declining, you may be faced with having little to no equity built up when it comes time for you to sell your current home.

Assuming you can buy a house in the first place leads to our second piece of advice: *Build up the equity in your house and don't borrow against it.* Don't be tempted by the tax advantages to borrowing against the equity in your home to pay off debts and to finance big-ticket purchases: almost none of these advantages is as good as the long-term advantage of building equity in the home. If you *do* borrow against the equity in your home, doing so to improve the home makes the most sense, and then through a home equity loan rather than a home equity line of credit. Be wary of home equity lines of credit that issue "credit cards" that draw funds from the equity in your house.

Collective Responses: As a Nation, We Can Do Better Than This

We can put our own economic houses in order, but the long-term solution to post-industrial peonage involves collective action. Collective action will be necessary to work toward an American society that links capital accumulation with the financial well-being of the middle class; that invests in families by providing stable jobs, good wages, healthcare, and pensions; and that acknowledges the corrosive effects of extreme inequality and the political influence that the wealthy can buy. Stagnant incomes, rising debts, higher taxes, productivity gains expropriated by others, the politics of anger . . . as a nation, we can do better than this!

Collectively there is an array of things we could do. Many of these require political courage we haven't yet mustered. Some will require changes in how we perceive ourselves. Let's start with the key perception.

Reevaluating the Successes of the Past

To confront our modern dilemma, we must finally admit that the middle-class prosperity of the 1950s and 1960s was an accident. The United States emerged from World War II the world's foremost economic and political power. Low fertility rates during the Depression, relatively low levels of immigration in the decades following the 1924 Immigration Act, and the push for women to return from the labor force to the homestead created a boom in jobs for males. The industrial economy had broken free from the Depression through the stimulus of wartime production. The economies of our opponents (the Germans and Japanese) and even our allies (the French and British) lay in ruins; years would pass before they were economically competitive with us again. Moreover, consumers had pent-up demand for items, such as cars and refrigerators, not widely available during the war. Under these conditions, it would have been a miracle if the middle class *hadn't* prospered.

The 1970s saw the beginning of a globally competitive marketplace. Since then, easy profits and productivity gains have slowly vanished, and with them the more or less automatic pay raises, job stability, and long-term commitments of 1950s and 1960s middle-class life. The goods once produced here are now produced elsewhere and shipped here, sold to consumers at lower prices.

The coherent rules that once governed middle-class life have not been replaced by equally coherent updated rules. And as fond as we are of recalling the middle-class heyday of the 1950s and 1960s (conservatives recall strong family values, while liberals recall strong economies with lower inequality and rising wages), we cannot return to this era by simply rolling back the clock. Collectively re-creating those cultural conditions is not only impossible, it is also not desirable in many respects

It seems that the middle class got it right once in our nation's history. If returning to our past is impossible, what can we do instead?

Reconnecting Capital Accumulation to Middle-Class Prosperity

One virtue of the industrial economy of the 1950s and 1960s was that the social classes needed each other. Investment occurred in tangible ways and tangible places. Work occurred at fixed worksites where employers and investors made extensive commitments. Investors and employers often lived in the same communities as average workers. In spite of the labor strife that this era is often remembered for, the classes needed each other and had to deal with each other if each was to prosper.

One reason for the plight of the post-industrial peasant is that capital accumulation is divorced from the economic prosperity and health of the middle class. The middle class of a prior age fueled the consumer economy by spending the rising wages they received from work. The post-industrial peasant fuels the consumer economy by borrowing money from the same financial elites that accumulate capital through financial manipulations, capital flight, and expropriating productivity gains.

Given the power that voters have in an electoral representative democracy, the question is whether or not we're willing to acknowledge that policies that benefit the wealthy do not trickle down to the rest of us. This leads to a broader question, one we must ask in an era in which massive assets can be accumulated through the manipulation of markets, financial instruments, and tax loopholes: Under what conditions do we want capital to accumulate, and how will we reward those who follow those rules? Under the present circumstances there are few if any rules, and the rules that do exist are not respected by people protected by extensive legal staffs, campaign contributions, and political action committees.

What should these rules be? We could start our answer with a very simple idea: In order to accumulate wealth in the United States, you have to take some of us with you as employees. There are presently almost no rewards for creating steady jobs that pay well—in fact, there are financial *penalties* for doing so. Would it be too much to ask to provide a substantial tax credit to corporations that employ a lot of people for long periods of time without laying them off? Given everything else you can get a tax break for, this sounds reasonable.

To help define what is acceptable, let's define what is *not* acceptable: the unbridled accumulation of wealth through market and tax manipulations that involve the relentless buying and selling of companies, laying off of workers, cutting of wages, elimination of benefits, and paying CEOs and investors from productivity gains that the overworked, downsized, perpetually frightened workforce produces. Simply acknowledging that this is not what we want would be a start.

If We Value Families, We Should Put Our Money Where Our Mouths Are

Much of what passes as "family values" rhetoric is a classic example of the politics of displacement. (You don't see the connection between teenage abstinence from sexual activity and falling middle-class wages? We don't either.) However, elements of our current cultural unrest about the state of the American family are not the manipulative invention of unscrupulous politicians. The divorce rate really is high, and child welfare, bad schools, and quality daycare and supervision for kids really are problems.

But just as we can't go back to the 1950s and 1960s, the political right can't do so either. In fact, as Giddens would point out,[3] exactly the opposite has to occur: If we value families, traditions, and communities, they must be sheltered from global market forces, not left to their mercy. No collective way to promote family values is rhetorical and costs us nothing economically. No amount of religious fundamentalism, personal transformation, sexual abstinence, forced marriages, or complaining about those who don't follow the rules will help people make the choices that promote the long-term health of families. These things won't work because the economic base is not there.

If we truly want to support the American family, in all its forms, we must provide the economic base. Here are three suggestions for altering the rhetorical discussion concerning family values:

1. *Good jobs at good wages are a family value.* The turmoil that ravages modern families is often driven by economics. Couples fight over money, and fight harder over money when they're in debt and they don't have any money. When both parents have to work longer hours for lower wages, children are not supervised. Children who are not supervised get into trouble. When parents have to work nonstandard hours, the problem is worse.

   Many on the political right claim that the problems of American families are caused by cultural decline. This decline, to the extent there is one, would be leveled by offering middle-class parents stable jobs, offered by employers that are rewarded for providing them; ready access to healthcare; affordable childcare; family leaves; reasonable work hours; and paid vacations. The present political system does not view this social experiment as worth the effort, and no politician is currently willing to make this the centerpiece of a political campaign.

2. *All types of work must be treated with dignity and respect.* As other commentators have suggested,[4] working poverty needs to be legislated out of existence, even at the cost of slightly higher unemployment. The tax system must provide those who earn income with some of the same tax breaks as those who make unearned income. Or, more justly perhaps, the tax system should treat both types of income the same way. The rhetorical claim that investment income is somehow tied to the prosperity of the middle class has not been true for the post-industrial economy of the past thirty years. Hence the tax breaks that favor all types of unearned income are not justified. Worse from a cultural standpoint, such provisions of the tax law penalize, and degrade, work.

   In short, if we're really interested in stopping cultural decline, those who work should not be poor. We should promote the work ethic for everybody.

3. *The government must provide national healthcare and a viable, portable pension system.* These would not only restore the basic dignity of work but would also reduce the anxiety of job instability. Pensions and mandatory contributions by employers and employees should be universal and portable. Employees should not be forced to invest 401(k) plans only in company stock, but should have control over retirement funds. These funds should be administered by responsible third parties to which employers don't have access.

A viable national healthcare system would eliminate healthcare crises caused by skyrocketing out-of-pocket expenses, a major source of bankruptcy among the middle class. Virtually no evidence suggests that we can't afford a national healthcare system, while plenty of evidence shows that we all pay a very high social cost for our present healthcare system. Every other industrialized nation in the world has national healthcare, so why can't we?

Finally, We Need to Acknowledge that Inequality Is a Social Problem

The issue of income and wealth inequality is much more fundamental than the old question of whether inequality motivates people to pursue economic opportunities. We must start a national dialogue on these issues as social problems. We aren't arguing that inequality at any level is bad, but how much of it do we need to promote the economic activities that make our economy prosperous?

 Three major problems arise for a society with high and rising levels of economic inequality:

1. *Those who have privileged access to wealth can buy political influence with it.* This access guarantees access to other forms of wealth accumulation and deprives those with less political clout of economic opportunities. The tax and wealth redistribution of the past twenty-five years and the relative weighing of the tax system toward earned income and away from unearned income provides substantial evidence that this has happened.

2. *The rest of us lose faith in the system.* As we discussed in Chapter 7, an economically harried, unstable, one-step-from-bankruptcy middle class is not a group on which peace and social harmony can be built. Not only will government not function well, but virtually all other areas of civic life are damaged as well. Economically stable people are generous and giving: economically unstable people might still give and might still pay, but they won't like it, and the system gives them

no reason to like it. None of this would matter, of course, if private organizations and private volunteering really did pick up the slack created by declines in government services. But the same money the middle class pays in taxes that don't provide these services is earned from unstable working hours and jobs in distant suburbs that leave no room for voluntary activities.

3. Extreme levels of inequality eliminate the possibility that we might think "There but for the grace of God go I." The wealthy and the superrich increasingly buy their way out of the social and personal problems they produce, hiring lawyers to extricate them from legal trouble, living in gated communities to shield themselves from urban decay, sending their children to private schools when public schools go downhill, hiring private physicians to attend to their healthcare needs and nannies to take care of their children. They hire employees in developing countries for 50 cents an hour and fire them without looking them in the face. Some can even buy helicopters and airplanes to avoid commuting gridlock, and install water purifiers and private sewer systems in their homes. What exactly is the connection between these elites and the rest of us?

Our bet is that politicians will not become interested in these issues until voters show that they are. The costs of not having a rational discussion about rising inequality and the declining fortunes of the middle class are simply more of the same—more tax cuts for the wealthy, more pseudo-cultural fights about everything from evolution in the public schools to gay marriage, and a middle class covered in mountains of debt and beholden to economic elites who work them ever longer hours for less money, poorer healthcare, and fewer retirement prospects, obsessed with where their next paycheck is coming from.

One way we suggest for middle-class Americans to get noticed is to (a) admit that there is a common good that we all benefit from, (b) admit that the middle class has a distinctive set of economic interests that are not synonymous with the rising unearned incomes of economic elites, (c) define political goals in concrete economic terms that actually put earned money in the pockets of the middle class in the here-and-now, and then (d) hold politicians and economic elites accountable for the economic health and well-being of the middle class.

So far, the only political message we've heard is that we should all aspire to emulate our economic elites. We think it is possible to do better, but we must first see through the illusions and rhetoric and recognize that the plight of the post-industrial peasant is real. Once we have done this, the middle-class revolution will begin.

Figure 3.1

Taxing Less and Getting More—The Laffer Curve in Supply-Side Economics

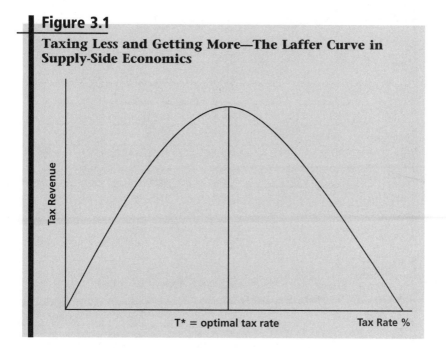

Figure 3.2

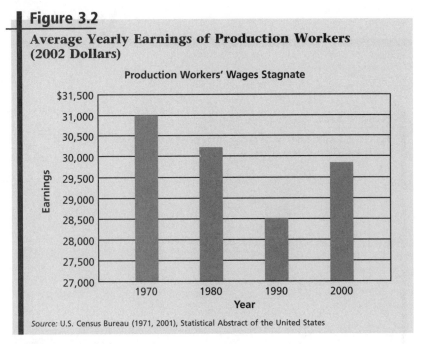

**Average Yearly Earnings of Production Workers
(2002 Dollars)**

Source: U.S. Census Bureau (1971, 2001), Statistical Abstract of the United States

Figure 3.3

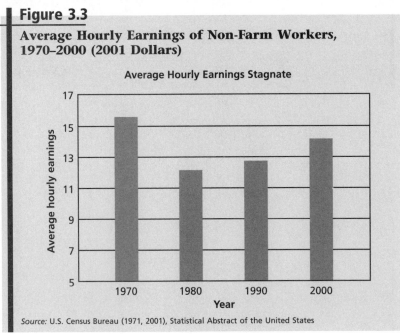

**Average Hourly Earnings of Non-Farm Workers,
1970–2000 (2001 Dollars)**

Source: U.S. Census Bureau (1971, 2001), Statistical Abstract of the United States

Figure 3.4

Ratio of the Middle Fifth Share of Household Income to the Top Two Fifths

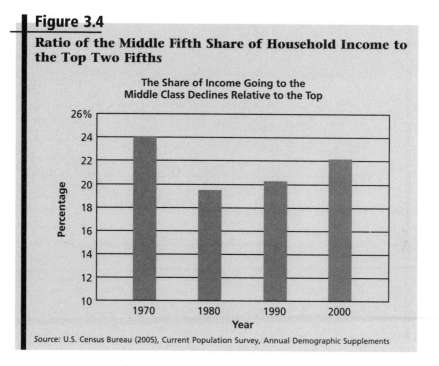

The Share of Income Going to the
Middle Class Declines Relative to the Top

Source: U.S. Census Bureau (2005), Current Population Survey, Annual Demographic Supplements

Figure 3.5

Difference between Mean and Median Family Income, 1969–2001 (2001 Dollars)

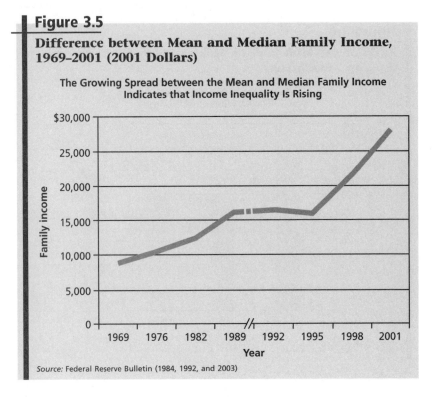

The Growing Spread between the Mean and Median Family Income Indicates that Income Inequality Is Rising

Source: Federal Reserve Bulletin (1984, 1992, and 2003)

Figure 3.6

Mass Layoffs per 1,000 Workers, 1996–2003

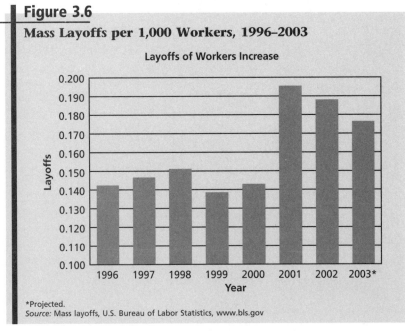

Layoffs of Workers Increase

*Projected.
Source: Mass layoffs, U.S. Bureau of Labor Statistics, www.bls.gov

Figure 3.7

U.S. Balance of Payments, 1970–2002 (Millions of Dollars)

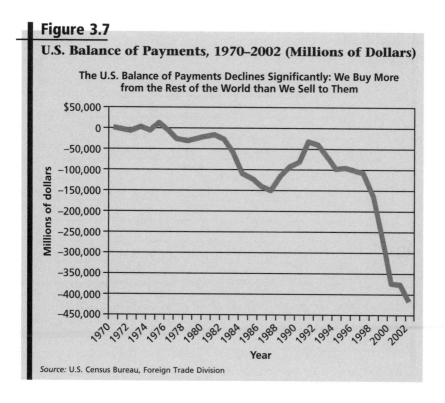

The U.S. Balance of Payments Declines Significantly: We Buy More from the Rest of the World than We Sell to Them

Source: U.S. Census Bureau, Foreign Trade Division

Figure 3.8

Balance of Payments as a Percentage of GDP, 1970–2002

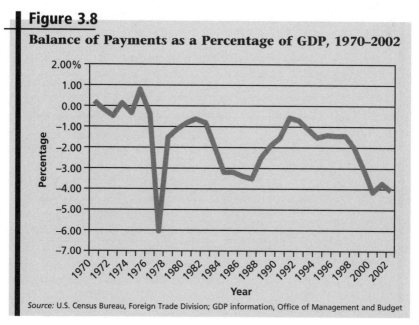

Source: U.S. Census Bureau, Foreign Trade Division; GDP information, Office of Management and Budget

Figure 3.9

Index of Aggregate Weekly Hours*

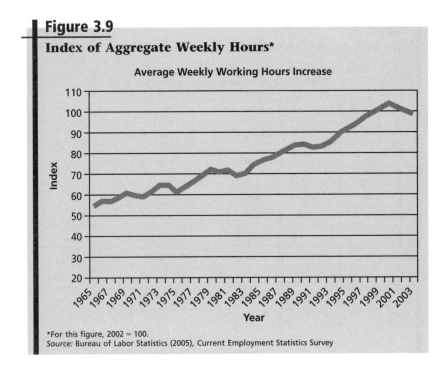

Average Weekly Working Hours Increase

*For this figure, 2002 = 100.
Source: Bureau of Labor Statistics (2005), Current Employment Statistics Survey

Figure 3.10

Married Couples Working 100 Hours or More of Paid Labor a Week, 1970–1997

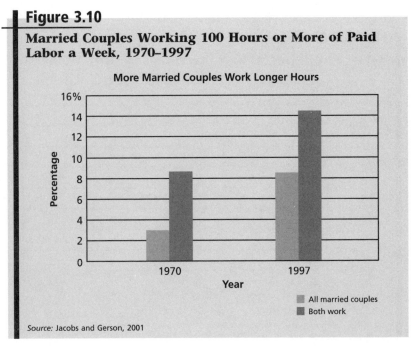

More Married Couples Work Longer Hours

All married couples
Both work

Source: Jacobs and Gerson, 2001

Figure 3.11

Percentage of Married Women in the Labor Force, 1950–2003

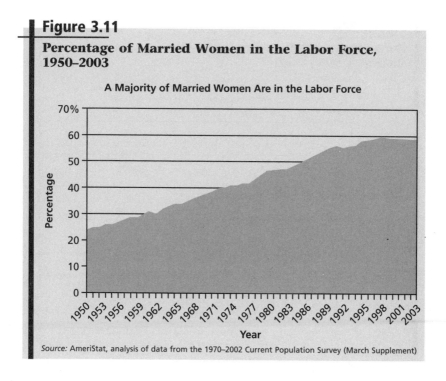

A Majority of Married Women Are in the Labor Force

Source: AmeriStat, analysis of data from the 1970–2002 Current Population Survey (March Supplement)

Figure 3.12

Average and Median Credit Card Debt per College Student, 1998–2001

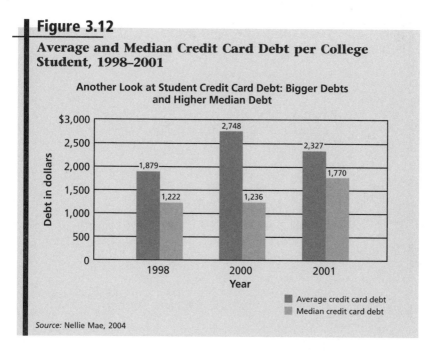

Another Look at Student Credit Card Debt: Bigger Debts and Higher Median Debt

Source: Nellie Mae, 2004

Figure 3.13

Percentage of College Students with Large Credit Card Balances, 1998–2001

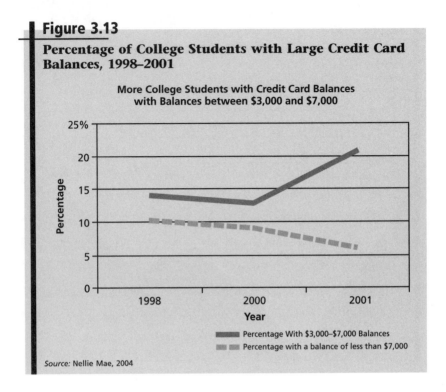

More College Students with Credit Card Balances with Balances between $3,000 and $7,000

Legend:
- Percentage With $3,000–$7,000 Balances
- Percentage with a balance of less than $7,000

Source: Nellie Mae, 2004

Figure 4.1

Hypothetical Differences in Productivity in Two Economies: One with Shifts toward Employment and One with Shifts in Output Shares

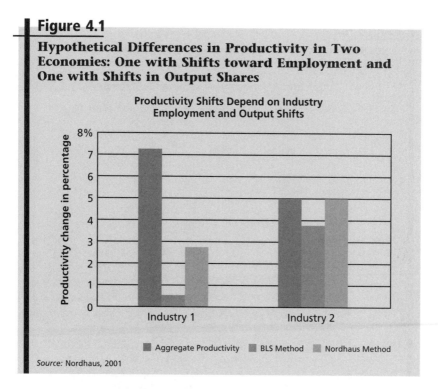

Source: Nordhaus, 2001

Figure 4.2

Alternative Productivity Indicies Calculated Using Different Data Sources, 1960–1979

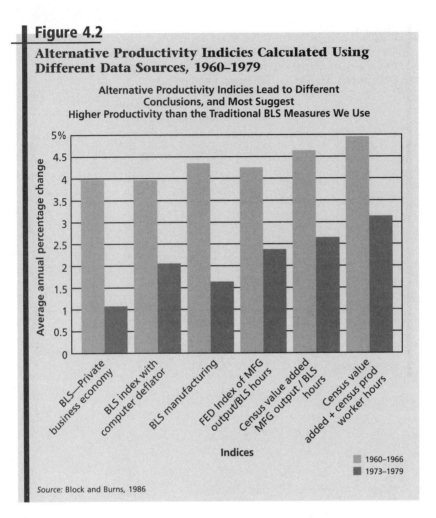

Alternative Productivity Indicies Lead to Different Conclusions, and Most Suggest Higher Productivity than the Traditional BLS Measures We Use

Average annual percentage change

Indices

■ 1960–1966
■ 1973–1979

Source: Block and Burns, 1986

Figure 4.3

Manufacturing Productivity: Annual Percentage Change in Output per Person

Productivity Cycles, but the General Trend Is Upward in the 1990s and 2000s

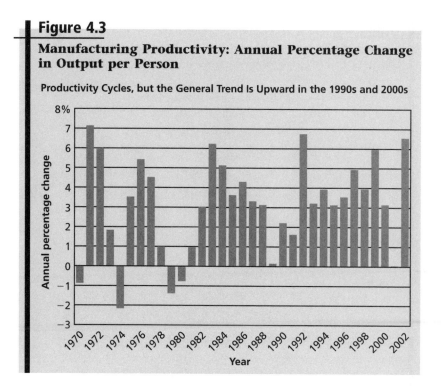

Figure 4.4

Non–Farm Business Productivity: Annual Percentage Change in Output per Person

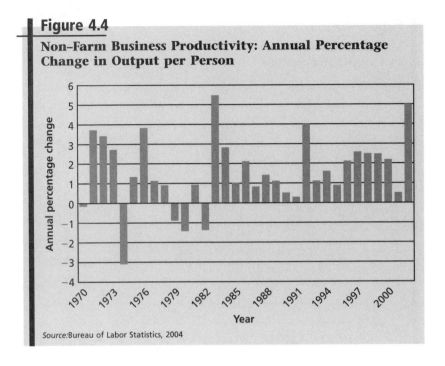

Source:Bureau of Labor Statistics, 2004

Figure 4.5

Dow Jones Industrial Average, 1970–2003

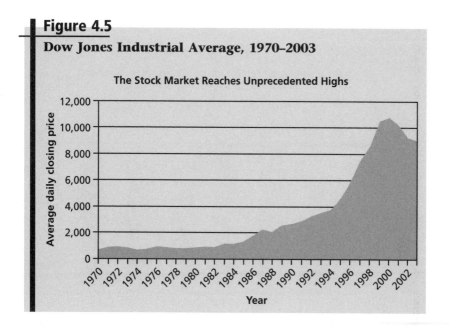

The Stock Market Reaches Unprecedented Highs

Figure 4.6

Standard & Poor's Composite Index, 1970–2003

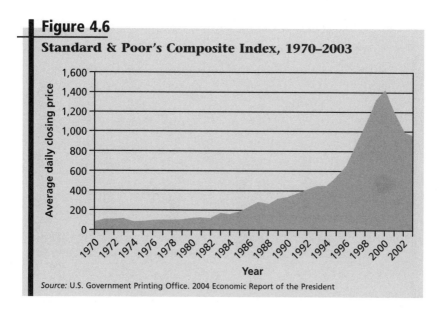

Source: U.S. Government Printing Office. 2004 Economic Report of the President

Figure 4.7

Percentage of U.S. Families That Own Stock

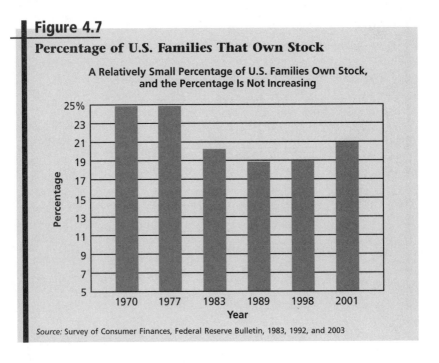

A Relatively Small Percentage of U.S. Families Own Stock,
and the Percentage Is Not Increasing

Source: Survey of Consumer Finances, Federal Reserve Bulletin, 1983, 1992, and 2003

Figure 4.8

Median Family Net Worth by Income Percentiles, 1989–2001 (Thousands of 2001 Dollars)

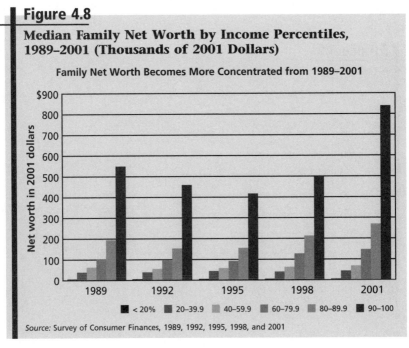

Family Net Worth Becomes More Concentrated from 1989–2001

Source: Survey of Consumer Finances, 1989, 1992, 1995, 1998, and 2001

Figure 4.9

Median Family Net Worth by Wealth Quintiles and Top 10 Percent, 1989–2001 (Thousands of 2001 Dollars)

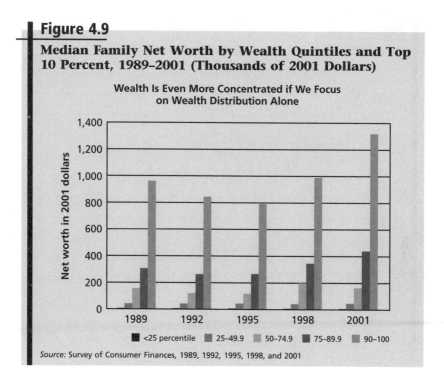

Wealth Is Even More Concentrated if We Focus on Wealth Distribution Alone

Legend: ■ <25 percentile ■ 25–49.9 ■ 50–74.9 ■ 75–89.9 ■ 90–100

Source: Survey of Consumer Finances, 1989, 1992, 1995, 1998, and 2001

Figure 4.10

Sales Growth of Luxury Retailers, 1969–2003

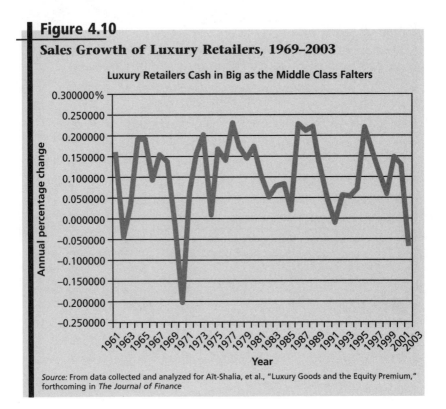

Luxury Retailers Cash in Big as the Middle Class Falters

Source: From data collected and analyzed for Aït-Shalia, et al., "Luxury Goods and the Equity Premium," forthcoming in *The Journal of Finance*

Figure 4.11

U.S. Cross-Border Transactions Top Ten Deals, 2004*

Rank	Value ($mm)†	Announce date	Seller	Unit sold
1	$57,402.19	01/14/04	BankOne Corp	
2	$54,131.38	02/11/04	Walt Disney	
3	$40,717.19	02/17/04	AT&T Wireless Services Inc.	
4	$8,601.57	01/23/04	Regions Financial Corp	
5	$6,133.97	02/17/04	GreenPoint Financial Corp	Wireless Latin American Operations of BellSouth
6	$5,850.00	03/08/04	BellSouth Corp	Cosmote Mobile Telecommunications SA
7	$3,851.20	02/26/04	Telenor ASA	
8	$3,816.15	02/09/04	NetScreen Technologies Inc.	
9	$2,603.10	03/17/04	Apogent Technologies Inc.	
10	$2,600.00	02/03/04	Peoples Bank	Credit Card Business of Peoples Bank

*Year-to-date is reflected as April 8, 2004. †Value is the base equity price offered.
Source: Mergerstat Free Reports, 2004, FactSet

Figure 4.12

M&A Deals, Top Industry Rankings, 2004*
(in Millions of Dollars)

Rank	Classification	Deals	Value ($mm)[†]
1	Banking & finance	114	$87,741.20
2	Leisure & entertainment	115	$64,585.80
3	Communications	114	$55,444.00
4	Computer software, supplies, & services	446	$13,674.50
5	Retail	93	$13,209.90
6	Beverages	20	$10,557.30
7	Oil & gas	27	$8,033.40
8	Drugs, medical supplies, & equipment	72	$7,302.90
9	Miscellaneous services	289	$5,858.40
10	Wholesale & distribution	98	$4,593.70
11	Brokerage, investment, & management consulting	123	$3,050.20
12	Chemicals, paints, & coatings	42	$2,994.40
13	Insurance	105	$2,949.50
14	Electric, gas, water, & sanitary services	49	$2,945.20
15	Electronics	43	$2,875.40
16	Broadcasting	188	$2,380.90
17	Energy services	14	$2,374.50
18	Instruments & photographic equipment	42	$1,808.60
19	Health services	52	$1,777.00
20	Food processing	46	$1,765.30

*Year-to-date is reflected as April 8, 2004. [†]Value is the base equity price offered.
Source: Mergerstat Free Reports, 2004, FactSet and Bureau of Labor Statistics, National Employment, Hours, and Earnings, www.bls.gov

Figure 4.14

Real Average Hourly Earnings (1992 Dollars) and Productivity Index*

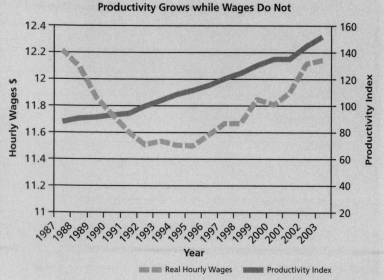

Productivity Grows while Wages Do Not

Real Hourly Wages   Productivity Index

*For this figure, 1992 = 100.
Source: Bureau of Labor Statistics, National Employment, Hours, and Earnings; Major Sector Productivity and Costs Index. www.bls.gov

Figure 4.13

Non–Farm Business Real Hourly Earnings (1992 Dollars)

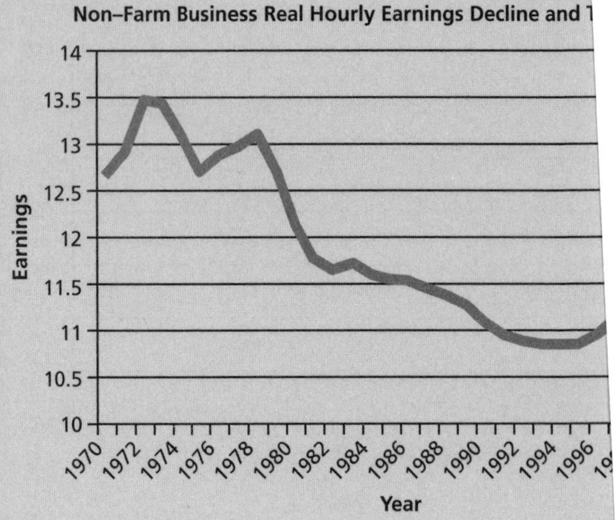

Non–Farm Business Real Hourly Earnings Decline and 1

Source: Bureau of Labor Statistics, National Employment, Hours, and Earnings, www.

Figure 4.15

Real Hourly Earnings for Manufacturing Workers, plus Productivity Enhanced Wages (1992 Dollars)

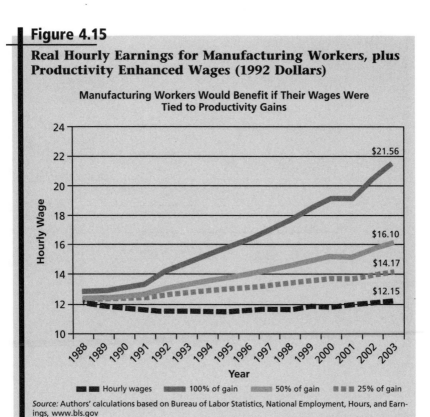

Manufacturing Workers Would Benefit if Their Wages Were Tied to Productivity Gains

Source: Authors' calculations based on Bureau of Labor Statistics, National Employment, Hours, and Earnings, www.bls.gov

Figure 5.1

Bank Mergers and Bank Assets Acquired, 1980–1998

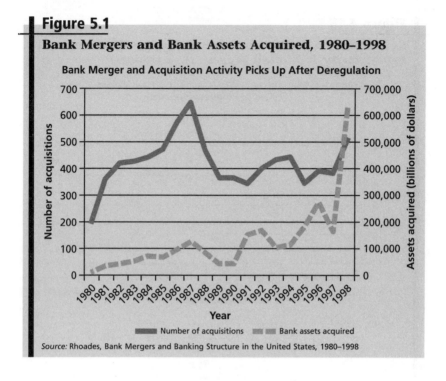

Bank Merger and Acquisition Activity Picks Up After Deregulation

Source: Rhoades, Bank Mergers and Banking Structure in the United States, 1980–1998

Figure 5.2

General Purpose Credit Card Users as a Percentage of All Families, 1970–2001

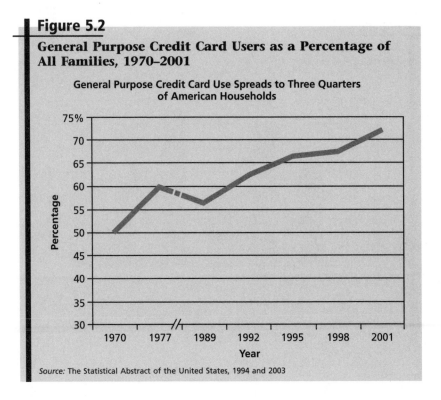

General Purpose Credit Card Use Spreads to Three Quarters
of American Households

Source: The Statistical Abstract of the United States, 1994 and 2003

Figure 5.3

Percentage of Users with Credit Card Balances by Income Category

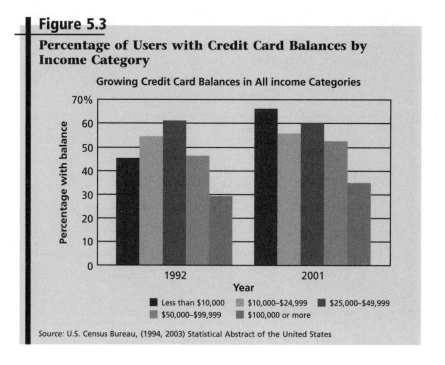

Growing Credit Card Balances in All income Categories

Legend:
- Less than $10,000
- $10,000–$24,999
- $25,000–$49,999
- $50,000–$99,999
- $100,000 or more

Source: U.S. Census Bureau, (1994, 2003) Statistical Abstract of the United States

Figure 5.4

Top 5 Most Requested Lease Vehicles (New and Used)*

New	Used
1 Infiniti G35	1 BMW 330 Series
2 Honda Accord	2 Porsche 911 Carrera
3 BMW 330 Series	3 BMW 5 Series
4 BMW 5 Series	4 Mercedes Benz CLK Class
5 Acura TL	5 Mercedes Benz E Class

* = 1st Quarter, 2004
Source: www.leaseguide.com citing and *Automobile Consumer Services, Inc* release

Figure 5.5

Percentage Households Leasing Vehicles, Total and by Household Income: 1989 to 2001

	Share of Households Leasing a Vehicle for Personal Use (%)				
	1989	**1992**	**1995**	**1998**	**2001**
All households		2.9	4.5	6.4	5.8
Household Income					
Less than $10,000	(z)	(z)	(z)	(z)	(z)
$10,000 to $24,999	(z)	(z)	1.5	4.0	1.8
$25,000 to $49,999	(z)	3.3	3.4	5.0	5.3
$50,000 to $99,999	6.1	4.1	9.4	9.5	7.6
$100,000 and over	5.0	9.6	14.2	14.8	12.9

z = Ten or fewer observations
Source: U.S. Census Bureau. Statistical Abstract of the United States: 2000, 2001

Figure 5.6

Consumer Credit Outstanding, Pools of Securitized Assets, 1989 to 2003

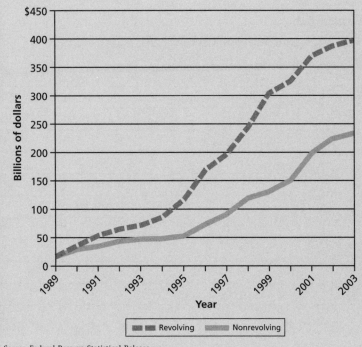

Source: Federal Reserve Statistical Release.

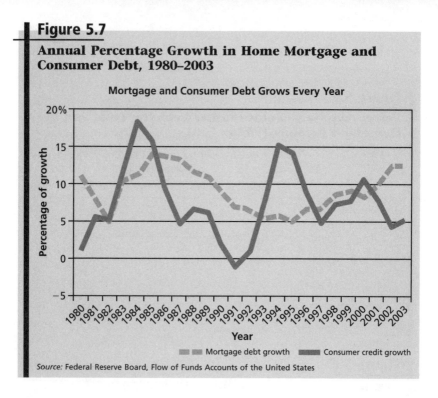

Figure 5.7

Annual Percentage Growth in Home Mortgage and Consumer Debt, 1980–2003

Mortgage and Consumer Debt Grows Every Year

Percentage of growth

Year

Mortgage debt growth   Consumer credit growth

Source: Federal Reserve Board, Flow of Funds Accounts of the United States

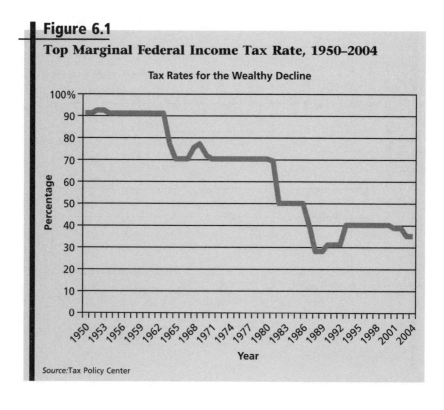

Figure 6.1

Top Marginal Federal Income Tax Rate, 1950–2004

Tax Rates for the Wealthy Decline

Percentage

Year

*Source:*Tax Policy Center

Figure 6.2

Shifts in Effective Federal Tax Rates by Population Income Decile, 1977–1988

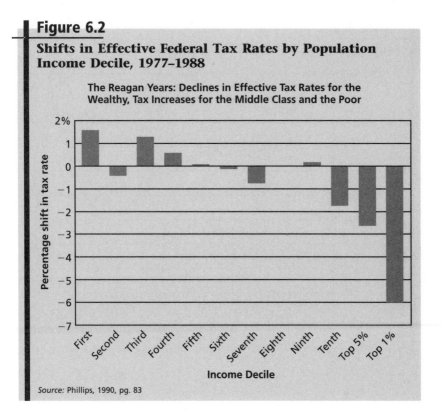

The Reagan Years: Declines in Effective Tax Rates for the Wealthy, Tax Increases for the Middle Class and the Poor

Source: Phillips, 1990, pg. 83

Figure 6.3

Federal Deficit, 1950–2004

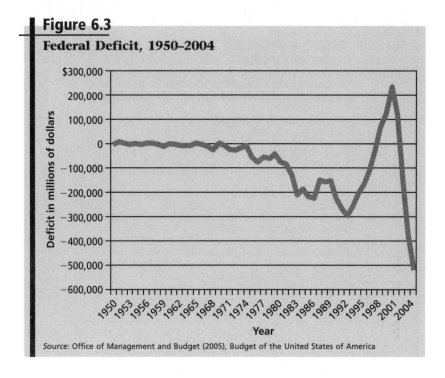

Source: Office of Management and Budget (2005), Budget of the United States of America

Figure 6.4

Total Taxes as a Percentage of GDP: The United States in Comparison with OECD Countries

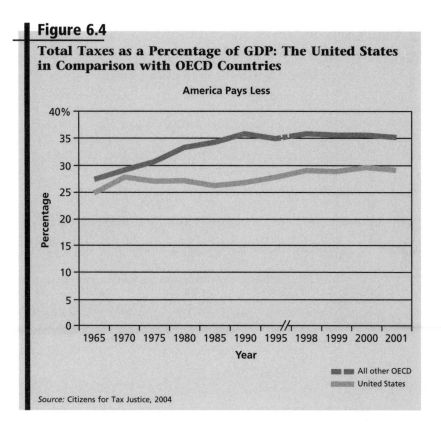

America Pays Less

Source: Citizens for Tax Justice, 2004

Figure 6.5

Growth in Corporate Tax Loopholes, 1970–1986

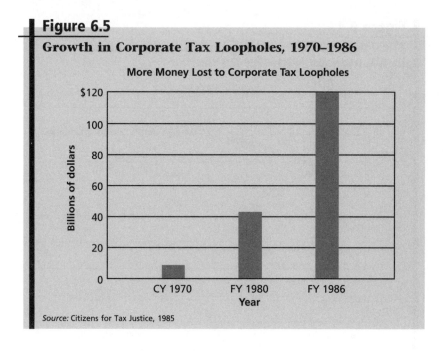

Source: Citizens for Tax Justice, 1985

Table 6.1

Overall Effective Tax Rates for 275 Major Corporations, 1981 to 1984

Year	Effective Rate
1981	16.5%
1982	11.8%
1983	14.9%
1984	16.6%
Average:	15%

Source: Citizens for Tax Justice, 1985

Figure 6.6

**Corporate Income Taxes as a Percentage of GDP:
The United States in Comparison with Other
OECD Countries**

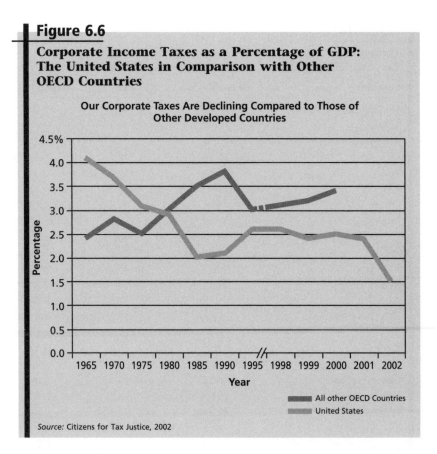

**Our Corporate Taxes Are Declining Compared to Those of
Other Developed Countries**

All other OECD Countries
United States

Source: Citizens for Tax Justice, 2002

Figure 6.7

Federal Income Taxes, 24 Companies Paying Less than Zero in 1998

Company	98 Profit	98 Tax	98 Rate
Lyondell Chemical	$80.00	$−44.0	−55.0%
Texaco	182	−67.7	−37.2%
Chevron	708	−186.8	−26.4%
CSX	386.6	−102.1	−26.4%
Tosco	227.4	−46.7	−20.6%
PepsiCo	1,583.00	−302.0	−19.1%
Owens & Minor	46.1	−7.9	−17.1%
Pfizer	1,197.60	−197.2	−16.5%
J. P. Morgan	481.1	−62.3	−12.9%
Saks	83	−7.9	−9.5%
Goodyear	400.7	−33.2	−8.3%
Ryder	227.5	−16.4	−7.2%
Enron	189	−12.5	−6.6%
Colgate-Palmolive	348.5	−19.6	−5.6%
MCI Worldcom	2,724.20	−112.6	−4.1%
Eaton	478.8	−18.0	−3.8%
Weyerhaeuser	405	−9.5	−2.3%
General Motors	952	−19.0	−2.0%
El Paso Energy	383.7	−3.0	−0.8%
WestPoint Stevens	142.6	−1.2	−0.8%
MedPartners	49.6	−0.4	−0.7%
Phillips Petroleum	145	−1.1	−0.7%
McKesson	234	−1.0	−0.4%
Northrop Grumman	297.7	−1.0	−0.3%
Totals	**$11,953.00**	**$−1,272.9**	**−10.6%**

Source: Institute on Taxation and Economic Policy, 2000

Figure 6.8

Taxes on Median-Earning One- and Two-Income Families as a Percentage of After-Tax Income, 1955–1998

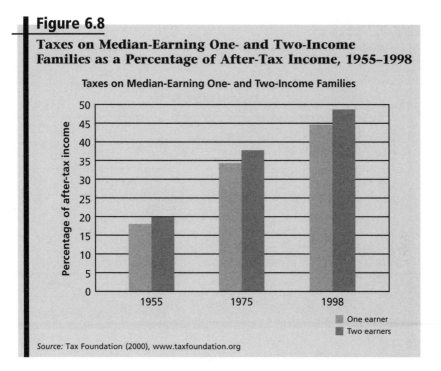

Taxes on Median-Earning One- and Two-Income Families

■ One earner
■ Two earners

Source: Tax Foundation (2000), www.taxfoundation.org

Figure 6.9

Changes in Federal, Payroll, and State and Local Tax Burdens on Median-Income Families, 1955–1998

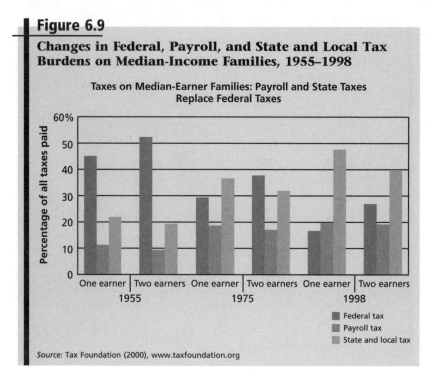

Taxes on Median-Earner Families: Payroll and State Taxes Replace Federal Taxes

Source: Tax Foundation (2000), www.taxfoundation.org

Figure 6.10

Average State and Local Taxes in 1995: State and Local Taxes Imposed on Residents as Shares of Family Income

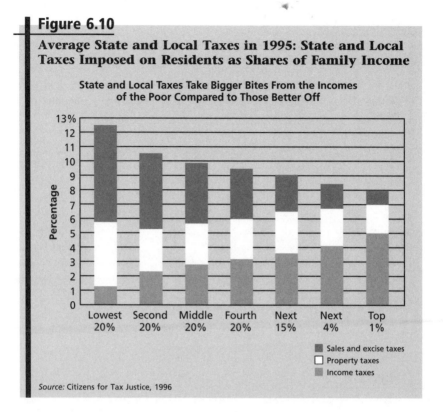

State and Local Taxes Take Bigger Bites From the Incomes
of the Poor Compared to Those Better Off

■ Sales and excise taxes
☐ Property taxes
▨ Income taxes

Source: Citizens for Tax Justice, 1996

Figure 6.11

The Ten Most Regressive State Tax Systems

Income Group	Taxes as a % of Income on			Ratio	
	Poorest 20%	Middle 60%	Top 1%	Poor/Top 1%	Middle/Top 1%
Washington	17.1%	10.5%	3.9%	435%	267%
Florida	14.0%	7.7%	3.6%	390%	216%
Texas	13.8%	8.5%	4.4%	314%	194%
South Dakota	11.7%	7.7%	2.9%	408%	269%
Tennessee	12.3%	7.5%	3.6%	340%	208%
Louisiana	13.4%	9.9%	6.0%	224%	167%
Pennsylvania	13.3%	10.2%	6.1%	220%	168%
Illinois	13.6%	9.8%	6.1%	223%	160%
Alabama	11.6%	9.0%	4.8%	242%	187%
Michigan	13.3%	10.6%	6.9%	193%	154%

Source: Citizens for Tax Justice, 1996

Figure 6.12

The 12 Most Regressive General Sales Taxes

Income Group	Sales Tax on Individuals			Sales Tax on Groceries?
	Lowest 20%	Middle 20%	Top 1%	
Tennessee	6.0%	4.1%	1.0%	Yes
Louisiana	7.6%	5.4%	1.3%	Yes
Arkansas	5.3%	3.5%	0.8%	Yes
Georgia	4.5%	2.8%	0.7%	Yes
Florida	4.4%	3.0%	0.7%	
Missouri	4.7%	3.0%	0.7%	Yes
New Mexico	7.3%	4.9%	1.4%	Yes
Mississippi	5.6%	3.9%	0.9%	Yes
California	4.2%	2.7%	0.7%	
Oklahoma	4.6%	3.1%	0.8%	Yes
Alabama	4.1%	2.6%	0.6%	Yes
Utah	4.7%	3.5%	0.8%	Yes

Source: Citizens for Tax Justice, 1996

Figure 6.13

Six States with Progressive Income Taxes

Income group	Lowest 20%	Middle 60%	Top 1%	Notes
California	0.1%	1.8%	8.2%	Highly graduated rates—for now
New Mexico	−0.8%	1.9%	5.8%	Graduated rates; refundable credits*
Rhode Island	0.6%	26.0%	7.1%	% of federal tax; refundable credits*
Vermont	−0.2%	2.2%	6.0%	% of federal tax; refundable credits*
Idaho	−0.1%	3.2%	6.3%	Highly graduated; refundable credits*
Maine	0.5%	3.0%	6.5%	Highly graduated rates

*Refundable credits are allowed even if they exceed a low-income family's income tax liability.
Source: Citizens for Tax Justice, 1996

Figure 6.14

Changes in Taxes and Tax Shares Under the First Three Bush Tax Cuts in 2010*

Income Group	% Tax Cut	Change in Share of Total Federal Taxes (Percentage Points)
Lowest 20%	−10%	+0.1%
Second 20%	−13%	+0.1%
Middle 20%	−9%	+0.7%
Fourth 20%	−8%	+1.5%
Next 15%	−11%	+1.4%
Next 4%	−21%	−1.0%
Top 1%	−25%	−2.7%
Addendum:		
All but top 5%	−10%	+3.8%

*Keep bonus depreciation and sec. 179 depreciation; keep dividend and capital gain tax cut; completely fix AMT.
Source: Citizens for Tax Justice, 2003

Figure 6.15

Taxpayers Getting Less Than $100 from 2003 Tax Cut Program, 2003–2006, by States

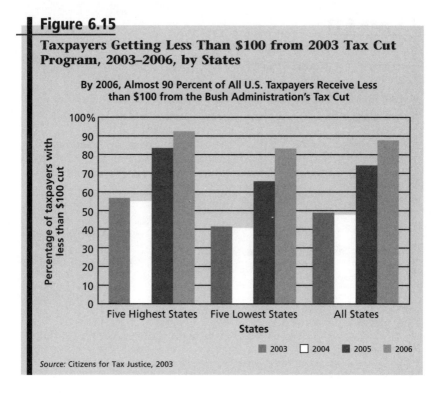

By 2006, Almost 90 Percent of All U.S. Taxpayers Receive Less than $100 from the Bush Administration's Tax Cut

Source: Citizens for Tax Justice, 2003

Figure 6.16

Effect of 2003 Tax Cuts by Family Type, 2003

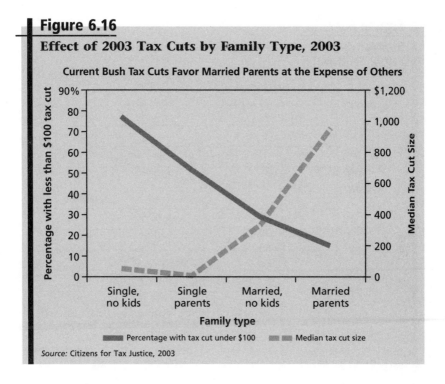

Current Bush Tax Cuts Favor Married Parents at the Expense of Others

Source: Citizens for Tax Justice, 2003

Figure 6.17

**Median New and Existing Home Sale Prices
(1992 Dollars)**

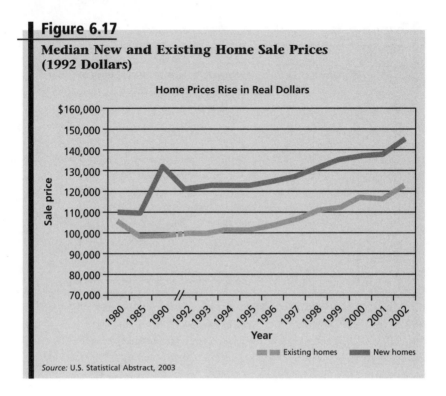

Home Prices Rise in Real Dollars

Source: U.S. Statistical Abstract, 2003

Figure 6.18

Median Price of New and Existing Homes, 1980–2002, in Current Dollars

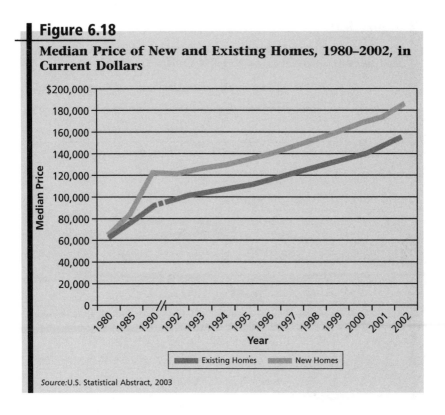

*Source:*U.S. Statistical Abstract, 2003

Figure 6.19

**Average Price of Domestic and Imported New Car Sales
in Current and Constant (1984 Dollars)**

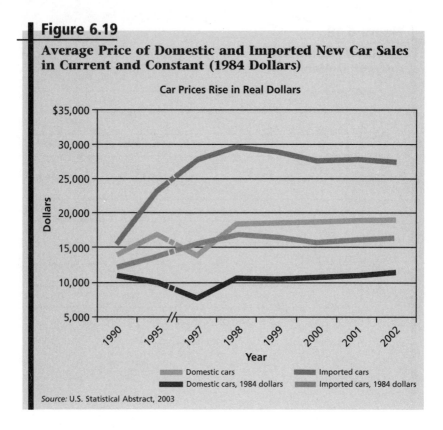

Car Prices Rise in Real Dollars

Source: U.S. Statistical Abstract, 2003

Figure 6.20

Trends in the Use of Grants and Loans for Student Aid (in 2001 Dollars)

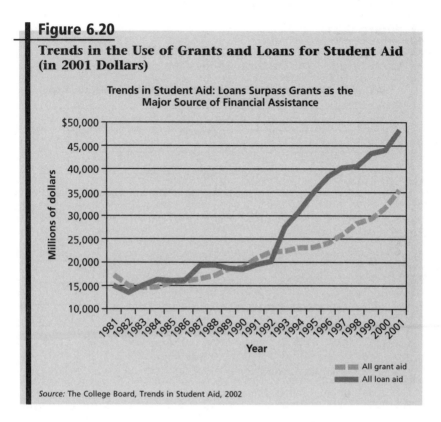

Trends in Student Aid: Loans Surpass Grants as the Major Source of Financial Assistance

Source: The College Board, Trends in Student Aid, 2002

Figure 6.21

Change in the Percentage of Public Higher Education Costs Funded by Tuition, 1980–1999

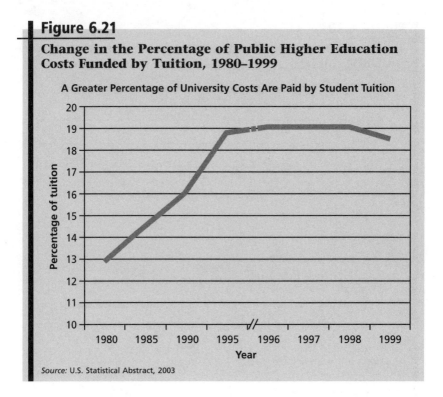

A Greater Percentage of University Costs Are Paid by Student Tuition

Source: U.S. Statistical Abstract, 2003

Figure 6.22

Change in the Price of Healthcare Relative to the Consumer Price Index, 1980–2002*

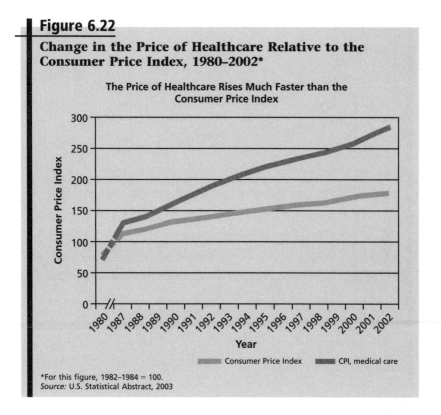

The Price of Healthcare Rises Much Faster than the Consumer Price Index

Consumer Price Index / Year

Legend: Consumer Price Index | CPI, medical care

*For this figure, 1982–1984 = 100.
Source: U.S. Statistical Abstract, 2003

Figure 6.23

Number of Americans Without Health Insurance, 1990–2001

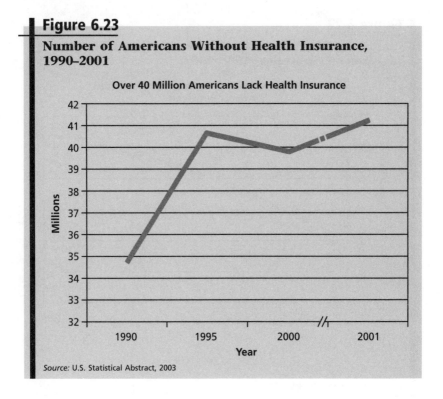

Over 40 Million Americans Lack Health Insurance

Source: U.S. Statistical Abstract, 2003

Figure 6.24

Number of Medicare and Medicaid Recipients, 1990–2005

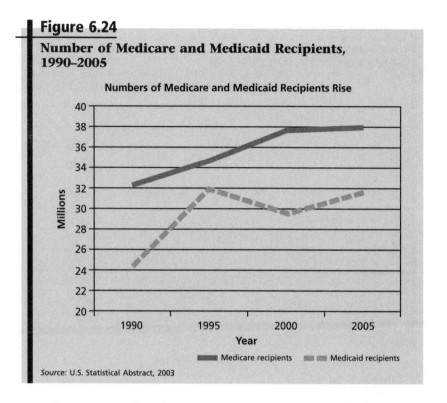

Numbers of Medicare and Medicaid Recipients Rise

Source: U.S. Statistical Abstract, 2003

Figure 6.25

Average Weekly Childcare Expenses for Children Under Five Years Old (1993 Dollars)

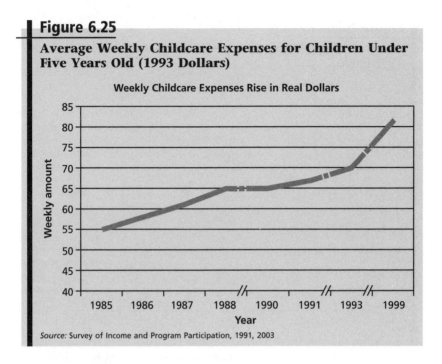

Weekly Childcare Expenses Rise in Real Dollars

Source: Survey of Income and Program Participation, 1991, 2003

Figure 6.26

The Work Force Has Grown, Pension Coverage Has Not

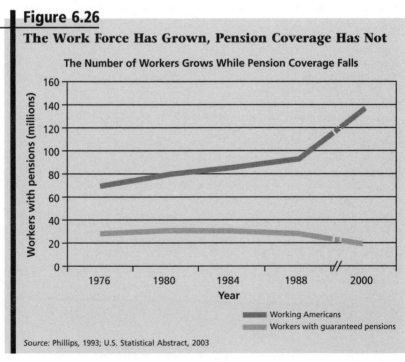

The Number of Workers Grows While Pension Coverage Falls

Working Americans
Workers with guaranteed pensions

Source: Phillips, 1993; U.S. Statistical Abstract, 2003

Notes

Chapter 1

1. 1997 Economic Report of the President, p. 7. Retrieved from www.umsl. edu/services/govdocs/erp/1997/clintlet.htm.
2. 2005 Economic Report of the President, p. 16. Retrieved from www. whitehouse.gov/cea/economic-agenda.html.
3. Mahler, Jonathan. 2003. "Commute to Nowhere." *New York Times,* April 23, pp. 46–47.
4. Moss, Michael. 2004. "Erase Debt Now. (Lose Your House Later.)" *New York Times,* October 10. Retrieved from www.nytimes.com/2004/10/ 10/business/yourmoney/10sub.html?ei=5090&en=e8573da3b340261 b&ex=1255147200&adxnnl=1&partner=rssuserland&adxnnlx=1111 486316-kF25AesAYNN02r7sUbMWKA.
5. Bayot, Jennifer. "As Bills Mount, Debts on Homes Rise for Elderly." *New York Times,* July 4. Retrieved from www.nytimes.com/2004/07/ 04/business/04DEBT.html?ex=1246593600&en=ae19d269f6206c03& ei=5090&partner=rssuserland.
6. For in-depth discussions of these issues, see, for example, Barbara Ehrenreich (1989), *Fear of Falling: The Inner Life of the Middle Class* (New York: Pantheon Books) and Alan Wolfe (1998), *One Nation, After All* (New York: Viking).
7. Skocpol, Theda. 2000. *The Missing Middle: Working Families and the Future of American Social Policy.* New York: W. W. Norton.
8. See, for example, Thomas Byrne and Mary D. Edsall (1992), *Chain Reaction: The Impact of Race, Rights, and Taxes on American Politics* (New York: W. W. Norton) and Jeff Manza and Clem Brooks (1999), *Social Cleavages and Political Change: Voter Alignments and U.S. Party Coalitions* (Oxford, UK: Oxford University Press).
9. See, for example, Robert D. Putnam (2000), *Bowling Alone: The Collapse and Revival of American Community* (New York: Simon and Schuster); Robert N. Bellah, Richard Madsen, William M. Sullivan, Ann Swidler, and Steven M. Tipton (1985), *Habits of the Heart: Individualism and Commitment in American Life* (Berkeley: University of California Press); and Amitai Etzioni (2001), *Next: The Road to the Good Society* (New York: Basic Books).

10. See Richard Sennett (1998), *The Corrosion of Character: The Personal Consequences of Work in the New Capitalism* (New York: W. W. Norton) and Beth A. Rubin (1996), *Shifts in the Social Contract: Understanding Change in American Society* (Thousand Oaks, CA: Pine Forge Press).

11. U.S. Census Bureau. 2003. Statistical Abstract of the United States. Washington, D.C.: U.S. Government Printing Office.

12. Rubin, *Shifts in the Social Contract*, p. 4.

13. Barlett, Donald L. and James B. Steele. 1992. *America: What Went Wrong?* Kansas City, MO: Andrews McMeel, p. xii.

14. Porter, Eduardo. 2004. "Hourly Pay in U.S. Not Keeping Pace with Price Rises." *New York Times*, July 18. Retrieved from www.nytimes.com/2004/07/18/business/18WAGES.html?position=&ei=5090&en=d165 cecaedae7891&ex=1247889600&adxnnl=1&partner=rssuserland& pagewanted=all&adxnnlx=1143932935-zq/RYqvnD0MfdJUT8Y5jcA.

15. Warren, Elizabeth and Amelia Warrent Tyagi. 2003. *The Two-Income Trap: Why Middle Class Mothers and Fathers Are Going Broke*. New York: Basic Books, p. 7.

16. See Kevin Phillips (1990), *The Politics of Rich and Poor: Wealth and the American Electorate in the Reagan Aftermath* (New York: Random House), p. 83, and (1993), *Boiling Point: Democrats, Republicans, and the Decline of Middle-Class Prosperity* (New York: Random House), pp. 103–29.

17. Giddens, Anthony. 1994. *Beyond Left and Right: The Future of Radical Politics*. Stanford, CA: Stanford University Press, p. 9.

18. See, for example, Anthony Giddens (1998), *The Third Way: The Renewal of Social Democracy* (Oxford, UK: Polity Press); Richard Harvey Brown (2005), *Culture, Capitalism, and Democracy in America* (New Haven: Yale University Press); Andrew E. G. Jonas (1996), "In Search of Order: Traditional Business Reformism and the Crisis of Neoliberalism in Massachusetts" in *Transactions of the Institute of British Geographers* 21: 617–34; Alejandro Portes (1996), "Neoliberalism and the Sociology of Development" in *Population and Development Review* 23: 229–59; Andreas Hasenclever, Peter Mayer, and Volker Rittberger (1996), "Interests, Power, and Knowledge: The Study of International Regimes" in *Mershon International Review* 40: 177–228.

19. Skocpol, *The Missing Middle*, pp. 22–58.

20. See, for example, David M. Gordon, Richard Edwards, and Michael Reich (1982), *Segmented Work, Divided Workers: The Historical Transformation of Labor in the United States* (New York: Cambridge University Press); Richard Edwards (1993), *Rights at Work: Employment Relations in the Post-Union Era* (Washington, D.C.: Brookings Institution); and Richard B. Freeman, ed. (1994), *Working Under Different Rules* (New York: Russell Sage Foundation).

21. See, for example, Kevin T. Leicht and Mary L. Fennell (2001), *Professional Work: A Sociological Approach* (Oxford, UK: Blackwell).

22. See, for example, Jeremy Rifkin (1995), *The End of Work: The Decline of the Global Labor Force and the Dawn of the Post-Market Era* (New York: Putnam); Thomas S. Moore (1996), *The Disposable Workforce: Worker Displacement and Employment Instability in America* (New York: Alden de Gruyter); William J. Baumol, Alan S. Blinder, and Edward N. Wolff (2003), *Downsizing in America: Reality, Causes, and Consequences* (New York: Russell Sage Foundation); and Martin Carnoy (2000), *Sustaining the New Economy: Work, Family, and Community in the Information Age* (Cambridge, MA: Harvard University Press).

23. Giddens, Anthony. 1987. *The Nation-State and Violence*. Berkeley: University of California Press, pp. 71–78.

24. Steve Lohr. 2005. "Cutting Here, but Hiring Over There." *New York Times*, June 25. Retrieved from www.nytimes.com/2005/06/24/technology/24blue.html?ei=5090&en=d74442b36081d4c2&ex=1277265600&partner=rssuserland&emc=rss&pagewanted=print.

Chapter 2

1. Green, Jennie. 2003. "Leaning On Their Parents, Again." *New York Times*, July 20.

2. Alan Wolfe. 1998. *One Nation, After All*. New York: Viking, p.1.

3. According to the U.S. Census Bureau (2005), the median family income in the United States in 2003 was $44,482. See www.census.gov/prod/2005pubs/p60-229.pdf.

4. Sørensen, Aage. 2000. "Toward a Sounder Basis for Class Analysis." *American Journal of Sociology*, 105:1525.

5. See also Jonathan Kay (2004), *Culture and Prosperity* (New York: HarperBusiness), pp. 22–30.

6. Tilly, Charles. 1998. *Durable Inequality*. Berkeley: University of California Press, pp. 147–69.

7. See Rubin (1996), pp. 9–13; U.S. Department of Commerce, Statistical Abstract of the United States, 2006, p. 436; and Castells (1996), pp. 277–278.

8. Bloch, Marc. 1961. *Feudal Society*. Chicago: University of Chicago Press, pp. 250–51.

9. Lenski, Gerhard E. 1966. *Power & Privilege: A Theory of Social Stratification*. New York: McGraw-Hill, p. 270.

10. Goldstone, Jack A. 1991. *Revolution and Rebellion in the Early Modern World*. Berkeley: University of California Press, pp. 285–347. See also William H. McNeill (1976), *Plagues and Peoples* (Garden City, NY: Anchor Press), pp. 1–10.

11. Moore, Barrington, Jr. 1966. *Social Origins of Dictatorship and Democracy: Lord and Peasant in the Making of the Modern World.* Boston: Beacon Press, pp. 451–83.

12. Lachmann, Richard. 2000. *Capitalists in Spite of Themselves: Elite Conflict and Economic Transitions in Early Modern Europe.* Oxford, UK: Oxford University Press, pp. 8–14.

13. Giddens, Anthony. 1987. *The Nation-State and Violence.* Berkeley: University of California Press, pp. 71–78.

14. For more on the ideology of such social inequality, see Max Weber (1968), *Economy and Society: An Outline of Interpretive Sociology,* ed. Guenther Roth and Claus Wittich (New York: Bedminster Press).

15. See James C. Scott (1976), *The Moral Economy of the Peasant: Rebellion and Subsistence in Southeast Asia* (New Haven: Yale University Press), pp. 1–12; Theda Skocpol (1979), *States and Social Revolutions: A Comparative Analysis of France, Russia and China* (Cambridge, UK: Cambridge University Press), pp. 14–19; Skocpol (1994), *Social Revolutions in the Modern World* (Cambridge, UK: Cambridge University Press), pp. 99–120; Moore, *Social Origins of Dictatorship and Democracy,* pp. 451–83; and Charles Tilly, Louis Tilly, and Richard Tilly (1975), *The Rebellious Century, 1830–1930* (Cambridge, MA: Harvard University Press), pp. 11–13.

16. For more detail, see Immanuel Wallerstein (1976), "From Feudalism to Capitalism: Transition or Transitions?" in *Social Forces* 55: 273–83.

17. Schwartz, Michael. 1976. *Radical Protest and Social Structure: The Southern Farmers' Alliance and Cotton Tenancy, 1880–1890.* New York: Academic Press.

18. James, David R. 1988. "The Transformation of the Southern Racial State: Class and Race Determinants of Local State Structures." *American Sociological Review* 53: 191–208.

19. Castells, Manuel. 1996. *The Rise of the Network Society.* Oxford, UK: Blackwell.

20. Castells, Manuel. 1997. *The Power of Identity.* Oxford, UK: Blackwell.

21. U.S. Census Bureau. 2004. www.census.gov/hhes/poverty/poverty03/table3.pdf.

22. See Elijah Anderson (1999), *Code of the Street* (New York: W.W. Norton); Jonathan Kozol (1992), *Savage Inequalities: Children in America's Schools* (New York: HarperPerennial); and William Julius Wilson (1996), *When Work Disappears: The World of the New Urban Poor* (New York: Knopf).

23. See Juliet B. Schor (1998), *The Overworked American: The Unexpected Decline of Leisure* (New York: Basic Books; and Schor).

Chapter 3

1. Steinhauer, Jennifer. 2005. "When the Joneses Wear Jeans." *New York Times*, May 29. Retrieved from www.nytimes.com/2005/05/29/national/class/CONSUMPTION-FINAL.html?ex=1275019200&en=795f7395856a9eb8&ei=5090&partner=rssuserland&emc=rss.

2. Even if they had this money, this is not always the wisest thing to do with it. In investment banking, investors may have only the stock and anticipated returns on the stock to show for their money. In this case, the "loan" to the company is akin to buying part of the company and betting that your investment will pay off in terms of greater value for the stock or dividends paid on the stock from the profits accruing to the investment.

3. Kennedy, David M. 1999. *Freedom from Fear: The American People in Depression and War, 1929–1945*. Oxford, UK: Oxford University Press, p. 166.

4. Weaver, Frederick S. 2002. *Economic Literacy: Basic Economics with an Attitude*. Lanham, MD: Rowman and Littlefield, p. 105.

5. Keynes, John Maynard. 1936, rpt. 1964. *The General Theory of Employment, Interest, and Money*. First Harbinger Edition. New York: Harcourt Brace Jovanovich.

6. For more on this tax cut, see Martin F. J. Prachowny (2000), "The Kennedy–Johnson Tax Cut: A Revisionist History" (Cheltenham, UK and Northampton, MA: Edward Elgar Publishing). Abstract retrieved from http://qed.econ.queensu.ca/faculty/prachowny/CEA.HTM.

7. Weaver, *Economic Literacy*, p. 105.

8. For one thing, if wages responded to government intervention directly, then many Keynesian assumptions about closing the "output gap" without increasing inflation were problematic. See Jerome L. Stein (1982), *Monetarist, Keynesian and New Classical Economics* (Oxford, UK: Blackwell), pp. 1–10.

9. See Stein, *Monetarist, Keynesian and New Classical Economics*, pp. 85–104.

10. Explaining persistent inflation in the face of high unemployment—the "stagflation" of the late 1970s—proved as difficult for monetarists as it had been for Keynesians. Monetarists could only suggest that slowing the growth in money supply would directly increase unemployment but that inflation remained high by past rates of monetary expansion and inertia caused by inflationary expectations.

11. Laffer, Arthur B. 2004. "The Laffer Curve: Past, Present, and Future." *Backgrounder*, No. 1765. The Heritage Foundation.

12. We'll avoid the question of whether the purpose of supply-side economics was to shrink the actual size of government by undermining the ability of government to fund itself. See, for example, David Stockman (1986), *The Triumph of Politics: How the Reagan Revolution Failed* (New York: Harper and Row), pp. 44–76, and Paul Krugman (1994), *Peddling Prosperity: Economic Sense and Nonsense in the Age of Diminished Expectations* (New York: W. W. Norton), pp. 151–169.

13. This assumes that the prior tax rate was on the "dysfunctional" side of the Laffer curve. Because taxes in the United States are among the lowest in the industrialized world, this strikes most economists as a dubious claim.

   Differences between supply-side economics weren't simply with the Keynesians. Unlike classical economists, supply-side economists believe that economic actors respond to government incentives and that fighting inflation will result in higher unemployment—in short, supply-side economics disregards the policy ineffectiveness hypothesis. And supply-side economics differed from monetarist economics as well. The money supply wasn't tightened during the Reagan years; instead, interest rates were increased to reduce incentives to borrow. Supply-side economics regulated money supply through interest rates, much as Keynesians did, and keeping the money supply in tight reign was not part of the program.

14. It's not as if each of these macroeconomic theories has nothing to offer the middle class. Monetarists offer steady prices, steady wages, and slow but steady economic growth—nothing flashy, but very predictable. New classical economics offers low inflation. Keynesian economics offers to increase purchasing power, and the demand multiplier effects from this should keep people employed and productive as long as potential output is above actual output. Keynesians also offer a hedge against hard times with a series of income maintenance programs that will help people if they get laid off or sick, or otherwise lose their jobs. Supply-side economics offers tax cuts, lower prices through deregulation, and productivity gains that in theory translate into higher wages.

15. See also U.S Government Printing Office (2005), www.whitehouse.gov/omb/budget/fy2003/hist.html.

16. See Kevin Phillips (1990), *The Politics of Rich and Poor: Wealth and the American Electorate in the Reagan Aftermath* (New York: Random House), p. 84, and (1993), *Boiling Point: Democrats, Republicans, and the Decline of Middle-Class Prosperity* (New York: Random House), pp. 114–22.

17. Krugman, Paul. 2003. *The Great Unraveling: Losing Our Way in the New Century*. New York: W. W. Norton, pp. 27–51, 101–24.

18. See Juliet B. Schor (1992), *The Overworked American: The Unexpected Decline of Leisure* (New York: Basic Books); Schor (1998), *The Overspent American: Upscaling, Downshifting, and the New Consumer* (New York: Basic Books); Teresa A. Sullivan, Elizabeth Warren, and Jay L. Westbrook (1999), *As We Forgive Our Debtors: Bankruptcy and Consumer Credit in America* (Washington, D.C: BeardBooks); Teresa A. Sullivan, Elizabeth Warren, and Jay L. Westbrook (2000), *The Fragile Middle Class: Americans in Debt* (New Haven: Yale University Press); Robert D. Manning (2000), *Credit Card Nation: The Consequences of America's Addiction to Credit* (New York: Basic Books); and Elizabeth Warren and Amelia Warrent Tyagi (2003), *The Two-Income Trap: Why Middle Class Mothers and Fathers Are Going Broke* (New York: Basic Books).

19. Congressional Budget Office. 2006. www.cbo.gov/ftpdocs/70xx/doc7027/01-26-BudgetOutlook.pdf.

20. See David Cay Johnston (2003), *Perfectly Legal: The Covert Campaign to Rig Our Tax System to Benefit the Super Rich—And Cheat Everybody Else* (New York: Portfolio Hardcover), pp. 1–70; Kevin Phillips (1995), *Arrogant Capital* (Boston: Back Bay Books), pp. 29–66; and Brian Reidl (2003), "Ten Common Myths about Taxes, Spending, and Budget Deficits" in *The Heritage Foundation Backgrounder*, June 13.

21. The New York Times Company. 1996. *The Downsizing of America*. New York: Three Rivers Press.

22. Barlett, Donald L. and James B. Steele. 1992. *America: What Went Wrong?* Kansas City, MO: Andrews McMeel, pp. v–xii.

23. U.S. Census Bureau. 1971. Statistical Abstract of the United States. Washington, D.C.: U.S. Government Printing Office. Also, U.S. Census Bureau. 2001. Statistical Abstract of the United States. Washington, D.C.: U.S. Government Printing Office.

24. Francis, David R. 2004. "Gap in Wages Grows Wider: Pay Rises for Well-Off, but Not for Others." *Christian Science Monitor*, February 12.

25. U.S. Census Bureau, www.census.gov/hhes/income/histinc/h02ar.html.

26. See Robert B. Avery, Gregory E. Ellihausen, Glenn B. Canner, and Thomas A. Gustafson (1984), "Survey of Consumer Finances, 1983," Federal Reserve Bulletin, September; Arthur Kennickell and Janice Shack-Marquez (1992), "Changes in Family Finances from 1983 to 1989: Evidence from the Survey of Conumer Finances," Federal Reserve Bulletin, January; and Ana M. Aizcorbe, Arthur B. Kennickell, and Kevin B. Moore (2003), "Recent Changes in U.S. Family Finances: Evidence from the 1998 and 2001 Survey of Consumer Finances," Federal Reserve Bulletin, January.

27. Leonhardt, David. 2004. "Time to Slay the Inequality Myth? Not So Fast." *New York Times*, January 25.

28. For arguments on the causes of these trends, see Krugman, *The Great Unraveling*, pp. 376–78; Joseph E. Stiglitz (2003), *The Roaring Nineties* (New York: W. W. Norton), pp. 180–202; David M. Gordon (1996), *Fat and Mean: The Corporate Squeeze of Working Americans and the Myth of Managerial Downsizing* (New York: Martin Kessler Books), pp. 15–33; and James K. Galbraith (1998), *Created Unequal: The Crisis in American Pay* (New York: Free Press), pp. 3–65.

29. Mandel, Michael. 1996. *The High-Risk Society: Peril and Promise in the New Economy.* New York: Times Business.

30. These include Gordon, *Fat and Mean*, pp. 61–94 and Kevin T. Leicht and Mary L. Fennell (2001), *Professional Work: A Sociological Approach* (Oxford, UK: Blackwell), pp. 96–112.

31. U.S. Census Bureau. 2003. Statistical Abstract of the United States. Washington, D.C.: U.S. Government Printing Office.

32. For example, see the New York Times Company, *The Downsizing of America*; Bill Moyers (2004), "Changing Face of Unemployment," retrieved from www.pbs.org./now/politics/unemployment.html; Manuel Castells (1996), *The Rise of the Network Society* (Oxford, UK: Blackwell), pp. 243–308; and Martin Carnoy (2000), *Sustaining the New Economy: Work, Family, and Community in the Information Age* (Cambridge, MA: Harvard University Press), pp. 56–105.

33. Hacker, Jacob. 2004. "Call It the Family Risk Factor." *New York Times,* January 11, quoting from the University of Michigan Panel Study of Income Dynamics, available online at psidonline.isr.umich.edu.

34. U.S. Census Bureau. 2003. Foreign Trade Division. Retrieved from www.census.gov/foreign-trade/www/press.html.

35. Jacobs, Jerry A. and Kathleen Gerson. 2001. "Overworked Individuals or Overworked Families? Explaining Trends in Work, Leisure, and Family Time." *Work and Occupations* 28: 40–63.

36. Warren, Elizabeth and Amelia Warrent Tyagi. 2003. *The Two-Income Trap: Why Middle Class Mothers and Fathers Are Going Broke.* New York: Basic Books.

37. CardWeb.com Inc.

38. O'Malley, Marie. 2004. "Educating Undergraduates on Using Credit Cards." Nellie Mae, www.nelliemae.com.

39. For more detail on this recent trend, see Patrick McGeehan (2004), "The Plastic Trap: The Debt That Binds," in the *New York Times,* November 21.

40. Take Charge America. 2005. "Credit Counseling Firm Warns Consumers of 'Perfect Financial Storm' Conditions." July 6. Retrieved from www.takechargeamerica.org/Pressroom/PerfectFinancialStorm.htm.

Chapter 4

1. Gasparino, Charles. 2005. "Good News: You're Fired." *Newsweek*, July 25. Retrieved from www.msnbc.msn.com/id/8598956/site/newsweek.
2. Nordhaus, William. 2001. "Alternative Methods for Measuring Productivity Growth." National Bureau of Economic Research. Working Paper 8095, pp. 1–20.
3. See, for example, Fred Block and Gene Burns (1986), "Productivity as a Social Problem: The Uses and Misuses of Social Indicators" in *American Sociological Review* 51: 767–80; Fred Block (1990), *Postindustrial Possibilities: A Critique of Economic Discourse* (Berkeley: University of California Press); and Erik Olin Wright (2000), "Working-Class Power, Capitalist-Class Interests, and Class Compromise" in *American Journal of Sociology* 105: 957–1002.
4. Block and Burns, "Productivity as a Social Problem."
5. Manser, Marilyn E. 2001. "The Bureau of Labor Statistics (BLS) Productivity Programs." Retrieved from www.nabe.com/publib/manser1.pdf.
6. 2005 Economic Report of the President, p. 394. Retrieved from www.gpoaccess.gov/usbudget/fy05/pdf/2004_erp.pdf.
7. Mishel, Lawrence, Jared Bernstein, and Sylvia Allegretto. 2005. *The State of Working America 2004/2005*. An Economic Policy Institute Book. Ithaca, NY: ILR Press, p. 10.
8. Wolff, Edward N. 2002. *Top Heavy: The Increasing Inequality in Wealth in America and What Can Be Done About It*, Second Edition. New York: The New Press.
9. See Arthur Kennickell and Janice Shack-Marquez (1992), "Changes in Family Finances from 1983 to 1989: Evidence from the Survey of Consumer Finances," Federal Reserve Bulletin, January; and Ana M. Aizcorbe, Arthur B. Kennickell, and Kevin B. Moore (2003), "Recent Changes in U.S. Family Finances: Evidence from the 1998 and 2001 Survey of Consumer Finances," Federal Reserve Bulletin, January.
10. Aüt-Shalia, Yacine, Jonathan Parker, and Motohiro Yogo. 2004. "Luxury Goods and the Equity Premium." *Journal of Finance*, vol. 59: 2186–2222.
11. Barlett, Donald L. and James B. Steele. 1992. *America: What Went Wrong?* Kansas City, MO: Andrews McMeel, pp. v–xii.
12. See David M. Gordon (1996), *Fat and Mean: The Corporate Squeeze of Working Americans and the Myth of Managerial Downsizing* (New York: Martin Kessler Books), pp. 204–37, and Barlett and Steele, *America: What Went Wrong?*, pp. v–xii.

13. Barlett and Steele, *America: What Went Wrong?*, pp. v–xii.
14. See, for example, James K. Glassman and Kevin A. Hassett (1999), *Dow 36,000: The New Strategy for Profiting from the Coming Rise in the Stock Market* (New York: Crown Business).
15. Stiglitz, Joseph E. 2003. *The Roaring Nineties*. New York: W. W. Norton, pp. 87–114.
16. See David Cay Johnston (2003), *Perfectly Legal: The Covert Campaign to Rig Our Tax System to Benefit the Super Rich—And Cheat Everybody Else* (New York: Portfolio Hardcover), pp. 215–28, and Stiglitz, *The Roaring Nineties*, pp.115–39.
17. Stiglitz, *The Roaring Nineties*, pp. 241–68.
18. Hightower, Jim. 2003. *Thieves in High Places: They've Stolen Our Country—and It's Time to Take it Back*. New York: Penguin Group, p. 56.
19. Bureau of Labor Statistics. 2005. Retrieved from www.bls.gov/bdm/total_private.gif.
20. Some economists would argue that productivity gains should be paid to marginal workers, not average workers. See, for example, Michael Mandel (1996), *The High-Risk Society: Peril and Promise in the New Economy* (New York: Times Business), pp. 23–74.
21. Manser, "The Bureau of Labor Statistics (BLS) Productivity Programs."
22. Bluestone, Barry and Bennett Harrison. 1982. *The Deindustrialization of America: Plant Closings, Community Abandonment, and the Dismantling of Basic Industry*. New York: Basic Books, pp. 25–48.
23. Block and Burns, "Productivity as a Social Problem," pp. 768–72.
24. Ruggles, Richard. 1983. "The United States National Income Accounts, 1947–1977: Their Conceptual Basis and Evolution" in *The U.S. National Income and Product Accounts*, ed. Murray F. Foss. Chicago: University of Chicago Press, pp. 15–104.
25. Manser, "The Bureau of Labor Statistics (BLS) Productivity Programs."
26. Nordhaus, "Alternative Methods for Measuring Productivity Growth," pp. 1–20.
27. University of Michigan. 2004. "More Jobs Unable to Offset Higher Inflation and Interest Rates." Retrieved from www.sca.isr.umich.edu.
28. U.S. Census Bureau, 2004–2005, Statistical Abstract of the United States, Washington, D.C., p. 104.

Chapter 5

1. Andrews, Edmund L. 2005. "A Hands-Off Policy on Mortgage Loans." *New York Times*, July 15. Retrieved from www.nytimes.com/2005/07/15/business/15mortgage.html?ei=5088&en=c7825db3a1a4835a&ex=1279080000&adxnnl=1&partner=rssnyt&emc=rss&adxnnlx=1146388184-sgrYmb23DRbdZ4ob1iG+PA.

2. University of Michigan. 2006. "Consumer Confidence Sinks Under Weight of High Gas Prices and Rising Interest Rates." May. Retrieved from www.sca.isr.umich.edu/press-release.php.

3. Ritzer, George. 1995. *Expressing America: A Critique of the Global Credit Card Society*. Thousand Oaks, CA: Pine Forge Press, p. 36.

4. Evans, David S. and Richard Schmalensee. 1999. *Paying with Plastic: The Digital Revolution in Buying and Borrowing*. Cambridge, Mass: MIT Press, pp. 61–77.

5. Manning, Robert D. 2000. *Credit Card Nation: The Consequences of America's Addiction to Credit*. New York: Basic Books, p. 4.

6. Ellis, Diane. 1998. "The Effect of Consumer Interest Rate Deregulation on Credit Card Volumes, Charge-Offs, and the Personal Bankruptcy Rate." *Bank Trends*. March. FDIC. Retrieved from www.fdic.gov/bank/analytical/bank/bt_9805.html.

7. Sullivan, Teresa A., Elizabeth Warren, and Jay L. Westbrook. 2000. *The Fragile Middle Class: Americans in Debt*. New Haven: Yale University Press, p. 18.

8. Shull, Bernard and Gerald A. Hanweck. 2001. *Bank Mergers in a Deregulated Environment: Promise and Peril*. Westport, CT: Quorum Books.

9. Evans and Schmalensee, *Paying with Plastic*, p. 42.

10. Dymski, Gary. 1999. *The Bank Merger Wave: The Economic Causes and Social Consequences of Financial Consolidation*. Armonk, N.Y.: M. E. Sharpe.

11. Rhoades, Stephen A. 2000. "Bank Mergers and Banking Structure in the United States, 1980–98." Federal Reserve Staff Study 174.

12. Evans and Schmalensee, *Paying with Plastic*, p. 45.

13. Dymski, *The Bank Merger Wave*, p. 51.

14. See Kevin Phillips (1990), *The Politics of Rich and Poor: Wealth and the American Electorate in the Reagan Aftermath* (New York: Random House) and Shull and Hanweck, *Bank Mergers in a Deregulated Environment*.

15. Phillips, *The Politics of Rich and Poor*, p. 97.

16. Ibid., p. 87.

17. For more on the Gramm–Leach–Bliley Act, see www.ftc.gov/privacy/privacyinitiatives/glbact.html.

18. Hudson, Michael. 1996. *Merchants of Misery: How Corporate America Profits from Poverty*. Monroe, ME: Common Courage Press, p. 29.

19. Manning, *Credit Card Nation*, p. 225.

20. Federal Reserve Board. 2003. "Remarks by Governor Edward M. Gramlich at the Texas Association of Bank Counsel 27th Annual Meeting." October 9. Retrieved from www.federalreserve.gov/BOARDDOCS/Speeches/2003/20031009/.

21. Hudson, *Merchants of Misery*, p. 3.

22. Manning, *Credit Card Nation*, p. 5.

23. Manning, Robert D. 2001. Prepared Statement for Hearing on "Giving Consumers Credit: How is the Credit Card Industry Treating Its Customers?" before the Subcommittee on Financial Institutions and Consumer Credit, U.S. House of Representatives, November 1, p. 3. Retrieved from www.creditcardnation.com/pdfs/110101rm.pdf.

24. See Manning, *Credit Card Nation* and (2003), Prepared Statement for Hearing on "The Role of FCRA in the Credit Granting Process" before the Subcommittee on Financial Institutions and Consumer Credit, U.S. House of Representatives, June 12. Retrieved from www.creditcardnation.com/pdfs/061203rm.pdf.

25. See Lewis Mandell (1999), "Our Vulnerable Youth: The Financial Literacy of American 12th Graders—A Failure by Any Measurement" in *Credit Union Magazine*, January; Manning, "The Role of FCRA in the Credit Granting Process"; and Manning (2005), Prepared Statement for Hearing on "Current Legal and Regulatory Requirements and Industry Practices for Card Issuers With Respect to Consumer Disclosures and Marketing Efforts" before the U.S. Senate Committee on Banking, Housing, and Urban Affairs, May 17, retrieved from http://banking.senate.gov/_files/manning.pdf.

26. Fabian, Elaine. 2005. "Bill Would Limit Credit for Students." *Daily Iowan*, August 25. Retrieved from www.uwire.com/content/topnews082505001.html.

27. Mandell, "Our Vulnerable Youth."

28. Mayer, Caroline E. 2004. "Girls Go from Hello Kitty to Hello Debit Card: Brand's Power Tapped to Reach Youth." *Washington Post*, October 3. Retrieved from www.washingtonpost.com/wp-dyn/articles/A2959-2004Oct2.html.

29. Manning, *Credit Card Nation*, p. 7.

30. Ibid., pp. 22–23.

31. Manning, "Current Legal and Regulatory Requirements . . .", p. 3.

32. Manning, *Credit Card Nation* and "Current Legal and Regulatory Requirements . . .", p. 3.

33. Bayot, Jennifer. 2003. "Surprise Jumps in Credit Rates Bring Scrutiny." *New York Times*. May 29.

34. Take Charge America. 2005. "Credit Counseling Firm Warns Consumers of 'Perfect Financial Storm' Conditions." July 6. Retrieved from www.takechargeamerica.org/Pressroom/PerfectFinancialStorm.htm.

35. Ritzer, *Expressing America*, p. 85.

36. Ibid., p. 60.

37. DeMong, Richard F. and John H. Lindgren Jr. 1999. "How Lenders Are Marketing Home Equity Products." *Journal of Retail Banking Services* Vol. XXI (1): 31–37.

38. Punch, Linda. 1998. "The Home Equity Threat." *Credit Card Management*, p. 113.
39. U.S. Census Bureau. 2000. Statistical Abstract of the United States, www.census.gov/prod/2001pubs/statab/sec16.pdf, p. 517.
40. Thomas Financial Inc. 1998. "Introduction and Summary." *Mortgage-Backed Securities Letter*. December, v. 13, p. 1.
41. Punch, "The Home Equity Threat," p. 116.
42. Ibid., p. 116.
43. DeMong and Lindgren, "How Lenders Are Marketing Home Equity Products."
44. Cleaver, Joanne. 2003. "Moving Up to the Top of the Pile." *Credit Card Management* Vol. 16 (2): 48–51.
45. Sullivan, Warren, Westbrook, *The Fragile Middle Class*, pp. 21–22.
46. Leonhardt, David and Motoko Rich. 2005. "The Trillion-Dollar Bet." *New York Times*, June 16. Retrieved from www.nytimes.com/2005/06/16/realestate/16arm.html?ei=5088&en=d4ea9a4dd01af4d5&ex=1276574400&partner=rssnyt&emc=rss&pagewanted=print.
47. Aizcorbe, Ana and Martha Starr-McCluer. 1996. "Vehicle Ownership, Vehicle Acquisition and the Growth of Auto Leasing: Evidence from Consumer Surveys." Federal Reserve Board of Governors. Retrieved at www.federalreserve.gov/PUBS/feds/1996/199635/199635pap.pdf.
48. Federal Reserve Board. 2004. "Vehicle Leasing: Quick Consumer Guide." May. Retrieved from www.federalreserve.gov/pubs/leasing/.
49. See Federal Deposit Insurance Corporation (2003), "Payday Lending," www.fdic.gov retrieved from www.fdic.gov/regulations/safety/payday/; and the Consumers Union (2003), "Payday Lenders Burden Working Families and the U.S. Armed Forces," retrieved from www.consumersunion.org/pdf/payday-703.pdf#search='Payday%20Lenders%20Burden%20Working%20Families%20'.
50. Consumers Union, "Payday Lenders Burden Working Families . . ."
51. Community Financial Services Association of America. 2004. "Payday Advance Industry Overview." Retrieved from www.cfsa.net/govrelat/PaydayAdvanceIndustryOverview.htm.
52. Cited in Manning, *Credit Card Nation*, p. 205.
53. Federal Deposit Insurance Corporation (2003), "Payday Lending," retrieved from www.fdic.gov/regulations/safety/payday/.
54. Consumers Union, "Payday Lenders Burden Working Families . . ."
55. Community Financial Services Association of America, "Payday Advance Industry Overview."
56. Consumers Union, "Payday Lenders Burden Working Families . . ."
57. Consumers Union. 2004. "Fact Sheet on Payday Loans." Retrieved from www.consumersunion.org/finance/paydayfact.htm.
58. Manning, *Credit Card Nation*, pp. 205–06.

59. The Association of Progressive Rental Organizations. 2006. "Industry Overview," retrieved from www.rtohq.org/About_rent-to-own/Industry_overview/index.aspx#industry.

60. Manning, *Credit Card Nation*, p. 215.

61. The Association of Progressive Rental Organizations. 2006. "Industry Overview," retrieved from www.rtohq.org/About_rent-to-own/Industry_overview/index.aspx#industry; see also Manning's discussion of results from the FTC study of rent-to-own businesses in *Credit Card Nation*, p. 210.

62. Manning, *Credit Card Nation*, p. 210.

63. Rent-A-Center. 2004. "Company Fact Sheet." Retrieved from http://www6.rentacenter.com/site/page/pg4425.html.

64. Manning, *Credit Card Nation*, p. 208.

65. Rosenthal, James A. and Juan M. Ocampo. 1988. *Securitization of Credit: Inside the New Technology of Finance*. New York: Wiley.

66. Furletti, Mark. 2002. "An Overview of Credit Card Asset-Backed Securities." Discussion Paper, Payment Cards Center. Federal Reserve Bank of Philadelphia. Retrieved from www.phil.frb.org/pcc/workshops/workshop11.pdf.

67. Rosenthal and Ocampo, *Securitization of Credit*.

68. Furletti, "An Overview of Credit Card Asset-Backed Securities."

69. Ibid.

70. Federal Reserve Statistical Release. Retrieved from www.federalreserve.gov/releases/g19/hist/cc_hist_r.html.

71. See George Ritzer (2001), *Explorations in the Sociology of Consumption: Fast Food, Credit Cards, and Casinos* (Thousand Oaks, CA: Sage Publications) and (2004), *The Globalization of Nothing* (Thousand Oaks, CA: Pine Forge Press).

72. Wolfe, Alan. 1998. *One Nation, After All*. New York: Viking, p. 118.

73. Schor, Juliet B. 1998. *The Overspent American: Upscaling, Downshifting, and the New Consumer*. New York: Basic Books, p. 73.

74. Warren, Elizabeth and Amelia Warrent Tyagi. 2003. *The Two-Income Trap: Why Middle Class Mothers and Fathers Are Going Broke*. New York: Basic Books.

75. For more on such communal and recreational activity, see Robert D. Putnam (2000), *Bowling Alone: The Collapse and Revival of American Community* (New York: Simon and Schuster).

Chapter 6

1. Krugman, Paul. 2003. *The Great Unraveling: Losing Our Way in the New Century*. New York: W. W. Norton, p. 457.

2. Kristol, William. 2004. "The Neoconservative Persuasion." In Irwin Stelzer, ed. *The Neocon Reader*. New York: Grove Press.

3. Reidl, Brian. 2003. "Ten Common Myths about Taxes, Spending, and Budget Deficits." In *The Heritage Foundation Backgrounder*, June 13, p. 4.

4. Ibid.

5. Stelzer, Irwin. 2003. "Neoconservatives and Their Critics: An Introduction." In Irwin Stelzer, ed. *The Neocon Reader*. New York: Grove Press, p. 21.

6. Ibid.

7. Phillips, Kevin. 1990. *The Politics of Rich and Poor: Wealth and the American Electorate in the Reagan Aftermath*. New York: Random House, pp. 32–51.

8. U.S. Department of Treasury Bureau of Public Debt. 2005. "Historical Debt Outstanding: 1950–2000." Retrieved from www.publicdebt.treas.gov/opd/opdhisto4.htm.

9. Phillips, *The Politics of Rich and Poor*, p. 120.

10. Johnston, David Cay. 2003. *Perfectly Legal: The Covert Campaign to Rig Our Tax System to Benefit the Super Rich—And Cheat Everybody Else*. New York: Portfolio Hardcover, p. 7.

11. Johnston, *Perfectly Legal*, p. 43.

12. Citizens for Tax Justice. 2002. "Corporate Income Taxes as a Percentage of GDP: The United States and Other OECD Countries." www.ctj.org/images/oecd1.gif.

13. Johnston, David Cay. 2003. *Perfectly Legal: The Covert Campaign to Rig Our Tax System to Benefit the Super Rich—And Cheat Everybody Else*. New York: Portfolio Hardcover, p. 222.

14. Source Watch. 2005. "Government-Industry Revolving Door." www.sourcewatch.org/index.php?title=Government-industry_revolving_door.

15. Hightower, Jim. 1997. *There's Nothing in the Middle of the Road but Yellow Stripes and Dead Armadillos*. New York: HarperCollins, p. 108.

16. Citizens for Tax Justice. 1996. *Who Pays? A Distributional Analysis of the Tax Systems in All 50 States*. Washington D.C.: Citizens for Tax Justice and the Institute on Taxation and Economic Policy.

17. Stiglitz, Joseph E. 2003. *The Roaring Nineties*. New York: W. W. Norton, pp. 39–41.

18. Ibid., 177.

19. U.S. Census Bureau. 2003. Statistical Abstract of the United States. Washington, D.C.: U.S. Government Printing Office.

20. Associated Press. 2006. "Federal Budget Deficit Sparks Worries." www.msnbc.msn.com/id/10868785/.

21. U.S. Census Bureau (2003), Statistical Abstract of the United States.

22. Greenspan, Alan, Sept. 26th, 2005. "Remarks by Chairman Alan Greenspan to the American Bankers Association Annual Convention, Palm Desert, California." www.federalreserve.gov/boarddocs/speeches/2005/200509262/default.htm.

23. For more on this, see Kevin T. Leicht and Mary L. Fennell (2001), *Professional Work: A Sociological Approach* (Oxford, UK: Blackwell), pp. 131–41.

24. Ibid., pp. 61–81.

25. Mandel, *The High-Risk Society*, pp. 53–74.

26. U.S. Census Bureau. 2004 and 2005. Statistical Abstracts of the United States.

27. Manning, Robert. 1999. "Credit Card Debt Imposes Huge Costs on Many College Students." Retrieved from www.consumerfed.org.

28. Ibid. pp. 3, 4–8.

29. McMurray, Coleen. 2004. "Health Costs Dominate American's Health Concerns." *Gallup Poll Tuesday Briefing*, February 3rd, 2004. Princeton, NJ: The Gallup Organization.

30. Bureau of Labor Statistics. 2003. "Employee Benefits in Private Industry, 2003." Retrieved from stats.bls.gov/newsrelease.

31. O'Donnell, Janne. 1999. Press conference, June 8. Retrieved from www.rsok.com/~sean/credit.html.

32. Giannarelli, Linda and James Barsimantov. 2000. "Child Care Expenses of America's Families." Occasional Paper Number 40: Assessing the New Federalism. Washington D.C.: The Urban Institute.

33. Schubert, Ruth. 2002. "Day Care a Huge Expense for Parents." *Seattle Post-Intelligencer*. June 24, 2002.

34. BLS, 2004. www.bls.gov/bls/peoplebox7.

35. For more on the precarious state of retirement planning, see Lauren Fox (2003), *Enron: The Rise and Fall* (Hoboken, N.J.: John Wiley and Sons); Stiglitz, *The Roaring Nineties*; and Mimi Swartz with Sheryl Watkins (2003), *Power Failure: The Inside Story of the Collapse of Enron* (New York: Doubleday).

36. Fox, *Enron*, p. 4.

37. Crutsinger, Martin. 2005. "Trustees: Social Security Broke in 2041." ABC News. March 23, 2005. Retrieved from http://abcnews.go.com/Politics/wireStory?id=607878&page=1.

38. Mary Williams Walsh. September 18th, 2005. "Whoops! There Goes Another Pension Plan." *New York Times*. Retrieved from www.nytimes.com/2005/09/18/business/18pensions.html?ex=1284696000&en=f0efc65d38b5829f&ei=5090&partner=rssuserland&emc=rss.

39. Holtz-Eakin, Douglas. 2005. "The Role of the Economy in the Outlook for Social Security." CBO Testimony before the Subcommittee on So-

cial Security Committee on Ways and Means, U.S. House of Representatives. June 21.

40. Morin, Richard and Jim VanderHei. 2005. "Social Security Plan's Support Dwindling." *Washington Post*, June 9. Retrieved from www.washingtonpost.com/wpdyn/content/article/2005/06/08/AR2005060801975.html.

Chapter 7

1. These analyses include Teresa A. Sullivan, Elizabeth Warren, and Jay L. Westbrook (1999), *As We Forgive Our Debtors: Bankruptcy and Consumer Credit in America* (Washington, D.C: BeardBooks); Teresa A. Sullivan, Elizabeth Warren, and Jay L. Westbrook (2000), *The Fragile Middle Class: Americans in Debt* (New Haven: Yale University Press); Elizabeth Warren and Amelia Warrent Tyagi (2003), *The Two-Income Trap: Why Middle Class Mothers and Fathers Are Going Broke* (New York: Basic Books); Robert N. Bellah, Richard Madsen, William M. Sullivan, Ann Swidler, and Steven M. Tipton (1985), *Habits of the Heart: Individualism and Commitment in American Life* (Berkeley: University of California Press); Robert D. Putnam (2000), *Bowling Alone: The Collapse and Revival of American Community* (New York: Simon and Schuster); and Jean Bethke Elshtain (1995), *Democracy on Trial* (New York: Basic Books).

2. Scott, James C. 1976. *The Moral Economy of the Peasant: Rebellion and Subsistence in Southeast Asia.* New Haven: Yale University Press.

3. Scott, *The Moral Economy of the Peasant*, p. 5.

4. Ibid., p. 10, emphasis added.

5. Mahler, Jonathan. 2003. "Commute to Nowhere." *New York Times Magazine*, April 13.

6. Witte, Griff. 2004. "As Income Gap Widens, Uncertainty Spreads." *The Washington Post*, September 20. Retrieved from www.washingtonpost.com/ac2/wp-dyn/A34235-2004Sep19?language=printer.

7. The anger that Scott and Robert feel toward politicians and others that seem to ignore their plight has been documented by, among others, Susan. J. Tolchin (1996), *The Angry American: How Voter Rage is Changing the Nation* (Boulder, Col.: Westview Press), and Thomas Frank (2004), *What's the Matter with Kansas? How Conservatives Won the Heart of America* (New York: Metropolitan Books).

8. Wolfe, Alan. 1998. *One Nation, After All.* New York: Viking.

9. Ibid., p. 251.

10. Roberts, Sam. 1997. "Another Kind of Middle-Class Squeeze." *The New York Times*, May 18, 1997. Retrieved from www.tenant.net/Alerts/Guide/press/nyt/sr051897.html.

11. Sullivan et al., *The Fragile Middle Class: Americans in Debt*; Warren and Tyagi, *The Two-Income Trap: Why Middle Class Mothers and Fathers Are Going Broke*.

12. Associated Press. 2005. "Change in Law Spurs Bankruptcy Filings." September 25. Retrieved from http://abcnews.go.com/Business/wireStory?id=1155754&CMP=OTC-RSSFeeds0312.

13. Giddens, Anthony. 1994. *Beyond Left and Right: The Future of Radical Politics*. Stanford, CA: Stanford University Press, p. 9.

14. Kesler, Charles. 1998. "What's Wrong with Conservatism." Speech for the American Enterprise Institute for Policy Research, June 8. Retrieved from www.aei.org/publications/pubID.16662,filter.all/pub_detail.asp.

15. Krugman, Paul. 2003. *The Great Unraveling: Losing Our Way in the New Century*. New York: W. W. Norton.

16. Giddens, *Beyond Left and Right*, p. 9.

17. See Kevin Phillips (1993), *Boiling Point: Democrats, Republicans, and the Decline of Middle-Class Prosperity* (New York: Random House), pp. 72–77.

18. Teixeira, Ruy A., and Joel Rogers. 2000. *America's Forgotten Majority: Why the White Working Class Still Matters*. New York: Basic Books, p. xi.

19. Bellah et al., *Habits of the Heart*, p. 250.

20. Putnam, Robert D. 2000. *Bowling Alone: The Collapse and Revival of American Community*. New York: Simon and Schuster.

21. For a transcript of this October 15, 2004 episode of "Crossfire," see http://transcripts.cnn.com/TRANSCRIPTS/0410/15/cf.01.html. For video, see www.ifilm.com/ifilmdetail/2652831.

22. Coulter, Ann. 2003. *Treason: Liberal Treachery from the Cold War to the War on Terrorism*. New York: Crown Forum, p. 1.

23. Hightower, Jim. 2003. *Thieves in High Places: They've Stolen Our Country—and It's Time to Take it Back*. New York: Penguin Group, p. xiii.

24. Hartmann, Thom. 2003. "Turn Your Radio On—The Unions' Answer to Right-Wing Static." Common Dreams News Center. August 11. Retrieved from www.commondreams.org/views03/0811-02.htm.

25. Anti-Defamation League. 2004. "The Quiet Retooling of the Militia Movement." Retrieved from www.adl.org/extremism/Militia/default.asp?m_flipmode=1.

26. Krugman, Paul. 2003. *The Great Unraveling: Losing Our Way in the New Century*. New York: W. W. Norton, p. 183.

27. See, for example, Thomas Byrne and Mary D. Edsall (1992), *Chain Reaction: The Impact of Race, Rights, and Taxes on American Politics* (New York: W. W. Norton); Kevin Phillips (1993), *Boiling Point: Democrats, Republicans, and the Decline of Middle-Class Prosperity* (New York: Random House); and Jeffrey C. Goldfarb (1991), *The Cynical Society: The*

Culture of Politics and the Politics of Culture in American Life. (Chicago, IL: University of Chicago Press).

28. Elshtain, *Democracy on Trial*, p. 53.

Chapter 8

1. Juliet Schor, personal communication.
2. Warren, Elizabeth and Amelia Warrent Tyagi. 2003. *The Two-Income Trap: Why Middle Class Mothers and Fathers Are Going Broke.* New York: Basic Books, pp. 123–62.
3. Giddens, Anthony. 1994. *Beyond Left and Right: The Future of Radical Politics.* Stanford, CA: Stanford University Press, pp. 22–50.
4. Skocpol, Theda. 2000. *The Missing Middle: Working Families and the Future of American Social Policy.* New York: W. W. Norton, pp. 140–71.

Further Readings

Anderson, Elijah. 1999. *Code of the Street: Decency, Violence, and the Moral Life of the Inner City*. New York: W. W. Norton.

Bourdieu, Pierre. 1984. *Distinction: A Social Critique of the Judgement of Taste*. London: Routledge & Kegan Paul.

Bureau of Labor Statistics. 2003. Employee Benefits in Private Industry, 2003. Retrieved from www.bls.gov/ncs/ebs/sp/ebbl0021.pdf.

CardWeb.com, Inc. 2004. "U.S. Marketshare by Brand." www.cardweb.com

Citizens for Tax Justice. 2003. "Final Tax Plan Tilts Even More Toward Richest." Washington, D.C.: Citizens for Tax Justice. May 22. Retrieved from www.ctj.org/pdf/sen0522.pdf.

Citizens for Tax Justice. 2003. "Most Taxpayers Get Little Help from Latest Bush Tax Plan." Washington, D.C.: Citizens for Tax Justice, May 30. Retrieved from www.ctj.org/pdf/2003statecut.pdf.

Citizens for Tax Justice. 2003. "Effects of First Three Bush Tax Cuts Charted." Washington, D.C: Citizens for Tax Justice, June 4. Retrieved from www.ctj.org/pdf/allbushcut.pdf.

The College Board. 2002. *Trends in Student Aid, 2002*. Retrieved from www.collegeboard.com/press/cost02/html/CBTrendsAid02.pdf.

Community Financial Services Association of America. 2004. "Payday Advance Customer Profile." Retrieved from www.cfsa.net/govrelat/pdf/Payday%20Advance%20Customer%20Profile.pdf.

Congressional Budget Office. 2005. "Budget Outlook, Fiscal Years 2004–2013." Retrieved from www.cbo.gov/showdoc.cfm?index=4032&sequence=0.

de Graaf, John, David Wann, and Thomas H. Naylor. 2001. *Affluenza: The All-Consuming Epidemic*. San Francisco, CA: Berrett-Koehler Publishers, Inc.

Francis, David R. 2004. "Gap in Wages Grows Wider: Pay Rises for Well-off, but Not for Others." *Christian Science Monitor*, February 12.

Hacker, Jacob. 2004. "Call It the Family Risk Factor." *New York Times*, January 11.

Leonhardt, David. 2004. "Time to Slay the Inequality Myth? Not So Fast." *New York Times*, January 23.

Manning, Robert. 2002. Prepared Statement on "The Importance of Financial Literacy Among College Students." September 5. Retrieved from http://banking.senate.gov/02_09hrg/090502/manning.htm.

McGeehan, Patrick. 2004. "Mountains of Interest Add to Pain of Credit Cards." *New York Times*, November 21.

McIntyre, Robert S. and David Wilhelm. 1985. "Corporate Taxpayers and Corporate Freeloaders: Four Years of Continuing, Legalized Tax Avoidance by America's Largest Corporations, 1981–84." Washington, D.C.: Citizens for Tax Justice. Retrieved from www.ctj.org/pdf/corp0885.pdf.

McIntyre, Robert S. and T. D. Coo Nguyen. 2000. "Corporate Income Taxes in the 1990s." Washington, D.C.: Institute on Taxation and Economic Policy.

Newman, Katherine. 1988. *Falling from Grace*. New York: The Free Press.

The New York Times. 2003. "The Budget Fight Is Now." *The New York Times* Editorial April 3.

Office of Management and Budget. 2004. Budget of the United States of America, Fiscal Year 2005. Retrieved from www.whitehouse.gov/omb/budget/fy2005/.

Peltzman, Sam and Clifford Winston, eds. 2000. *Deregulation of Network Industries: What's Next?* Washington D.C.: AEI-Brookings Joint Center for Regulatory Studies.

President's Commission to Strengthen Social Security. 2001. "Strengthening Social Security and Creating Personal Wealth for All Americans." Office of the Chief Actuary, Office of the Social Security Commission. Retrieved from www.csss.gov/reports/Final_report.pdf.

Public Agenda. 2005. "Social Security: People's Chief Concerns." Retrieved from www.publicagenda.org/issues/pcc_detail.cfm?issue_type=ss&list=7.

Social Security Administration. 2005. "Historical Development." Retrieved from www.ssa.gov/history/pdf/histdev.pdf.

Stanley, Harold W. and Richard G. Niemi, eds. *Vital Statistics on American Politics, 2005–2006*. Washington, D.C., CQ Press, 2005.

Stockman, David A. 1986. *The Triumph of Politics: How the Reagan Revolution Failed*. New York: Harper and Row.

Veblen, Thorstein. 1992. *Theory of the Leisure Class*. New Brunswick, NJ: Transaction Publishers. For a free online version of this text, see http://xroads.virginia.edu/~HYPER/VEBLEN/veb_toc.html.

Waldman, Amy. 2004 "India Takes Economic Spotlight, and Critics Are Unkind." *New York Times*, March 7.

Index